The Chronicle of Lanercost, 1272-1346

LANERCOST PRIORY

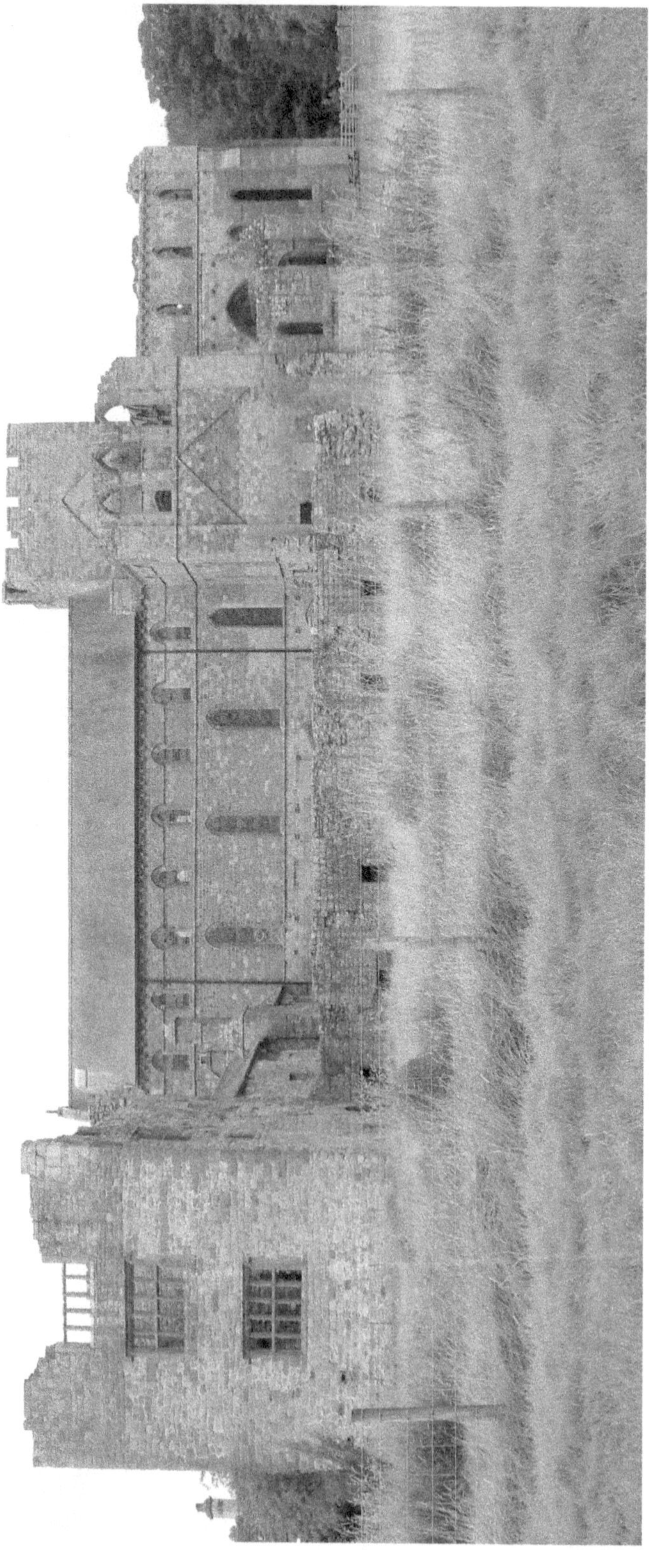

The Chronicle of Lanercost, 1272-1346

Translated, with Notes, by
Sir Herbert Maxwell
(1913)

The Grimsay Press

The Grimsay Press
An imprint of Zeticula
57, St Vincent Crescent
Glasgow
G3 8NQ
Scotland
http://www.thegrimsaypress.co.uk

First published by James Maclehose in Glasgow in 1913

This edition first published in 2010

ISBN 978-1-84530-094-4

Preface

STUDENTS of English and Scottish history in the thirteenth and fourteenth centuries have so long been familiar with the record known as *The Chronicle of Lanercost* that an English translation may seem to be a superfluity. But, whereas the tendency of modern education is to exchange the study of the classics for a diversity of other subjects reputed to be of greater utility, it is certain that a far smaller proportion of educated persons can read Latin easily in the twentieth century than could do so before that flexible language had ceased to be the common medium of scientific and literary intercourse. Now the writer or writers of this chronicle indulged in so many digressions from formal narrative, thereby casting so many sidelights upon the social conditions of his time, that an English translation may prove convenient for such readers as lack time for arduous historical research.

The Latin text was edited from the oldest extant MS.[1] by the late Joseph Stevenson with his usual acumen and fidelity, and printed for the Maitland and Bannatyne Clubs in 1839. 'The whole Chronicle,' wrote Stevenson in his preface, 'as it now stands has been reduced to its present form, about the

[1] British Museum, Cottonian MSS. Claudius D. vii.

latest period of which it treats, by a writer who had before him materials of a varied character and of unequal merit.' In this form it has been appended as a continuation to Roger de Hoveden's *Annals*.

In Stevenson's opinion there is no warrant for attributing the origin of this chronicle to the Priory of Lanercost. He judged from internal evidence that it was written by a Minorite Friar of Carlisle. That evidence has been analysed afresh by Dr. James Wilson, who has contributed an introductory chapter vindicating the claim in favour of the Augustinian Priory of Lanercost as the source of the chronicle. It still remains somewhat perplexing that an Austin Canon, or a succession of Austin Canons, should have been at the pains exhibited in this chronicle to exalt the renown of the Franciscan Order of Mendicants. The entire work covers the period from 1201 to 1346. The translation now presented only extends over the reigns of Edward I. and II. and part of the reign of Edward III., a period of perennial interest to Scotsmen, who, however, must not be offended at the bitter partisanship of a writer living just over the Border.

In preparing the translation for the press I have had the advantage of the literary acumen and historical erudition of Mr. George Neilson, LL.D., who, by undertaking the tedious task of reading my MS., has steered me clear of many pitfalls and pulled me out of others into which I had fallen.

HERBERT MAXWELL.

MONREITH,
1st *March*, 1913.

List of Illustrations

ERRATA

Page 29, note 1, Mr. Cleland Harvey has proved to me that *Ecclesia de Bothanis de Laodonia*, being dedicated, as the chronicler mentions, to S. Cuthbert, cannot be Abbey S. Bathans in Berwickshire, but was the parish church of S. Bothans in Haddingtonshire, mentioned in A.D. 1176 in the Register of the Priory of S. Andrews as *Ecclesia Sancti Bothani in Decanatu Laodonie*. On 12th April, 1421, it was erected by the Bishop of S. Andrews into a college for a provost and four chaplains, which was broken up during the Reformation, and the ancient title of the parish was altered to that of Yester or Gifford.

Page 95, note 1, read 'probably *mostellum*, a little tub.'

Page 170, note 3, read 'The Comte de Bar, who married Eleanor, daughter of Edward I.'

Page 332, line 16, for 'shattered the bones' read 'broke the gates.'

Authorship of the Chronicle of Lanercost[1]

By the Rev. JAMES WILSON, Dalston, Cumberland

THE authorship of the Chronicle of Lanercost, when the manuscript first came within the cognisance of literary men, was unhesitatingly ascribed to the canons of the house which bears its name, and such origin does not appear to have been doubted till the transcript in the Cotton collection was printed in 1839 as a joint-production of the Bannatyne and Maitland Clubs under the care of the Rev. Joseph Stevenson.

Nothing is known of the history of the manuscript of the Chronicle (Cotton MS. Claudius D. vii.) before the sixteenth century, when it came into the possession of Sir Henry Savile, who published his *Scriptores post Bedam* in 1596. There is little doubt that the manuscript belonged to him before it passed into the collection of Sir Robert Cotton. Not only is there a printed label bearing Sir Henry's name pasted on the fly-leaf, but traces of perusal by him may be ascertained from annotations in the margin. For example, the phrase 'in comitatu Roberti de Sabuil' on folio 97 is underlined in the text, and a note is placed in the margin to call attention to the early occurrence of the name.

[1] The references in footnotes, when not otherwise stated, apply to the pages of this translation.

Indications are not wanting on several folios that the manuscript was used by students and that attempts were made to disclose the constituent parts of the compilation.

The whole manuscript, which is bound in one volume, comprises 242 vellum leaves or 484 folios, arranged in double column and written in a hand apparently of the fourteenth or early fifteenth century. There is some evidence that the hand varies, but not perhaps more than may be ascribed to different sessions by the same writer. In the later portions of the manuscript, say from folio 66, which represents the year 1181, a new style of rubric and illumination begins. Perhaps a uniform style should not be assumed for any large sections of the narrative. The scribe did not always finish his folio before commencing the next. Several columns are blank, occasionally a whole folio. In one instance at least, he had just commenced a new folio (fol. 101) under the year 1190, but before he had proceeded far down the first column and had written 'Deinde Rex Anglie,' he stopped and commenced a new folio with the same words. When he had reached folio 21^b, the end of the introductory portions, he laid down his pen with the pious sentiment, 'finito libro benedicamus Domino,' leaving a whole leaf blank before he resumed. The abrupt ending of the manuscript has tempted some late student to remark that 'videtur hoc exemplar esse imperfectum.' It may be added that he was not the last to hold a similar opinion.

Students of the manuscript were under no delusion about its authorship. In various places the legend 'historia canonici de Lanercost in comitatu Northumbrie' is met with, which may be taken as the unauthorised interpolation of the reader. The owners, however, may be justly regarded as responsible for the index and table of contents, though not made at the same date or by the same person. The 'elenchus contentorum' appears to be the earlier. Referring to the beginning of the continuous narrative on folio 23, apart from the fragments with which the Chronicle is prefaced, we have 'Larga Anglie historia composita per canonicum de Lanercost in comitatu Northumbrie que descendit ad tempora Edwardi tertii.' The ignorance of the geography of Cumberland, which placed Lanercost in the neighbouring county, is very welcome, inasmuch as it shows that the compiler of the *elenchus* was not a local antiquary prejudiced in favour of the Lanercost authorship.

It is different, however, with the index at the end of the volume, the writing of which appears to be in a later hand, perhaps about the close of the seventeenth century. The compiler of the index was not only a north-countryman interested in northern history, but he held decided views on the authorship. In fact, the index was made for the sole use of historical students of the Border counties, but especially of the county of Cumberland. It embodies the principal local references, notably those relating to the priory of Lanercost and the barony of Gillesland, with very little reference to occurrences elsewhere except when they affected that neighbourhood. The index is entitled, 'Ex manuscripto per quemdam canonicum de Lanercost infra baroniam de Gillisland in comitatu Cumbrie composita.' In referring the reader to the visitation of the priory of Lanercost by the Bishop of Carlisle in 1281, which will be discussed presently, the index-maker remarked that 'constat fol. 206 authorem libri esse canonicum de Lanercost.' The compiler of this addition to the volume appears to have had no doubt about the authorship.

The first writer who printed portions of the manuscript, so far as we have ascertained, was Henry Wharton, librarian at Lambeth, who extracted from it the references to Bishop Grosteste of Lincoln, and published them in 1691 in the *Anglia Sacra* (ii. 341-3). The heading of the chapter indicates Wharton's view of the authorship: 'Vita Roberti Grosthed, ex Annalibus de Lanercost, in Bibliotheca Cottoniana, Claudius D. 7.' But in the preface he has given a more positive opinion. 'Among the unprinted chronicles,' he says,[1] 'the author of the Annals of Lanercost has commemorated (*celebravit*) Bishop Robert the most fully: I have therefore appended his account of Robert's life. The Annals of Lanercost are extant from the coming of the Saxons to the year 1347, exceedingly copious (*valde prolixi*), in the Cotton Library. The monastery of Lanercost is situated in the county of Cumberland near the borders of Scotland. Its annals were written by several persons in succession, as appears at the year 1245, where the writer states that he had committed to the earth the Elect of Glasgow.'

The value of the compilation was known to Dr. William Nicolson, Bishop of Carlisle (1702-1718), whose literary activities entitle him to rank among the laborious scholars who adorned the age in which he lived. Writing with his customary precision in 1708, he referred to 'the jingling rhyme on the building of the Roman Wall in the Chronicle of Lanercost[2] (MS. in Bibl. Cott. Claudius D. vii. fol. 14[a],)' and spoke of 'the learned Canon Regular who was the author of the Chronicle.' The same prelate had no misgivings about the authorship in 1713, when he urged Humfrey Wanley, the famous librarian of the Earl of Oxford,[3] to publish 'a Chronicle by some of the Canons of Lanercost in this diocese,' a manuscript 'in the Cotton Library, Claudius D. vii.' It was probably owing to the well-deserved reputation of Bishop Nicolson as a scholar of exceptional critical ability that the authorship had not been called in question till the publication of the manuscript by the Scottish Clubs.

Planta, when making a catalogue of the Cottonian collection in 1801 for the Record Commission, accepted the traditional authorship without demur. His account of the contents of the Chronicle is taken almost wholly from the *elenchus contentorum* of the Cotton manuscript. The introductory fragments are resolved

1 *Anglia Sacra*, ii. pref. xvii.

2 *Stukeley's Diaries and Letters* (Surtees Soc.), ii. 62.

3 *Chron. de Lanercost*, pp. xv-xviii.

into nine sections, which take up the first 21 folios of the manuscript, as already noticed. The Chronicle itself, beginning on folio 23, is described[1] as 'a history of the affairs of the kings of the Britons and the English from Cassibelanus to 1346, extracted by a canon of Lanercost in the county of Cumberland from William of Malmesbury, Henry archdeacon of Hereford, Gildas, Geoffrey of Monmouth and Helinand.' Though we cannot accept the sources here indicated, the statement is useful as expressing the opinion of the authorities of the Record Commission on the authorship in 1801. It was not till Stevenson had printed the manuscript that the origin of the Chronicle was ascribed to a Minorite friar of Carlisle.

As the manuscript bears no title, and as nothing is known of its early history, a discussion of the probable authorship must rest wholly on internal evidence. But it is difficult to make an exposition of the evidences intelligible to students of the printed text, owing to Stevenson's treatment of the manuscript. He regarded the portion issued by the Scottish[2] Clubs 'as a continuation to the Annals of Roger of Hoveden, beginning where the work of that writer terminates without a break of any description.' For this reason he started his edition of the Chronicle on folio 172^b in the middle of the column, where the transcriber or author left no mark to indicate a new work. Opinions may differ on the wisdom of such a step, but no authority for the arbitrary division is recognised in the manuscript. For our own part, we prefer the statement of Bishop Stubbs[3] that a copy of Hoveden was 'used as the basis of the Lanercost Chronicle,' that is, of the unprinted portion embracing folios 23-172. Students of the manuscript will agree with the Bishop rather than with the Editor.

Though the question of sources does not arise, it may be

[1] *Catalogue of the MSS. in the Cottonian Library*, p. 197.

[2] *Chronicon de Lanercost*, p. iii.

[3] Roger de Hoveden (R.S.), i. pref. lxxxiii.

permissible to notice a few incidents in order to show the author's historical equipment independent of his use of the exemplars he had before him. Few of the chroniclers, except the historians of Hexham, mention the battle of Clitheroe in 1138 and the subsequent proceedings at Carlisle for the alleviation of the atrocities of warfare. Certainly Hoveden has left these matters unrecorded. But our author on folio 60^b has meditated on that period to some purpose. 'William, son of Duncan, nephew of King David,' he narrates, 'vanquished the English army in Craven at Clitheroe, slaying very many and taking numerous prisoners. At the same time Alberic, a monk of Cluny, then Bishop of Ostia and Legate of the Apostolic See, who had been sent by Pope Innocent to England and Scotland, came to King David at Carlisle and reconciled (*pacificavit*) Bishop Adelulf to King David and restored him to his own (*proprie*) See, as also John Bishop of Glasgow. In addition he obtained from King David that in the feast of St. Martin they should bring all the English prisoners to Carlisle and there give them their freedom. When this was done that city was not inappropriately called *Cardolium*, which means *carens dolore*, because there *captivitas Anglorum caruit dolore*.' If this account is laid alongside what is known from other sources of the incidents of 1138, it will be observed how little the author followed the textual phraseology of the Hexham writers.[1] The etymological adaptation of *Cardolium* to suit the happy incident appears to be quite new to history.

Another passage, indicative of his independence of Hoveden, raises a question of considerable interest in the literary history of England and Scotland. So important is the text that it must be reproduced in the original.

Eodem anno, videlicet, anno domini m° c° ij°, Rex Henricus primus, ut dicitur, per consilium et industriam Matildis regine, constituit canonicos

[1] *Priory of Hexham* (Surtees Soc.), i. 82-3, 98-9, 117-21.

regulares in ecclesia Karleolensi. Quidam vero presbiter, ad conquestum Anglie cum Willelmo Bastardo veniens, hanc ecclesiam et alias plures et aliquas villas circumiacentes, pro rebus viriliter peractis, a rege Willelmo in sua susceperat, Walterus nomine. Henricus [episcopatum[1]] sancte Marie Karleolensis fundavit et non multo post in pace quievit. Cuius terras et possessiones Rex Henricus dedit canonicis [Rex H. *underlined for deletion*] regularibus et priorem eorum primum Adelwaldum, iuvenem quidem etate sed moribus senem, priorem sancti Oswaldi de Nosles constituit, quem postea corrupte Adulfum vocabant.

It is true that this statement is made in the form of a note at the bottom of folio 58[a], but it is not the interpolation of a subsequent writer. The note is introduced in the same hand and with the same ink as the text in a place reserved for it. The position on the folio only shows that the statement was not in the exemplar the scribe was following for that portion of the narrative. Its resemblance to the famous passage[2] in the *Scotichronicon* (i. 289) on the foundation of the priory of Carlisle will be recognised.

Other passages in the manuscript tell the same tale. The compressed account on folio 51[a] of William the Conqueror's visit to Durham, his foundation of the castle there, his attempted profanation of the tomb of St. Cuthbert, and his meticulous flight

[1] There has been an erasure here in a very contracted text, but perhaps of only one letter. A late hand has interlineated *ecclesiam*. As the bishopric was founded only a few years before King Henry's death, *episcopatum* was probably in the scribe's mind. The sentence has been misplaced: it should have been written at the end of the passage.

[2] If Abbot Bower of Inchcolm added this note to Fordun's work, as it is generally believed, from what source is it likely that the superior of a Scottish Augustinian house should have obtained such local information? The statement in the *Scotichronicon* that the priory of Carlisle was founded in 1102 was supposed to be unsupported till within recent years. It has now the countenance of an English as well as a French Chronicle. See *Hist. MSS. Com. Report*, vi. 354.

beyond the Tese, shows indebtedness to Simeon of Durham as well as to Hoveden. It is not necessary to multiply proofs of Bishop Stubbs' statement that the earlier portion of the manuscript is based on the Chronicle of Roger of Hoveden, and not a mere continuation of it, as Stevenson has suggested. In not a few instances the author has shown his independence by addition, omission, and compression.[1]

That Hoveden was the basis of the compilation for the twelfth century every student of the manuscript will acknowledge. From this circumstance alone we get an important sidelight on the authorship. It is stated in the manuscript on folio 103, under the year 1190, that David, brother of William King of Scotland, married *blank*, sister of Ranulf earl of Chester, and on folio 157 in the list of the bishops assembled in London in 1199 occurs the name of *blank*, Archbishop of Ragusa. Thanks to the masterly collation of the Hoveden manuscripts by Bishop Stubbs, we can identify from *lacunae* like these the actual text of Hoveden that the author of our chronicle had before him. It was the Laudian copy now in the Bodleian, where alone these two omissions in the same manuscript are found. The interest, however, is not confined to this point. The Laudian copy has on its fly leaves transcripts of four documents, all relating to Carlisle. These show, as Bishop Stubbs[2] remarked, that the manuscript 'was at one time, and that probably a very long time, in possession of either the city or the Bishop of Carlisle.' But as one of these deeds is a letter from Henry VI. to Bishop Lumley, dated

[1] The same discretion, used by the author when dealing with the Chronicle of Melrose as his exemplar, will be observed if a collation is made of the early pages of Stevenson's printed text with the corresponding passages of that chronicle. The author appropriated whole slices of the Chronicle of Melrose when they suited his purpose. He did the same with Hoveden for the twelfth century, but perhaps with more frequency and freedom.

[2] Roger de Hoveden (R.S.), i. pref. pp. lxxiv-lxxx.

23rd November, 1436, 'de custodia ville et castri Karlioli,' we need have no hesitation in ascribing the ownership of the manuscript to that prelate, who was then warden of the Western March. It probably formed part of the episcopal library at Rose Castle. The deeds of this nature, inserted in it, just cover the period of the episcopal residence there up to Bishop Lumley's day. This identification, so far as our inquiry is concerned, localizes the production of our chronicle to the district of Carlisle,[1] the area of the bishop's jurisdiction.

Turning now to Stevenson's printed text, and especially to that portion of it translated by Sir Herbert Maxwell, when we are approaching the *floruit* of the author, no reader can help feeling that, like works of this nature, the Chronicle is a compilation from various sources, and that the materials, which make up the narrative, are of unequal historical value. It cannot be said that the compiler was a skilled artist in the use of his sources. There is no attempt to write continuous history, though a fair semblance of chronological arrangement has been maintained. Duplicate entries are frequent, many of which have been pointed out by the translator, and need not be repeated here. This repetition is evidence enough, if nothing else existed, that the Chronicle at this period was a sort of journal or literary scrap-book for the purpose of jotting down historical events as information had reached the authorities. An entry was made from perhaps imperfect knowledge, either from a written source or oral intelligence: later details arrived or a fuller account was found, and a more

[1] But it does far more than this. The scholar, who undertakes to identify the sources of the chronicle on the lines of those issued in the Rolls Series, will have to define its relationship to the *Cronica de Karleolo*, compiled for Edward I. in 1291 by the canons of Carlisle, as well as to Bishop Lumley's copy of Hoveden. It will be an interesting study, and will result in the probable discovery that the Carlisle copy of Hoveden was lent to the canons of Carlisle in 1291, as well as to the canons of Lanercost.

extended record of the incident was afterwards made without expunging the previous entry. In most of the duplicate passages it will be found that the second carries with it more particulars than the first.

The method of the compiler comes into view in the manipulation of his sources about 1290. In dealing with the plutocrat[1] of Milan, 'it pleases me,' he says, 'to add in this place what ought to have found a convenient place in the beginning of the eighth part, forasmuch as it happened at that time, although I did not receive timely notice of this matter.' Passages of this sort furnish some evidence that the work was not undertaken and carried out by the same person at the period in which the story draws to a close. But if the printed portion of the Chronicle was mainly compiled from written sources, to which assumption there is much antagonistic evidence, the duplicate passages offer indubitable proof of the writer's unskilfulness in his craft.

There is strong reason for believing that the body of the Chronicle was not put together in or after 1346. In various passages noticed by the translator, contemporary allusions are made at long distant periods quite incompatible with a single authorship after the close of the work. A few instances must suffice. Under 1293 there is recorded a story[2] from Wells about 'what I know to have happened nine years ago' to a prebendary of that church. 'This event,' the chronicler relates, 'took place in the year (19 March, 1285-6) when Alexander, King of Scotland, departed this life, and was told to our congregation by a brother who at that time belonged to the convent of Bristol.' There is no reasonable doubt that the entry was made in the year to which it refers when the story came to hand. Another incident, not included in this translation, is equally conclusive. It is well known[3] that Nicholas of Moffat was made archdeacon of Teviotdale in 1245, and though twice elected Bishop of Glasgow he

[1] P. 67. [2] Pp. 101-102. [3] Dowden, *Bishops of Scotland*, pp. 304-6.

died unconsecrated in 1270. With this neglected churchman the author of this portion of the Chronicle was so familiar, that he says he officiated at his funeral.[1] Contemporaneous allusions like these go a long way to show that the compilation was built up continuously, period by period, and cannot be the work of a single compiler in the middle of the fourteenth century.

But it is not so easy to form a definite opinion of the nature of the institution responsible for the continuous production of such a work. It seems to be agreed that the Chronicle emanated from some religious house on the English side of the Border. The tone of the composition in its acrimonious hostility to Scottish interests betrays its English origin : the historical setting of the narrative is similarly conclusive of its localisation to the Border counties. The ecclesiastical colour of the incidents cannot be mistaken : the lightning of the churchman coruscates on every page. As these general considerations will be conceded, the difficulty lies in the identification of the particular religious house in which the work was done.

It was a bold and praiseworthy venture of Stevenson to cut himself adrift from the traditional view that the Chronicle emanated from the priory of Lanercost, and to suggest the Grey-friar House in Carlisle as the more probable source. With much acumen has he marshalled his evidence, and with all the moderation of conviction has he defended his own discovery. Without going over in detail the formidable list of evidences in support of the Minorite authorship, it may be here acknowledged that no critical student can fail to be impressed with the cogency of his arguments. The narrative bristles with the exploits and virtues of the Friars Minor. One would think that it was specially composed in glorification of that Order. The passages are too numerous for special discussion: they are all of the same character: on every occasion, in season and out of season,

[1] *Chron. de Lanercost*, p. 53.

the merits of the brothers of St. Francis are lauded to the skies.

While this much is admitted without reserve, the weak side of Stevenson's proposition, as it would seem, presents itself when he attempts to identify the Franciscan habitation in which he locates the Chronicle. If the work is due to Minorite authorship, internal evidence gives little encouragement to make Carlisle the headquarters of the particular congregation that gave it birth. So much of the narrative is taken up with affairs, political and ecclesiastical, in the neighbourhood of that city, that the editor was constrained, as it may be permissible to believe, to fix on that place, in spite of the evidence, as the local habitation. The overwhelming evidence for a Greyfriar authorship is more conclusively in favour of Berwick than of Carlisle.

It will be observed that the references to this Mendicant Order are for the most part very general. News about the Order came from all points of the compass in the shape of prattle and legend: in very few instances can it be said to be local. When local news protrudes itself, the scene is at Berwick or elsewhere, not at Carlisle. Some specific instances of the compiler's connexion with Berwick are very striking. In his vision [1] after Mass on the Lord's Day in 1296, 'as I was composing my limbs to rest,' he saw an angel with a drawn sword, 'brandishing it against the bookcase in the library, where the books of the friars were stored, indicating by this gesture that which afterwards I saw with my eyes, viz. the nefarious pillaging, incredibly swift, of the books, vestments and materials of the friars.'

At the following Easter King Edward sacked Berwick, when a most circumstantial account is given of the siege and slaughter. 'I myself,' the chronicler [2] adds, 'beheld an immense number of men told off to bury the bodies of the fallen.' The description of the siege of Berwick by Bruce in 1312 is equally personal and

[1] Pp. 132-3. [2] Pp. 134-5.

explicit. It is unmistakably the account of an eye-witness. The Scottish scaling-ladders, he says,[1] were of wonderful construction, 'as I myself, who write these lines, beheld with my own eyes.' Personal testimony[2] is again advanced in the description of the battle at the same town in 1333. If the authorship is exclusively the work of the Minorites, its localisation, on the face of the evidence, must be transferred from Carlisle to Berwick. The former place supplies no local or personal touches to the narrative beyond a few isolated facts, with little bearing on the authorship, which can be explained in another way.

But a new order of things is introduced when we approach the local affairs of the priory of Lanercost. Their prominence in the Chronicle after 1280 can scarcely be explained without assuming that the author or successive authors were connected with the house, or had some annals or domestic memoranda of the institution at hand. The internal affairs of the priory loom largely in the narrative. It is not merely great events touching the place, like those of Berwick, that are recorded, events known to fame and of general interest, but the local colour is more clearly manifested by incidental remarks, quite undesigned, let fall as it were by chance, known to very few and of no particular concern, which betray the locality. No external writer could be the mouthpiece of such minute intelligence, nor is it likely, had it come to his knowledge, that he would have thought it worthy of record. Some of these incidental allusions will be noticed later on.

Without following Stevenson throughout his category of allusions to Lanercost, it may be here said that the influence of the canons on the authorship is not to be estimated by a single incident or a number of incidents of a general nature, but by the particular attention which the compiler or compilers gave to that house as compared with similar institutions or localities in the

[1] P. 201. [2] Pp. 278-80.

Border district. No other place or immediate neighbourhood has had the same search-light from the author's pen thrown upon it. One of these incidents evidently puzzled Stevenson, and though he tried valiantly to make it fit his hypothesis, it must be acknowledged that he has grievously failed. The year 1280-81 was memorable in the annals of the house. It signalised a victory for the canons in the local baronial court: witnessed a gracious visit of King Edward and Queen Eleanor: and brought Ralf of Ireton, the new Bishop of Carlisle, on a visitation of the priory. In the record of these events we have, it is true, no gushing or embroidered narrative, but we have particulars in abundance to connote the interested spectator. The very day on which the local court declared the immunity of the canons from manorial taxation is recorded:[1] the canonical dress of the prior and his brethren, when the royal party was received at the gate of the priory, and the nature of the royal bounty are duly described. The contents of the King's game-bag, which helped to get Stevenson out of his difficulty, need give no trouble. It was naturally recorded on hearsay evidence, and was thrown in with the account of the royal visit on the gossip of the community.

The Bishop's visitation of the convent has even more personal notice. It took place on 22 March, 1281: he was met at the gate like the King and Queen: he first gave the benediction and then the kiss of peace to all the brethren: after his hand had been first kissed he gave them a kiss on the lips. Then the Bishop entered the chapter-house and preached: the very text of his discourse has been preserved. At the conclusion of the sermon, he proceeded with his visitation, the object of his presence there, 'in which we were compelled (*coacti sumus*),' says[2] the narrator, 'to accept new constitutions.' It is only candour to say that Stevenson misunderstood the procedure of an episcopal visitation of an Augustinian house. It had nothing to do with a general visita-

[1] Pp. 23-4. [2] P. 25.

tion of the diocese. It was when the preaching was ended that the visitation began—inquiry into the mode of doing divine service, ministrations in their parochial churches, their conduct of the secular affairs of the community, the hearing of complaints and the adjusting of irregularities. Other visitations of Lanercost are on record, and the mode of procedure is well known. The graphic touches of the simple narrative could only come from one who took part in the function and who could describe its successive phases with ceremonial exactness.

On the previous page of the printed book, but on the same folio of the manuscript, another personal allusion, overlooked by Stevenson, is equally conclusive against Minorite authorship. On 24 October, 1280, the narrator[1] tells that 'a convocation was held in Carlisle Cathedral by Bishop Ralf, and a tenth of the churches was granted to him by the clergy for two years according to the true valuation, to be paid in the new money within a year: wherefore we paid (*solvimus*) him in all twenty-four pounds.' The writer of this passage was clearly subject to ecclesiastical taxation, whereas the friars, having no material resources except the actual buildings they inhabited, were exempt from episcopal subsidies and all kinds of assessment. It was different with the canons, who bore their share of such impositions in common with the parochial clergy. The special assessment here mentioned was a subsidy granted to an incoming Bishop by the clergy, parochial and collegiate, of his diocese. The poet of the Chronicle gave vent to his feelings about the exaction in pungent metre:

> Poor sheep, bereft of ghostly father,
> Should not be shorn: but pampered rather.
> Poor sheep! with cares already worn,
> You should be comforted, not shorn.
> But if the shepherd must have wool,
> He should be tender, just and cool.[2]

[1] P. 23. [2] Pp. 23-4.

If the amount of the subsidy be compared with the value of the revenues of Lanercost, as assessed for taxation ten years[1] afterwards, no doubt will be entertained that the *solvimus* of the record exactly tallies with the taxable capacity of the canons of that house.

Though Stevensón was sincere in his exposition of the Lanercost evidence,[2] and enumerated some of the most conspicuous allusions to it in the Chronicle, he has omitted one of the most important, as evidential of the interested onlooker, the account of the pillage of the priory by King David *cum diabolo* in 1346, the year in which the Chronicle ends. The touch of personal indignation in his description of the Scottish King is only of a piece with the account of the arrogance of his soldiery in the devastation of the sanctuary: they threw out the vessels of the church, plundered the treasury, smashed the doors, stole the jewels and annihilated everything they could lay hands on.[3]

It is not, however, in the record of great events, likely to attract general attention, but in the trifles of language and incident, where the student will find his embarrassment if he quarrels with the traditional authorship. The phraseology touching Lanercost, from its first introduction to its last mention, presupposes the local

[1] *Taxatio Ecclesiastica* (Rec. Com.), pp. 318-20.

[2] In fact, Stevenson missed the significance of all the Lanercost allusions. For example, the chronicler has much to say about Macdoual's doings in Galloway in 1307, including the capture of Bruce's two brothers and the decapitation of the Irish kinglet and the lord of Cantyre, and the sending of the spoils, quick and dead, to King Edward at Lanercost. But he did not tell that the spoils were first exhibited to the Prince of Wales, then sojourning at Wetheral near Carlisle, on their gruesome pilgrimage to the King (*Register of Wetherhal*, p. 402, ed. J. E. Prescott). The inference is obvious.

[3] *Chron. de Lanercost*, p. 346.

resident. One word only is used to designate a journey to that place. In 1280 King Edward and Queen Eleanor came (*venerunt*) to Lanercost: in 1281 Bishop Ireton came (*venit*): in 1306 King Edward came (*venit*): in 1311 King Robert came (*venit*) with a great army: and in 1346 King David and his rascal rout came (*venerunt*) to the priory of Lanercost and went off (*exierunt*) by way of Naworth Castle. Though the narrator is liberal in his use of the word in expressing locomotion, he frequently interlards the usage with 'went' (*adivit*) or 'passed' (*transivit*) in respect of other places. But so far as Lanercost is concerned there is no variation: always *came*, never *went*, as if the author was resident there.

The migration of brothers from one house to another, an incident of infinitesimal interest outside an ecclesiastical enclosure, is not without instruction. The house from which the brother was transferred is never mentioned. The reticence is such as might be expected if the narrator was an inmate. In all cases, so far as we have observed, intercommunication was restricted to Augustinian communities. Nicholas of Carlisle was sent in 1281 to reside at Gisburn[1] and became an inmate (*professus est*) there. Incidental allusion to another migration is more significant still. In 1288 we are told that brother N. de Mor received the canonical habit, and in 1307 that he was sent by the Queen to Oseney, another Augustinian house.[2] But it is not stated in what house he took the canon's profession nor from what house he was transferred to Oseney. The nature of the profession, however, predicates the canon and not the friar. But when we know that Queen Margaret spent quite half of the latter year at Lanercost, the veil falls from the transaction. Similar mystery hangs over the conventual apostacy of John of Newcastle, who took the monastic habit in the neighbouring Cistercian house of Holmcultram. In this instance there is no mention of transference, but the renunciation of his

[1] P. 28. [2] Pp. 55, 181.

first vows brought forth the contemptuous gibe of the Lanercost poet, that

> With altered habit, habits too must alter,
> Much need that John with sin no more should palter.
> Unless to mend his ways he doth not fail,
> White gown and snowy cowl will nought avail.[1]

Isolated incidents like these are eloquent of the local chronicler and his mode of record. His familiarity, too, with occurrences in the Austin houses of Gisburn, Oseney, Hexham, and Markby points in the same direction.

The poet of the Chronicle deserves honourable mention. His effusions, always diverting, if not always in the best of metre, are quoted under the name of Brother H., or Henry, or Henry de Burgo. Few readers will gainsay the suggestion that he was first canon and afterwards prior of Lanercost. In 1287 William Grynerig came to live in the community (*inter nos*), and his habits as a vegetarian were a source of perplexity to the house. Brother Henry hit off the situation thus :

> You may not seek a canon's dress to wear
> Who cannot feed yourself on common fare.[2]

The poet let the cat out of the bag when he revealed the *vestis canonicalis* employed *inter nos* : a friar did not wear the canonical habit. Perhaps the most striking of the undesigned coincidences supplied by Henry's muse in favour of Lanercost occurs in his use of the word *garcifer* to express a youth. The chronicler in the same folio uses *garcio* and *garcifer*, which Sir Herbert Maxwell distinguishes in his translation as *page* and *young fellow* ; but it was *garcifer* that Brother Henry adopted for his verse. It is a singular coincidence, as showing the currency of this rare word among the canons of Lanercost, the chartulary of whose house abounds in rare words, that shortly before 1280, when William

[1] P. 28. [2] P. 52.

garcifer was slain on one of his moonlight expeditions, the same word was used by one of the canons of that house in his sworn depositions touching a local dispute. Richard, the cook of Lanercost, alleged on oath that a *garcifer* in the kitchen, afterwards chief cook, had oftentimes gone with the canons to the vale of Gelt to receive the disputed tithes.[1] If this is a mere linguistic coincidence, accidents of this kind seem only to happen at Lanercost.

In 1300 Henry de Burgo, canon of Lanercost, was the bearer of a gift from Edward I. to the high altar of that church[2]: on 14 March, 1303-4, Henry, canon of Lanercost, appeared as proctor for his house in an act before Archdeacon Peter de Insula of Carlisle[3]: he was elected prior about 1310, and died in 1315.[4] As Henry rose in favour among his brethren, and as years lent gravity to his demeanour, it may be permissible to assume that his versification took a similar turn. His rhymes between 1280 and 1290 may be regarded as his best for piquancy and fun. After his elevation to the priorate, verses in his name cease in the Chronicle, and verses with any pretension to local colour vanish altogether after his death.

No discussion of authorship would be complete without reference to the prominence in the Chronicle given to the lords of Gillesland. No franchise, ecclesiastical or secular, receives such attention. In fact the descent of the lordship in the family of Multon is not only unique in the territorial history of the Border counties, but it is singularly accurate. No other lordship has mention of its successive owners. This feature is so obvious that it needs no elaboration. It is odd that Stevenson should have singled out one of those references as incompatible with the Lanercost authorship, whereas the very mention of a paltry

[1] Chartulary of Lanercost, MS. xiii. 10.

[2] *Liber Quot. Garder.* (Soc. of Antiq.), p. 40.

[3] Chartulary of Lanercost, MS. xiv. 11.

[4] P. 216.

suit[1] in the court of Irthington, the capital messuage of Gillesland in 1280, would seem to suggest the opposite. Though the local verdict was of immense interest to the canons, a glorification of the victory over their neighbour and patron, which Stevenson expected, would have been imprudent, not to say dangerous, if the record had ever met his eye. The canons of Lanercost were well aware of the power of their patrons over them, as we know from the history of that house.

From another quarter a charge of inaccuracy has been brought against the chronicler for his account of the territorial descent of Gillesland. In the same year, we are told,[2] died 'Thomas de Multona secundus,' then lord of Holbeach. It is unlikely, says the objector, that a canon of Lanercost should have fallen into this mistake, as the Thomas de Multon, who died at that time, was the third and not the second who was lord of Gillesland. The objection wholly fails, inasmuch as the Thomas de Multon, who came between the Thomas *primus* and the Thomas *secundus* in the family tree, was never lord of Gillesland at all, his mother, through whom the barony came to that family, having outlived him.[3] Misinterpretation of disjointed entries in this Chronicle has led to much confused chronology. The account[4] of the espousal of the heiress of the last of the Multons in 1313 and her subsequent rape from the castle of Warwick by the first of the Dacres of Gillesland is so picturesque in detail that scholars have worried themselves over the exact meaning of some of its phraseology.

How came the Chronicle to be so full of Lincolnshire news? After describing the avarice of the canons of Markby in 1289, some features of which he had hesitation to explain in detail, the narrator states that he was unwilling to believe the story till he had the particulars from the lips of a nobleman[5] who lived not

[1] P. 23. [2] P. 111. [3] Fine Roll, 12 Edw. I. m. 11.
[4] P. 205. [5] Pp. 56-8.

more than three miles from the place under discussion. Who was this nobleman? Can there be a doubt that Thomas de Multon, lord of Holbeach, who lived in that neighbourhood, was retailer of the news? In keeping with this we have the accounts of sundry occurrences in Lincolnshire, some of them of little interest beyond the ambit of the county, the communication of which may be ascribed to that family.

In holding an even balance between the rival claims to authorship, the geographical and business relationships of Lanercost should not be omitted. The situation was on one of the highways between England and Scotland. To this circumstance alone may be ascribed many of the sufferings it endured. There was no religious house in Cumberland that was more frequently burned by the Scots, and no district that underwent more pillage than Gillesland. In times of peace Scotsmen came into England by the Maiden Way, the old Roman highway from Roxburgh to Cumberland and the valley of the Eden, for the purpose of trade, as did Fighting Charlie in the days of the Wizard of the North. In recording one of these raids, the chronicler shows how much Lanercost occupied his mind when he tells that the Scots passed near the priory of Lanercost on their return to Scotland.[1]

By reason of its business connexions the house had unrivalled opportunities for gathering news relating to the Border districts. Apart from the advantages of its geographical situation, the canons had property in Carlisle, Dumfries, Hexham, Newcastle, and Mitford near Morpeth. From 1202 they were obliged to attend the yearly fair of Roxburgh on St James' Day to pay a pension to the monks of Kelso, issuing from the church of Lazonby, in Cumberland, in which they had a joint interest. Some of their property in Carlisle and Newcastle, not to speak of Dumfries, lay alongside the friaries of the Minorites in these towns. The direct road from Lanercost to Berwick, a town which

[1] P. 211.

figures largely in the narrative, passed near Roxburgh and through Kelso,[1] and if a return journey was made to visit their Northumberland estates, Berwick would inevitably be a halting-place. It will be seen, therefore, that within the area of the Lanercost connexions many of the scenes depicted in the printed portion of the Chronicle took place.

If it be admitted that the Chronicle bears evidence of continuous production as the work of more than one author, the presumptions in favour of Lanercost are difficult to set aside. The canon of an Augustinian priory belonged to his house: he was the member of a corporation with historic succession: like a family, his house inherited ancestral traditions. If attachment to the house of his profession was a feature of his rule, the direct opposite was the characteristic of the friar's calling. The friar did not belong to a house: local detachment was his glory: his individuality was lost in his province. He was a wanderer, a sort of parochial assistant, who went about from place to place under the Bishop's licence to give clerical help where required. Like John Wesley in his palmy days, the friar was incapable of localisation: the world was his parish. In addition, the Austin canons in the North of England had a well-deserved reputation as patrons of learning and students of history, for which their constitution well fitted them. Nearly half of their houses in the North produced chronicles, the value of which is appreciated at the present day. Who is not acquainted with the work of John and Richard of Hexham, Alan Frisington of Carlisle, William of Newburgh, Peter Langtoft, Walter of Hemingburgh, John of Bridlington, Stephen Edeson of Wartre, Walter Hilton of Thurgarton, George Ripley, and Robert the Scribe, scholars who shed lustre on the Augustinian institute in Northern England? The Chronicle of Lanercost betrays many symptoms of learning and scholarship in agreement with Augustinian traditions. It requires

[1] *Britannia Depicta* (1720), pp. 160-162.

a robust faith to predicate in the mendicant friar a knowledge of Beda, Chrysostom, Ambrose, Justin Martyr, Gregory, and Augustine, leaving out the Theodosian Code,[1] as the quotation is in some doubt. Whatever imperfections the composition may contain, and nobody wishes to conceal them, the authors may reasonably be acquitted of ignorance of patristic learning. Literary touches of various forms brighten up the dull catena of miracle and legend.

In the light of what has been already stated, it would be hazardous to offer a dogmatic view of the authorship of the Chronicle, but it seems quite reasonable to hold that the preponderance of evidence favours the Augustinian house. In the early vicissitudes of the friars in the Border counties, opportunities for undertaking and continuing such a work simply did not exist. The sources of the Chronicle, so far as they can be conjectured, are a strange mixture of written history and oral tale. Many of the stories there recorded, some of them being in glorification of the Mendicant Orders, were taken down from the lips of a narrator. An Augustinian house with the geographical advantages of Lanercost was well adapted to serve as an emporium of news, and the ubiquitous friars, who often assisted the canons in parochial administration, were convenient agents to collect the supply. But the corpus of the Chronicle, taken as it exists in manuscript, was compiled from written sources, and the institution from which it emanated was well supplied with some of the best materials for the period to which it relates.

JAMES WILSON.

[1] The phrase, *teste theodocto,* which puzzled Sir Herbert Maxwell (p. 128), should be compared with *teste Ezechiele* (p. 126) and *teste Chrysostomo* (p. 135) as clearly correlative. Stevenson should have printed *theodocto* as a proper name, but the spelling is probably corrupt. The print, however, corresponds with the text of the manuscript. The quotation savours of the style of the Theodosian Code.

THE CHRONICLE OF LANERCOST

REIGN OF EDWARD I.

AFTER the Church's three years widowhood, as it was called,[1] when all men were laughing at the College of Cardinals, the Archdeacon of Liége, who had accompanied [our] Lord Edward in his journey to the Holy Land, was elected Pope, and was named Gregory the Tenth. He sat for four years and ten days, and the seat was vacant for ten days. In the third year of his pontificate he held a solemn council at Lyons of five hundred bishops, six hundred abbots and three thousand other prelates, for the good of the Church and especially of the Holy Land, which he desired to visit at another time; at which council, among many other excellent acts, it was decreed that whensoever the name of Jesus should happen to be heard in church, every head, whether of layman or cleric, should be bowed, or, at least, every one should do adoration in thought. A.D. 1272.

[1] The Papal throne was vacant for two years and nine months, 1268-71.

The Greek official delegates were present with the Patriarch at this Council, and solemnly affirmed, by singing in their own language, the creed of the Holy Spirit proceeding both from the Father and the Son, to which [doctrine] they had not assented previously to that time. There were present also Tartar delegates, asking on behalf of their own people for teachers of the Christian faith, in token whereof they returned to their own [country] having been catechised and baptised.

In this Council the Orders both of Preachers and Minorites were approved and confirmed for the Colleges of Mendicants. But it would be a long matter to mention all the good things which were settled there.

And so in the year of the Consecration of this Pope, there arose, as is reported, a great dispute in the Curia over the election of William Wishart,[1] many of them raising so many objections that the Head of the Church himself, having examined the objections set forth in writing, vowed by Saint Peter that if a moiety of the allegations were brought against himself, he never would seek to be Pope. At length, by intervention of the grace and piety of Edward, he [Wishart] was consecrated under the Pope's dispensation. For the sake of example I do not hesitate to insert here what befel him later when he applied himself to his cure. Indeed, it is an evil far too common throughout the world that many persons, undertaking the correction of others, are very negligent about their own [conduct], and, while condemning the light offences of simple folk, condone the graver ones of great men.

There was a certain vicar, of a verity lewd and notorious,

[1] To the see of St. Andrews in 1271.

who, although often penalised on account of a concubine whom he kept, did not on that account desist from sinning. But when the bishop arrived on his ordinary visitation, the wretch was suspended and made subject to the prelate's mercy. Overcome with confusion, he returned home and beholding his doxy, poured forth his sorrows, attributing his mishap to the woman. Enquiring further, she learnt the cause of his agitation and became bitterly aware that she was to be cast out. 'Put away that notion,' quoth she to cheer him up, 'and I will get the better of the bishop.'

On the morrow as the bishop was hastening to his [the vicar's] church, she met him on the way laden with pudding,[1] chickens and eggs, and, on his drawing near, she saluted him reverently with bowed head. When the prelate enquired whence she came and whither she was going, she replied: 'My lord, I am the vicar's concubine, and I am hastening to MS.
the bishop's sweetheart, who was lately brought to bed, and fo. 189b
I wish to be as much comfort to her as I can.' This pricked his conscience; straightway he resumed his progress to the church, and, meeting the vicar, desired him to prepare for celebrating. The other reminded him of his suspension, and he [the bishop] stretched out his hand and gave him absolution. The sacrament having been performed, the bishop hastened away from the place without another word.[2]

About this time there departed this life a certain prebendary of Howden church named John, a man of honourable life,

[1] *Pultæ* = broth, pap or porridge, seems to have been used in the plural just as 'porridge' and 'brose' are so used in Lowland Scots at this day.

[2] *Quasi mutus.*

passing his days modestly and without ostentation, skilled in astrology, given to hospitality and works of mercy. He began [to build] a new choir to the church at his own expense, and foretold that the rest should be finished after his death; which [saying] we [now] perceive more clearly in the light; for, having been buried in a stately tomb in the middle of the choir itself, he is revered as a saint, and we have beheld, not only in the choir, but the wide and elaborate nave of the church completed through the oblations of people resorting [thither].

In the same church there lived at that time another master, called Richard of Barneby, a true and pure man, who, having surrendered his private means, was residing at Gisburn in return for his money.[1] He was formerly well known in the kingdom of Scotland as a cleric of the religious community of Kelso. On leaving that kingdom he commended his nephew, who is still living, to Sir Patrick Edgar, knight, for education and service. After a lapse of years, at the above-mentioned time, he ended his life in a fatal manner, when his nephew in Scotland, [feeling] his bed shaken, was putting on [his] garments or shoes. And behold, a bird of the size of a dove, but differing in appearance by its variety of colour, entered by the chimney of the house and attacked the said youth with its wings, striking him with so much noise, that the people in the kitchen wondered at the sound of blows, and the lad [thus] belaboured sat still as though stunned. This [the bird] did thrice, retiring each time to the beams of the roof. After about the space of a

[1] *Perhendebat*, a verb form from *perendinus*, the day after to-morrow.

There was a canonry at Gisburn, in Yorkshire, valued, says Matthew Paris, 'at 628 poundes yearlye.'

month had elapsed, the youth went on business to Kelso, and on drawing near, heard all the bells of the monastery sounding. Entering within the walls, he asked what was the cause of bell-ringing. 'Do you not know,' they said, 'that your uncle, our clerk, has died at Gisburn, on such and such a day and hour? The abbot received the news yesterday, and to-day is commemorating him.'

What lesson such an apparition was intended to convey, let him who readeth explain.

In the same year Richard King of Germany died.

In the same year died the Earl of Cornwall, brother of King Henry of England.[1]

In the same year Friar Robert of Kilwardby, of the Order of Preachers, was consecrated Archbishop of Canterbury.

Boniface Archbishop of Canterbury died, and in his place was elected the Prior of Holy Trinity; but on coming before the Sacred College his election was quashed, and his dignity conferred by the Pope upon Robert of Kilwardby, A.D. 1273. Prior Provincial of Preaching Friars in England. This person, a man of honourable life, a doctor of divinity, devoted to the study of God's Word, ruled and corrected the clergy as firmly as the laity, as his treatise on heresy and his condemnation of Oxford show by themselves.[2]

[1] These two entries refer to one and the same person, viz. Richard, Earl of Cornwall, brother of Henry III., elected King of the Romans by four out of seven electors in 1257; but the minority having elected Alphonso X. of Castile, Richard failed to establish his authority, and returned to England in 1260.

[2] Excellent work, no doubt; but it had been better if, when appointed Cardinal-Bishop of Porto and Santa-Rufina in 1278, he had not removed all the registers and political records of Canterbury to Italy, whence they never returned.

Also at this time King Henry of England, devout servant of God and the Church, departed from this world, on the feast day of Saint Edmund, Archbishop of Canterbury,[1] after he had ruled over England fifty-six years and four months. He was buried at Westminster, and the absence of his son[2] caused the coronation to be deferred.

In the time of this Henry a boy named Hugh was crucified in Lincoln by impious Jews, in derision of Christ and Christians, nor were they able to conceal him by any device.

Now in the beginning of King Henry's reign, Louis, son of the King of France, invaded England with Frenchmen at the instigation of some people of the country, as has been aforesaid; but afterwards intestinal war broke out at Lincoln between the English and French, where the French were beaten and Thomas Count of Perch was slain with many others. But the son of the King of France narrowly escaped in great terror, wherefore after his escape some Frenchman composed this rhyme:

> 'Enthroned in La Rochelle, our king never quails
> Before Englishmen armed, for he broke all their tails.'[3]

To which an Englishman replied thus:

> 'Lincoln can tell and the French King bewails
> How the rope bound his people to Englishmen's tails.'[4]

This King Henry in his youth, at the instigation of Peter, Count of Brittany, crossed the channel to Brittany to recover the

[1] 20th November, 1272.

[2] On the last Crusade.

[3] *Rex in Rupella regnat, et amodo bella*
Non timet Anglorum, quia caudas fregit eorum.
The taunt of *Angli caudati* is ancient and well known.

[4] *Ad nostras caudas Francos, ductos ut alaudas,*
Perstrinxit restis superest Lincolnia testis.

territory owned and lost by his predecessors; but failing altogether of success in his undertaking, returned [home] luckless and empty-handed.

In truth, whereas diligence in evil seldom has a good issue, it pleases one to relate an instance rather for the sake of justice than from ill-will to an individual. Queen Margaret of Scotland, deeply distressed by her various trials, chiefly by the death of her father[1] and by anxiety about the return of her brother,[2] went forth one beautiful evening after supper from Kinclavin to take the air on the banks of the Tay, accompanied by esquires and maidens, but in particular by her confessor, who related to me what took place. There was present among others a certain pompous esquire with his page, who had been recommended to him by his brother in the presence of his superiors. And as they were sitting under the brow of the bank, he [the esquire] went down to wash his hands, which he had soiled with clay in playing. As he stood thus bending over, one of the maids, prompted by the Queen, went up secretly and pushed him into the river-bed.

'What care I?' cried he, enjoying the joke and taking it kindly, 'even were I further in, I know how to swim.'

Wading about thus in the channel, while the others applauded, he felt his body unexpectedly sucked into an eddy, and, though he shouted for help, there was none who would go to him except his little page-boy who was playing near at hand, and, hearing the clamour of the bystanders, rushed into the deep, and both were swallowed up in a moment before the eyes of all. Thus did the enemy of Simon and satellite of Satan, who declared that he had been the cause of that gallant knight's destruction, perish

[1] Henry III. [2] Edward I. who was on his journey home from the Crusade.

in sight of all; and the matron, led away unduly by affection
MS. fo. 190 for her parents,[1] received rebuke for her selfish love, and showed herself before all men wounded to the heart by overpowering anguish.

From the Beginning of the World 6470 years.

In beginning the eighth part of our work and, as it were, the peace of our age with a new king, I deem it meet to put this foremost in our desires, that, as the renewer of the old Adam,
A.D. 1274. seated in the paternal throne, said—'Behold, I make all things new, so he (the king) may induce new growth of virtues [to spring] in the Church, and that new joys may be bestowed upon us through the king and in time following, whereof now we have undertaken to treat.

Accordingly, messengers were sent to the Council assembled, as aforesaid at Lyons, whereat the heir of England attended, urging him to return to his country and restore the condition of the desolate realm. Returning accordingly to England in the same year, being thirty-five years and two months of age, he was received in most honourable manner by the whole nation, [and] was solemnly anointed and crowned on the 14th of the kalends of September[2] by the Archbishop of Canterbury, Brother Robert of Kilwardby. The nobles of the land attended the ceremony with a countless multitude, redoubling the display of their magnificence in honour of the new king. But my lord Alexander King of Scotland, who attended with his consort and

[1] Or spoilt by the undue affection of her parents [*nimis affectu parentum seducta*]. The construction of the last paragraph and the moral are alike obscure.

[2] 19th August, 1274.

a train of his nobility, exceeded all others in lavish hospitality and gifts.

Before the date of this coronation, Robert of Stichell, Bishop of Durham, died on his return journey from the Council, about two days' journey on this side of Lyons. He had besought from the Pope letters and license for his resignation, [because] he disliked to be mixed up in worldly trouble. In dying, however, he suffered the greatest remorse of conscience because he had deprived the burgesses of Durham city of liberty of pasture, and bestowed it upon those who needed nothing. Therefore in proof of penitence and in token of his desire for reconciliation with St. Cuthbert, he gave his ring to his confessor to be carried to the shrine of the saint, vowing that, should he recover health, he would annul that gift.

In this year Margaret, Queen of Scotland and sister of the King of England, died on the fourth of the kalends of March.[1] She was a woman of great beauty, chastity, and humility—three [qualities] seldom united in one individual. When her strength was failing many abbots as well as bishops collected to visit her, to all of whom she refused entrance to her chamber; nor from the time that she had received all the sacraments from her confessor, a Minorite Friar, until her soul passed away, did she admit any other to discourse, unless perhaps her husband happened to be present. She left behind her three children—Alexander and David and a daughter Margaret, all of whom followed their mother in a short time, owing, it is believed, to the sin of their father.

[1] Feb. 27, 1274, or, according to our reckoning 1275; but in the Calendar then prevailing in Britain the year began on 25 March.

Richard of Inverkeithing, Bishop of Dunkeld, departed from the world, treacherously poisoned, as is affirmed, and it is believed by many that the aforesaid Queen [perished] in the same manner. For, after the death of the aforesaid man, a certain [fellow] author of this plot,[1] drawing near to death, declared that he had sold poison in this place and that, and that a full bottle thereof still remained in Scotland. And seeing that the movables of bishops dying in that kingdom devolve upon the king, he [the Bishop of Dunkeld] only and one other named Robert de la Provender, Bishop of Dublin, whom we remember above all others, so made a virtue of necessity at the point of death by distributing their goods, that they left scarcely anything to satisfy the cupidity of royal personages.

A.D. 1275.

About the same time in England there lived in Hartlepool William Bishop of Orkney, an honourable man and a lover of letters, who related many wonderful things about the islands subject to Norway, whereof I here insert a few lest they should be forgotten. He said that in some place in Iceland the sea burns for the space of one mile, leaving behind it black and filthy ashes. In another place fire bursts from the earth at a fixed time—every seven or five years—and without warning burns towns and all their contents, and can neither be extinguished nor driven off except by holy water consecrated by the hand of a priest. And, what is still more wonderful, he said that they can hear plainly in that fire the cries of souls tormented therein.

In the same year there [fell] a general plague upon the whole stock of sheep in England.

[1] *Hujus confectionis.*

In this year, on the seventh day of the month of October, the King of Scotland's fleet steered into the port of Ronaldsway. Straightway Lord John de Vesci and the king's chief men with their forces, landed on Saint Michael's Isle,[1] the Manxmen being arrayed for war under Godred the son of Magnus, whom shortly before they had made their king. But the nobles and chieftains of the King of Scotland sent to treat for peace with Godred and the people of Man, offering them the peace of God and of the King of Scotland, provided they would desist from their most foolish presumption and submit in future to the king and his chief men. But as Godred and certain of his perverse counsellors would not agree to the treaty of peace, on the following day before sunrise, when the shades were still upon the land and the minds of foolish men were darkened, a conflict took place and the wretched Manxmen, turning their backs, were terribly routed.

Pope Gregory died and was succeeded by Innocent the Fifth, a native of Burgundy, whose previous name was Peter of Taranto, of the Order of Preachers. He was formerly Doctor in Holy Writ, then Archbishop of Lyons, and afterwards Cardinal of Ostia. He sat but for five months and two days and the seat was vacant for eighteen days. To him succeeded Adrian the Fifth, and sat for one month and nine days. He suspended the constitution of my lord Gregory regarding the election[2] of Cardinals, intending to substitute another. After

A.D. 1276.

[1] Near Castletown, Isle of Man. S. Michael, having been set to guard the gate of Eden after the expulsion of Adam, is commonly the patron of extra-mural churches and of islands, such as Mont-Saint-Michel and S. Michael's Mount.

[2] *De inclusione.*

him in the same year John the Twenty-first was elected, formerly called Peter the Spaniard. He sat for eight months and one day, and the seat was vacant for twenty-eight days. Through want of attention he altogether destroyed the constitution which his predecessor had suspended. Expecting greatly to prolong MS. fo. 190b his life, for he excelled in skill as a physician, he caused a new vault to be built at Viterbo, supported by a single column. In this [vault] when it fell, whether by treachery, as some say, or by accident, he alone was crushed, and, having received the sacraments, he survived for six days; and, albeit he was a physician, he did not heal himself.

There lived in Rome about this time a certain very rich man, notoriously a usurer, who, although often admonished for his sin, died at length excommunicate. His friends having assembled, preparation was made for his sepulture, and, in accordance with the customs of his country, he was placed on an open bier adorned with all his garments, and carried to the place of the Minorite Friars in the Capitol, the Church of S. Maria in the Ara Cœli, which used to be the chamber of Octavian, to be buried there. The Rector of the Friars there would not permit the wrong to be done of burying a vessel of Satan, a person excommunicated by the Pope, within the sacred walls; [so] his [the dead man's] insolent friends [and] poor dependents forced the priest to the altar, so that he should begin the mass by their command, [while] they opened the pavement of the church to dig a grave. And lo! an enormous parti-coloured wolf appeared at the door of the church, and, showing no fear of so great a gathering, seized the corpse in the presence of them all, and carried it out of the church without hindrance from anybody; nor is it known to this day what became of a hair of its head.[1] This was reported by one who was present in the church at the time.

Nicholas the Third, who was previously called John of Gaeta, a Roman by birth, was created Pope and sat for four years. He was so devoted to the blessed Francis that he caused to be painted above the altar in his chapel Saint Nicholas drawing him to heaven and St. Francis pushing him from behind. Also he caused the general chapter of the brethren of Assisi to be summoned to his presence in Rome by the Cardinal Legate, whereat he [the Pope] personally attended. Besides this he issued a famous bull, expounding the rule of Saint Francis —[a bull] so glorious as would [have] amazed all previous ages. A.D. 1277.

At this time Robert de Coquina[2] was created Bishop of Durham, being a monk of that house.

Also, Philip King of the French marched with a picked army against Spain, no doubt for the following reason. The eldest son of the King of Spain[3] had married the King of France's sister [Blanche], and, having had two sons by her, was carried off by an early death before his father. That father, utterly unmindful of [his] dead [son] endeavoured to supplant the sons of the defunct [prince] by putting forward

[1] *Quo vel capillus capitis devenerit:* an idiomatic phrase which I do not recognise.

[2] History repeats itself: the present Dean of Durham is the Very Rev. G. W. Kitchin, D.D.

[3] Ferdinand, son of Alfonso X. of Castile, killed in battle with the Moors, 1275.

the surviving brother. When the King of Aragon became aware of this, he had the boys brought [to him] and took care of them in one castle, while his mother passed the time with [her brother] the King of France. Roused by this [proceeding], the King of Castile (who is the principal lord of Spain) determined to break into the castle where the boys were guarded. [The King of France] having advanced in this manner with an immense army three days march into Spain to the aid of the King of Aragon and the boys, [his people] could find nothing to sustain life, [so they] returned within their frontier.[1]

I shall insert here as a joke a certain anecdote made known to me by Sir Robert of Roberstone, one of the King of Scotland's knights, which at my request he related before many trustworthy persons. The said noble gentleman owned a town in Annandale, in the diocese of Glasgow, which he let in farm to the inhabitants thereof.

These people, waxing lewd through their wealth and giving way to wantonness, on leaving the tavern, used to violate each other's wives or seduce each other's daughters, and by such practice would frequently replenish the archdeacon's purse, and, by repeating the offence, they were almost continually upon his roll. But when the landlord required the rent of his farm, they either pled poverty or besought delay. That kindly and just man said to them—'Why should you not pay me my annual rent, any less than my other tenants? If [the land] is let to you at too dear a rent, I can reduce it; if you are unable to cultivate it, give it back to me.'

[1] *Ora conclusi.*

'No, my lord,' quoth a comical fellow among them with a loud laugh, 'none of these things which you mention is really the cause; but our incontinence is so great, and it exhausts us so much, that it re-acts both upon us and upon you, our lord.'

Thereupon the landlord said—'I make this law among you, that any man who commits adultery shall relinquish my land forthwith.'

Taking alarm at this and deterred by the penalty, they refrained from illicit intercourse, applied themselves to labour and agriculture and began to make money unexpectedly, although day by day their names disappeared from the Archdeacon's list.[1] And when he [the Archdeacon] enquired one day why he did not find the men of that village [entered] in his list, it was explained to him what the landlord had laid down as a law for them. He was indignant at this, and, meeting the knight upon the road one day, exclaimed with a haughty countenance—'Pray, Sir Robert, who has appointed you either Archdeacon or official?'

Sir Robert denied [that he was either one or other], whereupon the Archdeacon replied—'Undoubtedly you exercise that office when you coerce your tenants by penal laws.'—'I made a rule about my lands, not about offences,' said Sir Robert; 'but you absorbed the rents of my farms [in exactions] for the discharge of crimes. I perceive that so long as you can fill your purse, it does not concern you who gets the souls!'

[1] *In rotulo Officialis, i.e.* the Archdeacon in his capacity as episcopal judge in the consistorial court, the nature of which office is explained in the preface to *Liber Officialis S. Andree*, published by the Abbotsford Club in 1845.

After this the assessor of crimes and lover of transgressors held his peace.[1]

At this time began the first war in Wales by King Edward, with whom Llewellyn made peace, having paid the king 50,000 pounds of silver.

A scutage was again imposed in England.

A.D. 1278. Brother Robert [of Kilwardby] my lord Archbishop of Canterbury, having been summoned to the Curia, there to be made a cardinal, Friar John of Peckham, Provincial Minister of the Minorite Friars of England, who, after [occupying] the chair of Paris and Oxford, where he presided in the faculty of Theology de Quolibet, was summoned to the Curia and exalted the reputation of the science of divinity and of his own Order; and, after a couple of years of controversy which he sustained mostly every day against sundry heretics, dissipating their arguments and answers, he was proclaimed Archbishop of Canterbury by Pope Nicholas in a public oration on [the day of] the Conversion of Saint Paul,[2] having been previously appointed. How humbly, sincerely, and industriously he afterwards discharged that office, tongues do testify and consciences applaud.

Also in this year Robert Wishart, Bishop of Glasgow, *effectus*;[3] he survives in health to the present time. But in October MS. fo. 191 Robert de Chalize, Bishop of Carlisle, died; [he was] eager for

[1] It is significant of the condition of the church at this time, that a story like this should be repeated as a joke—*causa ludi*—not by a layman, but by a cleric.

[2] 25th January, 1278-9.

[3] The meaning of *effectus* is obscure. He was made Bishop of Glasgow in 1271 and died in 1316. Either the chronicler has mistaken the year, or the word should be *affectus*, *i.e.* sick.

the honour of God, philanthropic and ready in urbanity; the world may testify without our assurance how bountiful and liberal he was. He used often to relate, in reproach of himself, what at this day may often be repeated in rebuke of others.

'I used to be,' said he, 'physician in ordinary to the Lady Eleonora, mother of the king, and another cleric, whose affection was dear to me, served as notary. It came to pass that our noble mistress, wishing to reward [our] services, bestowed upon me a benefice of one hundred marks and upon him one of thirty marks a year. Having been promoted, impelled by conscience, he soon determined to serve God exclusively, and, having obtained license and left the court, applied himself entirely to the cure of the souls committed to him. I [however], bound down by habit, adhered to the vanity which I had undertaken. As years went by a longing stirred me for the absent one—that I might enjoy the sight and conversation of him whom I bore in my mind, and, having obtained leave, I started to go to him, and found him on the Lord's day performing the dominical office in the church. He was astonished [to see] me; I embraced him, and the affairs of God having been performed, we proceeded to his dwelling to refresh our bodies. While we rested and rejoiced, there came to us some who brought the offerings of the neighbours, and he, for my pleasure, added to the delicacy of the dishes. And as we left the table I asked this man how he was able to live upon such an income.—"Perfectly," quoth he, "and every day as you have seen to-day; I am neither embarrassed by debts, nor am I diverted from ruling [my] parish."—"Your income," said I, "is a very modest one, but mine is ample; and in the court of my mistress I am maintained in her general expenses, nor do I profit at all from the fruits of my church." To which the other replied piously, with a bland smile[1]—"Do you know that God is a faithful friend?"—"Undoubtedly," said I, "I understand [that]."—"This is the character of a faithful and true friend," he replied, "that he is all in all to him who loves him truly. Wherefore, as I think, God is with me because I give myself up to perform his service; but it is otherwise with you, so he is not with you."'

To him [Bishop Robert] succeeded Ralph, Prior of Gisburn, a shrewd and provident person, but somewhat covetous, who turned the visitation of the churches into a whirlpool of exactions, and extorted from honest priests at their anniversaries throughout his diocese an unfair tax for building the roof of the principal church of his see.

At this time the coinage was changed; pennies and farthings were made round, and Jews were hanged for clipping coins. In the same year Robert, Lord Bishop of Carlisle, lost the presentation to the church of Rothbury.

In the same [year], on the morrow of All Souls, the Itinerant Justiciaries sat in Carlisle—to wit, Sir John de Vallibus,[2] Sir John de Metyngham, Sir William de Seaham, and Master Thomas de Suttrington.

In the same [year], on the day of S. Lucia Virgin,[3] the canons of Carlisle elected as bishop Master William de Rothelfeld, Dean of York, who utterly declined [to take] office; wherefore on the following day they elected as bishop my lord Ralph, Prior of

[1] *Caste subridens et catholice respondens.*

[2] Vaus, which, by an ancient clerical error, is now written Vans.

[3] 13th December.

Gisburne. To which the king would not give assent, being angry with the Prior and Chapter of Carlisle because they had twice elected without license; wherefore my lord Ralph betook himself to the Roman Court.

Walter, Archbishop of York died, an elegant cleric, chaste, sociable and free handed, but fretful and feeble because of his corpulence. To him succeeded William of Wykeham,[1] who, on the contrary, was lean, harsh and niggardly, but certainly so far as could be known out of doors, just in judgment and most tender of conscience. For, as I shall set forth later, according to the rules set by the holy fathers, it is held and ordained that diocesans and their monks shall be visited by the metropolitan. Concerning which matter Walter, his [Wykeham's] predecessor twice informed him who presided over that church of his coming; but, when he was proceeding on his perambulation, the Prior of Durham cunningly inveigled him out of the city to his own lodgings, [where] he might divert him from his purpose by more sumptuous fare and by oblations. On arriving there he [Bishop Walter] did not yield to the stratagem, but performed the ordinary visitation, so that if they had anything to plead for themselves or anything upon their conscience to be lightened, they should not delay putting it before him. But as they responded neither in law nor prudence, but closed the windows of the church and even shut the public gates of the city [against him], he set a chair for himself in the open space before the gates, in official vestments addressed the populace with words of life, and, explaining the object of his

A.D. 1279.

[1] Not the famous founder of Winchester College, who was not born till 1324.

coming and pronounced sentence of excommunication upon the rebels. This gave rise to troubles, lawsuits and expenses which are not yet settled, even in the days of his successor.

At this time there died [1] at Morebattle William Wishart, Bishop of S. Andrew's, and was buried at his see; to whom succeeded William Fraser, king's chancellor also, who still survives.

In the same year died Walter Giffard, Archbishop of York, of good memory; and in the same year Oliver was consecrated Bishop of Lincoln on S. Dunstan's day. [2]

Item—a great fire at S. Botolph's at fair time.

Item—in the aforesaid year began the second war in Wales by Llewellyn and his brother David.

At midsummer there took place the burning of Norwich Cathedral, and nearly all the convent, from the following cause.

A.D. 1280.

While we consider how poverty is the guardian of holiness, it is equally certain that affluence is the mother of insolence, and that, as Daniel prophesied of Antichrist, of all things wealth destroys most men. Accordingly the monks [of Norwich], enriched by their possessions, and puffed up in spirit, deposed their prior, a virtuous, but aged, man, and elected a haughty youth, who forthwith multiplied for himself stables and carriages, not even denying himself a lodging for his whore within the walls of the convent, after the example of infatuated Solomon. And, forasmuch as deep calleth unto deep, and sin leads on to further sinning, so this presumptuous prior infringed the liberties of the burgesses in the matter of

[1] *Recessit e seculo.*

[2] 21st October. This is one of the duplicate passages tending to show that the chronicle was compiled from several sources.

their property and pasture. The community being roused [thereby], there followed waste of money, wrath of minds and strife of words. It grew at length to this, that they prepared to fight against each other, and, while the Prior's men in the church tower had prepared Greek fire to discharge upon the town, and those on the other side were striving to set fire to the abbey gates (strong as they were and richly wrought), those stationed within assembled to defend them, when a fire broke out which, being foolishly neglected, first consumed the bell-tower, and then the entire church with all its contents; which notwithstanding they continued fighting fiercely outside and burning houses. Thus did the heedlessness of this rash Prior lead to the dishonour of the Creative Trinity, and later to the sacrifice in a horrible death of many citizens by royal justice. MS. fo. 191b

At this time the King of Norway died, leaving as successor his son called Magnus;[1] who hearing that the King of Scotland had an amiable, beautiful and attractive[2] daughter, a virgin, of suitable age for himself (being a handsome youth of about eighteen years), could not rest until a formal mission, divines as well as nobles, had been sent twice to obtain her as his spouse in marriage and consort on the throne. But before I bring to an end the narrative of this marriage, let me relate to the praise of God and his servant, what was told by one of the emissaries about his king [to show] to what height human affection may be carried.

The father of this king being deeply attached to the religion of S. Francis, encouraged the [Franciscan] brethren above all others, and interested himself diligently in their schools of sacred

[1] Eric II. (Magnusson). [2] *Morigerosam*, cf. Lucretius, iv. 1277.

theology, where, also, he set up for himself a mausoleum. It happened that the Queen brought forth her first-born on the said saint's day,[1] to the shame rather than to the joy, of the realm, [for it] resembled more the offspring of a bear than a man, as it were a formless lump of flesh. When this was announced to the king, strong in faith, he said, 'Wrap it in clean linen and place it on the altar of S. Francis at the time of the celebration.'

Which having been fulfilled, when they came at the end of the service to take away what they had placed there, they found a lovely boy crying, and joyfully returned thanks to God and to the saint. This [child] having grown up, sought the damsel in marriage, as aforesaid; and, although the union was very distasteful to the maiden, as also to her relations and friends (seeing that she might wed elsewhere much more easily and honourably), yet it was at the sole instance of her father, the king, that the bargain was made that he should give her a dowry 17,000 merks, primarily for the contract of marriage, but secondarily for the redemption of the right to the Isles.

On the morrow of S. Laurence[2] she embarked at . . .[3] with much pomp and many servants, and after imminent peril to life which they ran on the night of the Assumption of the Holy Virgin,[4] at daybreak on the said festival they lowered their sails at Bergen. Shortly afterwards she was solemnly crowned and proclaimed before all men by a distinguished company of kinsmen. She comported herself so graciously towards the king and his people that she altered their manners for the better, taught them the French and English languages,

[1] 16th July. [2] 11th August; but the year was 1281 not 1280.

[3] Blank in MS. [4] 15th August.

and set the fashion of more seemly dress and food. He only had one daughter by her, who survived her mother but a short time.

On the day before the nones of October[1] [occurred] the translation of the blessed Hugh Bishop of Lincoln, which translation Master Thomas de Bek was the means of obtaining and liberally discharged all expenses. On the same day he was consecrated Bishop of S. David's by Friar John of Peckham, of the Order of Minorites, Archbishop of Canterbury, in the presence of Edward King of England and his Queen.

From the beginning of the world 6080 years, to wit, in the year of our Lord 1280, on S. Mark the Evangelist's day,[2] it was decided in the court of Irthington that an attachment upon the elemosynary land of the prior and convent of Lanercost was null and void.

Item—My lord Ralph came to England about Ascension Day,[3] consecrated as Bishop of Carlisle by the Roman Court. In the same year, on Thursday the ninth of the calends of November,[4] a convocation was held by my lord Bishop Ralph in the principal church of Carlisle, and there was granted to him by the clergy a tithe of the churches for two years according to their actual value, to be paid in the new money within a year, wherefore we paid him in all twenty-four pounds. Wherefore H[5] said as follows about that transaction :

'Poor sheep; bereft of ghostly father;
Should not be shorn; but pampered rather.

---

[1] 6th October. [2] 25th April. [3] 30th May. [4] 24th October.

[5] Perhaps the chronicler himself. Dr. James Wilson identifies this Brother H. with Henry de Burgo, who became Prior of Lanercost in 1310. Verses cease to appear in the chronicle after 1315, the year of Prior Henry's death.

Poor sheep! with cares already worn,
You should be comforted; not shorn.
But if the shepherd must have wool,
He should be tender, just and cool.'[1]

In the same year my lord . . . [2] received the canonical dress, on the day of St. Agapitus Martyr.[3]

In the same year, on the third of the Ides of September[4] my lord Edward King of England and Queen Eleanor came to Lanercost, and the prior and convent met them at the gate in their capes.[5] Item, the king presented a silken robe, and the king in his hunting took, as was said, two hundred stags and hinds in Inglewood.

At that time some box of a certain page was broken [into], whereat H. said as follows:

'A pilfered chest yields shameful booty,
The thief, when caught, must learn his duty;
Ill-gotten gains return no profit,
Who steals his wealth makes nothing of it.'[6]

About the same time a certain young fellow was killed, about whom H. said:

'William, poor fellow, has proved by his fate,
He is wanting in prudence who stays out too late.'[7]

---

[1] *Grex desolatus, pastore diu viduatus,*
Sic cito tondere, non indiget, immo foveri;
Grex desolatus, nimis hactenus extenuatus,
Jam comfortairi debet, non excoriari.
Sed si pastor oves habeat tendere necesse,
Debet ei pietas, modus et moderamem inesse.

[2] Blank in MS. [3] 18th August. [4] 11th September. [5] *In Cappis.*

[6] *Res, cista fracta, surrepta fuit male nacta;*
Juste surreptus fuerat male census adeptus;
Finitur foeda prave saepissime praeda;
Raro dives erit thesaurum qui male quaerit.

[7] *Garcifer occisus Willelmus testificatur*
Quod non est sapiens nimium qui nocte vagatur.

LANERCOST PRIORY CHURCH

FROM THE SOUTH EAST

In the same year, on Sunday, the eleventh of the Kalends of April,[1] Ralph, Lord Bishop of Carlisle, first came to Lanercost on a visitation, and the monks met him in the manner described above for the king, and afterwards he gave [them] benediction, and received all the brethren to the kiss of peace, and after his hand had first been kissed, he gave them a kiss on the lips; and having himself entered the chapter house, he preached, saying—'Behold I myself shall require.' The preaching being finished, he proceeded with his visitation, in which we were compelled to accept new constitutions.

Martin the Fourth, a native of Touraine, succeeded to Pope Nicholas, and sat for four years. In his time, Peter, King of Aragon, took Sicily, having expelled Charles, and held it against all the power of the Pope and of the King of France, a crusade made against him taking little effect. A.D. 1281.

This [Pope] was named Simon, and was sent as special legate to France, but particularly to Paris, to allay discord among the scholars; for Satan had sown among them something of a schism, and every nation was striving for the highest place in the university. The legate having arrived and hearkened to the controversy, promulgated the law that the English had priority in that university; for, said he, Baeda went to Rome, and, coming to Paris, held classes before anybody else, founding sacred theology upon the gospel of S. John, and, by first teaching regularly, opened the way to all other sciences after him.[2] MS. fo. 192.

He [the Pope], being under vows to S. Francis, on the

[1] 22nd March.

[2] The Legate's ruling may have been right, but his argument was wrong, for Bede himself tells us that he never was out of England.

feast of Pentecost, without any suggestion (unless it were that of the Holy Ghost), decreed and bestowed upon [the Franciscans] by his plenary power the privilege of preaching the word of God, and hearing the confessions of all and sundry, not without [exciting] the wonder of many and the indignation of great persons. For at that time the friars in various provinces had been prohibited by twenty-one bishops from the exercise of the aforesaid [offices]. When he was dying he directed that he should be buried at the feet of S. Francis ; nevertheless, contrary to his wishes, he was interred at Viterbo.

At this time the King of England, intending to hunt in parts of Westmorland, prepared to set out for Gascony [provisioned] with all kinds of game, because Gaston de Biern, once loyal, but now a rebel, drawing back from his allegiance. In a short time he forced them [to desist] from their rash purpose, and returned home.[1]

It happened in the same year that two Minorite Friars of the convent of Dumfries were travelling the country of Annandale to preach at the holy Nativity of the Lord.[2] Howbeit, there was near where they passed the steward of a certain church and overseer of the rector's glebe, who, being oppressed with infirmity, felt obliged to make confession, but, intending not to do so honestly, concealed twenty gold pieces[3] which he had

[1] This passage must have been misplaced by the compiler. King Edward did not go to Gascony in 1281, and the reference is probably to his expedition in 1286-89, though the facts are very inaccurately stated.

[2] Christmas.

[3] *Solidos.* The term in late Roman coinage denoted a gold piece, the older *aureus* ; but in this place it may have signified 'shillings.'

embezzled from his master. Having received from his master the rector instructions to prepare the house for his coming, the sick man quitted the hall wherein he had lain until that time, and moved into a wattled barn, where a single girl ministered to the needs of his ailment. But one of these nights when these [two] were resting apart, there came some satellites of Satan, who entered the house about cock-crow, lit a fire, placed upon it a cauldron, and poured in water to heat it. A little afterwards two of these devils were sent to the bed of the sick man, lifted him out, soused him in the boiling water,[1] and then bound him dripping to the cross-beam of the house, tearing him with their nails, and jeering at him with—'Take that for the twenty pieces of gold.' This was done three times in succession, the woman all the time witnessing the punishment and listening to the accusation. Having perpetrated the cruelty which God permitted, his tormentors carried the wretched man back to bed. Then one of them exclaimed—'What shall be done to that woman lying there?' To whom the leader replied, 'That water is not suitable for her. She is the priest's whore, and hotter water will suit her better.'[2]

When he said this, they all departed; and the woman went to the sick man, and asked with trembling how he was, who answered her—'You beheld my torments; need you ask how I am? but, for the fear of God, let a priest come to me, and seek safety for yourself.'

Therefore when it was light she went a distance of five miles

[1] *Lixa aqua.*

[2] The meaning seems to be that devils are afraid of hot water, as explained by one of them in an episode described in the *Chronicle*, ad ann. 1257.

to Annan, where, having confessed herself, she found plenty of hot water.

In this year Sir John of Newcastle took the monk's dress at Holmcultram, upon which H. observed:

'With altered habit, habits too must alter,
Much need that John with sin no more should palter.
Unless to mend his ways he doth not fail,
White gown and snowy cowl will nought avail.'[1]

In the same year Sir Nicholas of Carlisle was sent to reside at Gisburn, and became a monk there.

A.D. 1282.

The Friars of the Cross who inhabit the land of Robert de Chartersborough, and raise pleasant buildings there, having carried architectural work[2] through the middle of the church, were preparing for themselves a lower choir, where lies the body of that just man, leaving the lower part to pilgrims, [who come] thither in order to perform vigils and burn candles. The spirit of the just man resented this and a tremendous flood, such as no man there remembers, carried the waters of the Nidd into the upper part and the middle of the church, destroying the vaulted work in the night, and [the spirit of the just man, Robert] allowed [the friars] to stand together, not as his masters but as his comrades, on the pavement which was raised only a little [above the flood].[3]

[1] *Mutatis pannis mutetur vita Johannis*
Ut melioretur et ei constantia detur.
Si tibi sit pulla capa, forte, vel alba cucalla
Et virtus nulla, merces tibi non datur ulla.

[2] *Arvali opere* in Dr. Stevenson's edition, which Mr. Neilson reasonably suggests is a misreading of *arcuali.*

[3] This passage is very obscure: but Mr. Neilson has elucidated it by revising the punctuation, and showing that *aqua de Nith* is not the Scottish Nith but the Yorkshire Nidd.

About the same time the rector of the church of Bothans[1] in Lothian caused the woodwork of his choir to be carved during Lent, to the honour of S. Cuthbert, whose church it is and for the credit of the place. But when the work was finished, on the vigil of the Saint,[2] while the rector was worrying himself about how the scaffolding, made of huge, rough beams, which the workmen had erected on the ground, could be removed so that it should be no impediment to the celebration, one of the workmen went up and loosed the upper lashings so that the supports threatened to fall down. And while the artizan was at a loss how to get down, suddenly the whole scaffolding collapsed, carrying him with it. A great shout arose, for the men supposed that he was crushed [to death], seeing that he had fallen upon a stone pavement; [but], on removing the beams they found the man not a bit the worse, even making fun of it with his rescuers. Thus did the Saint renew his ancient miracles [performed] at the time of his translation in the scaffolding of vaulted building.

About this time, in Easter week, the parish priest of Inverkeithing, named John, revived the profane rites of Priapus, collecting young girls from the villages, and compelling them to dance in circles to [the honour of] Father Bacchus. When he had these females in a troop, out of sheer wantonness, he led the dance, carrying in front on a pole a representation of the human organs of reproduction, and singing and dancing himself like a mime, he viewed them all and stirred them to lust by filthy language. Those who held respectable matrimony in honour were scandalised by such a shameless performance,

[1] Abbey S. Bathans. [2] 19th March.

although they respected the parson because of the dignity of his rank. If anybody remonstrated kindly with him, he [the priest] became worse [than before], violently reviling him.

MS. fo. 192b And [whereas] the iniquity of some men manifestly brings them to justice, [so] in the same year, when his parishioners assembled according to custom in the church at dawn in Penance Week, at the hour of discipline he would insist that certain persons should prick with goads [others] stripped for penance. The burgesses, resenting the indignity inflicted upon them, turned upon its author; who, while he as author was defending his nefarious work, fell the same night pierced by a knife, God thus awarding him what he deserved for his wickedness.

In the same year Sir Hugh of Ireland obtained a license to enter stricter religion in his country; but in the same year he suffered rejection because of discord between the Prior and the Convent. Wherefore H. remarked:

'What profits it to leap and thus to fall?
No son of man prevails to conquer all.
Better, sometimes, to halt than forward press;
Virtue may profit e'en from ill success.
A change of scene proves often no bad leech;
One hankers less for what seems out of reach.'[1]

In the same year Henry de Burgh was arrested at Durham

[1] *Quid prodest facere saltum et sic resilire?*
In nullo genere genus est quod circuit omne.
Sed quando tantum est casus causa salutis;
Robur virtutis passum dat saepe gravamen.
Est medicinalis mutatio saepe localis;
Res minus optatur prope si non esse sciatur.

and confined for three days in the castle because of an execution which he had performed for the Archbishop of York, wherefore he wrote to Master R. Avenel as follows:

'Robert! if legates pass their way
With privilege, as all men say,
Then let me out this very day
From prison walls wherein I stay.
Cloisters, not towers like these, befit me,
Thus prison rules the harder hit me;
Wherefore to pray your grace permit me,
Command my jailors to demit me.
God's House to all should aye be free
To come and go. I cannot see
Why I, who canon am professed,
Should thus in person be oppressed;
The benefit we clergy boast of
Is what at present I lack most of.
Guiltless I languish in this cell.
God help me! Who dost all things well.'

Hugh de Burgh[1] wrote thus to the Archbishop:

'O Primate of York! 'twas for you that I paid
With my freedom in Durham. They did me upbraid,
And maltreat my person. My servants departed
And left me the victim of men evil-hearted.
Three days I remained in that horrible tower,
Forbidden to leave it, alone hour by hour.
Holy Sire! if you do not avenge such an outrage,
Nor clergy nor brethren can brook it without rage.
Thus study to rule us, upholding the law,
Keeping good men in safety and rebels in awe.'

In the same year Llewellyn, Prince of Wales, was captured in a skirmish and beheaded incontinently.[2]

[1] Henry and Hugh must have been the same monk.

[2] He was slain in the field.

On the day following the feast of S. Agnes,[1] the King of Scotland's son, Alexander, was taken from this world, being only twenty years of age, dying on his birthday, changing the rejoicing for his birth into lamentation for his death; forasmuch as, had he lived, he would have been the light of his country and the joy of his kindred. He was carried off in Cupar-in-Fife by a lingering illness, with which he suffered a degree of mental aberration; [but], coming to his senses late on Thursday evening, he foretold regarding his death, on the morrow at sunrise should set the sun of Scotland; and for King Edward of England he said: 'My uncle shall fight three battles; twice he will conquer; in the third he will be overthrown.' These things I learnt from information of those who were with him when he died, whereof one was a knight and his tutor, the other was rector of the church and his priest.

A.D. 1283.

In like manner his sister, the Queen of Norway, took the way of death in the following month of February, only thirty days later, in order that God's long-suffering should by many afflictions soften to a proper [degree of] penitence[2] the heart of the father through whose wrong doing these things came to pass.[3]

In the unlucky course of that year, the Welsh nation, unable to pass their lives in peace, broke over their borders on Palm Sunday, carrying fire and sword among the people engaged in

[1] He died on 28th January. St. Agnes' day is the 21st, which was his birthday.

[2] *Patientia*, which Mr. Neilson suggests may be a misreading for *penitentia*.

[3] Certain clerics never wearied of imputing to Alexander III., the best king that the Scots ever had, responsibility for all the calamities which befel both his country and his family.

procession, and even laid siege [to some places]; whose Prince Llewellyn, deceived (more's the pity!) by the advice of his brother David, fiercely attacked his lord the King; as we read written about Christ, 'him whom I loved most hath set himself against me.' For the King had given his own niece, only daughter of the Earl of Montfort, a lady of noble birth [endowed] with the ample possessions of her father, in marriage to Llewellyn, by whom he had two sons. But David was so much in the king's confidence that he got himself appointed guardian of his [the King's] head in place of the great David ap Udachis.[1] And forasmuch as nothing is so deadly as an enemy within the household, he persuaded his brother to rebel, trusting after the act to conciliate the king by his [David's] proved devotion. Having therefore raised an army, the King went in person to Wales, accompanied by gallant men; where, albeit at great expense and loss of men, he first occupied the land of Anglesey [which was] fertile, abounding in all good things. Which [island] he divided among English farmers, removing the Abbey of Aberconway and founding it elsewhere; but in that place[2] because of its suitability he built a town, a castle and a spacious harbour, the ditch surrounding the castle with the tide.

At this time the head of Llewellyn, who had been slain by the treachery of his own people, was sent to the King, although he would not have approved of this being done.[3] However, it

[1] Obscure. Stevenson's edition reads *vice magni David apud achis*, which is unintelligible.

[2] At the mouth of the Conway.

[3] The fate of Llewellyn ap Gruffudd has been briefly noted already *ad ann.* 1282.

was taken to the Tower of London, and fixed upon a stake. Arising out of these events, the King took proceedings against the traitor David; for, having returned to Hereford, he intended to revisit the seat of his government, when fresh rumours reached him that the author of perfidy could not desist from adding to his iniquity. The King therefore resumed the campaign, and, determined to exterminate the whole people of that nation, he caused them to be beset by land and sea in the district of Snowdon with a great fleet, so that by famine he might crush those stoney hearts which relied upon [safety in] stones and rocks.

MS. fo. 193 At length [David], having been conquered through privation, surrendered, and the King sent him forward to the Tower of London with wife and children; and, having built Flint Castle, received the common people to mercy, having appointed his own bailiffs and [made] many new laws. He also possessed himself of the ancient and secret treasures of that people, [dating], as is believed, from the time of Arthur; among which he found a most beautiful piece of the Holy Cross, carved into a portable cross, which was the glory of their dominion and [carried] the presage of their doom. Which [cross], it is said, Helena kept after the Invention as a special portion, and brought with her when she returned to Britain with her husband. The Welsh had been accustomed to call it, after the fashion of their own language, 'Crosnaith.'

Thus the King returned from the said campaign about the Nativity of the Glorious Virgin,[1] bringing with him as proof of

[1] 8th September.

his triumph the ensign of salvation of the human race; and, with a great procession of nobles, bishops and clergy, brought that monument of our redemption to London to be adored by the citizens.

David's children were condemned to perpetual imprisonment, but David himself was first drawn as a traitor, then hanged as a thief; thirdly, he was beheaded alive, and his entrails burnt as an incendiary and homicide; fourthly, his limbs were cut into four parts as the penalty of a rebel,[1] and exposed in four of the ceremonial places in England as a spectacle; to wit—the right arm with a ring on the finger in York; the left arm in Bristol; the right leg and hip at Northampton; the left [leg] at Hereford. But the villain's head was bound with iron, lest it should fall to pieces from putrefaction, and set conspicuously upon a long spear-shaft for the mockery of London. Just as the holy Jeremiah composed metrical dirges for the desolation of Judaea, so the Welsh nation composed a heroic elegy upon the death of their Prince and the desolation of their nation, at the end whereof they always commemorate David with curses, forasmuch as he was the author of this misfortune, whereon H. spoke these lines:

'David of Wales, a thief and traitor,
Slayer of men, of Church a hater,
A fourfold criminal in life
Now dies by horse, fire, rope and knife.
The ruffian thus deprived of breath
Most meetly dies by fourfold death.'[2]

[1] *Depellatoris*, probably an error for *debellatoris*.

[2] *David Walensis, equus, ignis, funis et ensis,*
Infelix, fatum tibi dant recis et cruciatum.
Es nece quadrifida—fur, proditor ac homicida,
Hostis et ecclesiae debes de jure perire.

In the same year, John, Prior of Lanercost, resigned, for whom adequate provision was granted and confirmed under the seal of Bishop Ralph.[1] In the same year, on the morrow of the Assumption of the Blessed Mary,[2] Simon of Driffield was elected Prior.

Item, in the same year, on the fifth of the Ides of January,[3] William, Archbishop of York, was translated, whose translation was procured and the expenses thereof borne by Sir Antony Bek, who, in the same [year], was consecrated Bishop of Durham, in the presence of the King and chief men of the country.

In the same year, Edward the Fifth, son of Edward the Fourth, was born at Carnarvon.[4]

At the feast of Holy Trinity,[5] Robert de Coquina, Bishop of Durham, died, and when he was about to be interred in the

A.D. 1284. chapter house of that place, those who were making the grave impinged upon the tomb of a bishop unknown to them, Turgot, who had been Prior of Durham, and afterwards Bishop of St. Andrews in Scotland, but returning to Durham, ended his life in that place. By this time he had lain in the depth of the earth eight score and nine years, yet he was not only found entire in his body, but also in his vestments, the diggers having accidentally broken the case containing his pastoral staff. Having therefore shown the unchanged remains of this venerable man to several persons, they filled in

[1] Ralph de Ireton, Bishop of Carlisle.

[2] 16th August.

[3] 9th January.

[4] The chronicler reckons the Saxon kings named Edward in the list of English kings.

[5] 4th June.

the place with the earth that had been thrown out, and prepared elsewhere a grave befitting such remains.

We have seen this man, about whose funeral we are now speaking, in life bountiful enough and merry, also quite facetious enough at table. It occurred to me once to extract a meaning from his sport, by way of example. For instance, he kept in his court, after the custom of modern prelates, as some relief from their cares, a couple of monkeys—an old and a young one. One day at the end of dinner, desiring to be refreshed by amusement rather than by food, [the bishop] caused a silver spoon with whitened almonds to be placed in the enclosure of the younger monkey, the bigger one being kept away [from it]. She [the little monkey], seeing the coveted food, and wishing to avoid being despoiled by the bigger one, made every endeavour to stuff all the contents of the spoon into her left cheek, which she managed to do. Then, just as she thought to escape with the spoil, the older monkey was released, and ran to her, seized the right cheek of the loudly screaming little one, drew out all that was stuffed into the left cheek, as if out of a little bag, and refreshed itself, until not a single [almond] was left. Everybody who saw this burst out laughing, but I perceived therein an image of the covetous of this world, calling to mind that proverb of Solomon in the twenty-second [chapter]: 'He that oppresseth the poor to increase his riches, shall himself give to a richer man and come to want.'[1]

At the feast of All Saints in this year, Alexander, King of

[1] The vulgate here differs in sense from the authorised version, where the passage runs, 'and he that giveth to the rich.'

Scotland, took a second wife, Yoleta by name, daughter of the Comte de Dreux, to his own sorrow, and to the almost perpetual injury of his kingdom, as will be repeatedly made clear.

In the same year [a son] was born to King Edward at Carnarvon in Snowdon, upon whom was bestowed his father's name on S. Mark the Evangelist's day.[1]

During that war in Wales a bridge of boats was made in the place called Menai, that is, between Snowdon and Anglesey, where Sir William de Audley, Lucas Tanay, Roger de Clifford and many others, old and young, were drowned.

In the same year there was granted to my lord the King of England a twentieth of all the churches of England.

Pope Martin departed from this world, to whom succeeded

A.D. 1285. Honorius the Fourth, who sat for two years. Feeble and gouty, he was made Pope from [being] Cardinal, and being able neither to walk nor stand, made for himself a revolving chair. On the day of his consecration, one of the cardinals made these verses upon him at the instance of certain brethren :

> 'They place a wretched hulk in Peter's seat,
> Maimed of both hands and lamed in both his feet.'[2]

Howbeit, he did one good thing in publicly reproving [all] false apostles, *orbanibulos* and ribald persons who had started in the city itself without authority from the Roman see, and in issuing
MS. fo. 193b written orders that if any such persons were apprehended, they should first be warned to relinquish their sect and enter the cloister of holy religion, and if they did not comply with this,

[1] 25th April.

[2] *Ponitur in Petri monstrum miserabile sede,*
Mancus utroque manu, truncus utroque pede.

they should be handed over to the public authority. In connection with this a certain trustworthy burgess of Hartlepool declared on his return from Rome that he knew of a dozen of these fellows being beheaded in one day. Two of them also were arrested in Berwick, with their wives and children, and were found to be carrying long daggers at their hips and purses full of silver.

In the course of this year King Alexander of Scotland was removed by sudden death from the world after he had reigned thirty-six years and nine months. He departed from the world on the fourteenth of the kalends of April,[1] late on Monday night, being the vigil of S. Cuthbert, Bishop and Confessor, the liberties and bounds of whose Bishopric he [Alexander] had violated for three years past. And whereas it was held by the superior [clergy][2] that the Lord would remove from the world both his children and his wife during his own lifetime for his chastisement, and [whereas] that did not cause him to reform, any one may perceive how there was fulfilled in him holy Job's prophecy, which saith: 'God will visit upon his children the sorrow of the father, and when he has accomplished [this] he shall know it.'

Of a truth it was foretold to him by just men that the Lord had shaken His sword against him, that He had bent and made ready His bow against him, and had prepared many arrows against him, etc. Besides all this there was repeated in the province throughout the whole of that year a fatal saying by the Scots, that at that time should come the Judgment Day, at which many trembled and a few scoffed.

[1] 19th March.

[2] *Superioribus*, perhaps meaning 'old people.'

In December preceding, next before these [events], under the sign of Capricorn, many terrible thunderings were heard and lightning was seen, which, in the opinion of wise men, presaged the overthrow of princes, who were [thus] warned to take heed to themselves. But whereas all these and other warnings were of no avail to enlighten his [Alexander's] mind, God punished him by the means He appointed. For he [Alexander] used never to forbear on account of season or storm, nor for perils of flood or rocky cliffs, but would visit, not too creditably [both] matrons and nuns, virgins and widows, by day or by night as the fancy seized him, sometimes in disguise, often accompanied by a single follower. On that very day, then, when judgment was imminent (though he suspected it not) there arose such a mighty tempest that to me and most men it seemed disagreeable to expose one's face to the north wind, rain and snow. On which day, he [Alexander] was holding a council in the lofty Castrum Puellarum[1] with a great assembly of the nobles of the land, for the purpose of replying to the emissaries of the King of England, who were due at Norham on the third day [after] with the bodily presence of Thomas of Galloway, whose release from prison was besought at that time by Sir John de Baliol, the son of the older Baliol.

When they had sat down to dinner, he [Alexander] sent a present of fresh lampreys[2] to a certain baron, bidding him by an esquire to make the party merry, for he should know that this was the Judgment Day. He [the baron], after returning thanks, facetiously replied to his lord: 'If

[1] Edinburgh. [2] *De murena recenti.*

this be the Judgment Day, we shall soon rise with full bellies.'

The protracted feast having come to an end, he [Alexander] would neither be deterred by stress of weather nor yield to the persuasion of his nobles, but straightway hurried along the road to Queensferry, in order to visit his bride, that is to say Yoleta, daughter of the Comte de Dru, whom shortly before he had brought from over the sea, to his own sorrow and the perpetual injury of the whole province. For she was then staying at Kinghorn. Many people declare that, before her engagement beyond the sea, she had changed her dress in a convent of nuns, but that she had altered her mind with the levity of a woman's heart and through ambition for a kingdom.

When he arrived at the village near the crossing, the ferry-master warned him of the danger, and advised him to go back; but when [the King] asked him in return whether he was afraid to die with him: 'By no means,' quoth he, 'it would be a great honour to share the fate of your father's son.' Thus he arrived at the burgh of Inverkeithing, in profound darkness, accompanied only by three esquires. The manager of his saltpans, a married man of that town, recognising him by his voice, called out: 'My lord, what are you doing here in such a storm and such darkness? Often have I tried to persuade you that your nocturnal rambles will bring you no good. Stay with us, and we will provide you with decent fare and all that you want till morning light.' 'No need for that,' said the other with a laugh, 'but provide me with a couple of bondmen, to go afoot as guides to the way.'

And it came to pass that when they had proceeded two

miles, one and all lost all knowledge of the way, owing to the darkness; only the horses, by natural instinct, picked out the hard road. While they were thus separated from each other, the esquires took the right road; [but] he, at length (that I may make a long story short), fell from his horse, and bade farewell to his kingdom in the sleep of Sisara. To him Solomon's proverb applies: 'Wo unto him who, when he falls, has no man to raise him up.' He lies at Dunfermline alone in the south aisle, buried near the presbytery. Whence [comes it] that, while we may see the populace bewailing his sudden death as deeply as the desolation of the realm, those only who adhered to him most closely in life for his friendship and favours, wet not their cheeks with tears?

But, whereas a chronicle which strews its course with extinguished cinders will be deemed too dry, I shall here relate, to the praise of the incorrupt Virgin, what befel on the Annunciation[1] immediately after this event. In that kingdom there is a village called Stanehouse[2] on this side of the burgh of Stirling, wherein a farmer, not sufficiently respecting the feast of the Conception of the Son of God,[3] went to the plough, yoked his team, and, having set his own son to drive the animals, began to plough the turf. But as the oxen did not go fast enough, and by avoiding [the yoke] drew a crooked furrow, the obstinate fellow cried to his son to goad them, and shouted curses on the beasts. At length, wrought into a fury, he seized a plough staff, and, meaning to deal a

[1] 25th March. [2] Stenhouse in Larbert parish.

[3] *I.e.* the Annunciation. Father Stevenson, confusing it with the Conception of the Virgin, noted it as 8th December.

heavy blow on the restive one of the oxen, he aimed amiss, and struck the head of his own son, who fell dead. Thus he became the murderer of his own offspring, an outlaw from his own people, obnoxious to the Author of Salvation, and the betrayer of his own [cause].[1]

After so evil a fate as the death of their king, the magnates of the realm of Scotland, adopting sound counsel for themselves, elected from the prelates as well as the nobles, Guardians of the Peace for the community, until such time as it should be made clear by deliberation what person should be accepted for such rule. They governed the country for six years, transacting the affairs of the people, and, before all, of the Lady Queen, widow of Alexander, assigning a portion as her terce. But she, resorting to feminine craft, was pretending to be pregnant, in order to cause patriots to postpone their decision, and that she might more readily attract popularity to herself. But just as a woman's cunning always turns out wretchedly in the end, so she disquieted the land with her pretences from the day of the King's death till the feast of the Purification,[2] nor would she admit respectable matrons to examine her condition ; [and], in order that she might return ignominy upon those from whom she had received reverence and honour, she determined to deceive the nation for ever by foisting on herself the child of another. She caused a new font to be made of white marble, and she

MS. fo. 194

A.D. 1285.

[1] It was by tales like these, diligently circulated, that the clergy terrified their flocks into due observance of holy days ; but in this instance the moral had been more apparent if the punishment had fallen upon the impious father instead of the innocent son.

[2] 2nd February.

contrived to have the son of a play-actor to be brought [to her] so that it might pass for hers; and when as many as collected to dance by license [in honour of] so important an accouchement had come to Stirling (the place where the aforesaid lady was staying) at the time for her to be brought to bed (which she herself had arranged beforehand), her fraud was detected and revealed by the sagacity of William of Buchan, to the confusion of all present, and to all those willing to trust her who heard of it afterwards.[1] Thus did she, who was first attracted from over the sea only by the prospect of wealth and was united to the King in marriage, depart from the country with shame. That I have said so much about the fidelity of women is my reason for adding another instance in a different matter.

Four years before this time there befel something else which, out of reverence for God's name and worship, must not be concealed. Certain scholars, residing at Oxford for the purpose of study, yielded themselves to sleep one of these days after supper. One of them, less careful about his comfort than the rest, but as merry and lively as the rest, went to his usual bed in some upper chamber. About midnight his companions were alarmed to hear him shouting, striking and gnashing his teeth, and roused their fellow-lodgers. Hastening to his bed-side they found the man speechless, behaving as if on the point of death; but, which is very wonderful, his whole body presented such a horrible appearance that you would have believed him to be a filthy Ethiopian rather than a Christian. And so, as all of them thought that his peril was urgent,

[1] For *confodere* in Stevenson's text read *confidere*.

one of them of more fervid faith than the others, exclaimed: 'Let one of us begin the holy gospel of God according to John, and I hope it will relieve the sick man.' Whereupon the others, stimulated by faith, began to recite the holy gospel in parts, because they did not know the whole of it; and lo! the evil spirit having gone out of him, in the hearing of them all, shook to the ground the great stone stair which led to the door of the chamber, leaving after his exit such a stench that they almost thought they would be suffocated. The sick man, however, restored to life by the sound of the holy words, shortly afterwards returned from the sooty appearance to his natural looks. This was related by a trustworthy person who was among them, and saw, heard and noted [the occurrence], and first of all pronounced [the words of] the gospel.

In the same year, on the sixth day of the week before the nativity of S. John the Baptist,[1] there occurred at Bywell, near Newcastle, something which ought to be remembered. There was in that place a married man, steward to the Lady of *Vallnor*, who under cover of his office had acquired many things dishonestly, and enriched himself from the property of others. Arriving at the close of life, he was advised by a priest that, among other things to be settled by the dying man, he should provide out of his property for the redemption of his soul. The one firmly insisted upon this, and the other on the contrary denied it, besides swearing falsely that he had nothing to make a will about, and could scarcely be persuaded to bestow sparingly part of each of his different kinds of property, saying: 'Whatever is over I commend to Satan.'

[1] 19th June.

After the close of his life, while his body was being carried to the church, and the funeral feast was being made ready in the house for the neighbours by the son and the servants, suddenly fire burst out from his house, which was towards the western part of the town, and consumed the whole buildings on either side of the street, following the body towards the east so swiftly that the mass to be celebrated for him could scarcely be fully performed, nor could the wretched corpse be committed to the grave with the proper rites. Nay, but the devouring flame even consumed two large and beautiful parish churches, all their contents being burnt, one [being] S. Peter's, where he [the dead man] was committed to the earth, the other, S. Andrew's. And inasmuch as the wind had increased in violence, a ball of fire crossed the adjacent river and reduced to ashes two villages distant half a league. These facts were known to the whole country, and to myself also, who shortly afterwards beheld the traces of conflagration, and was instructed very fully about the event by the inhabitants.[1]

About the same time, or a little before, it happened in Lunedale, in the diocese of York, that a certain widower, who was called Clerk of the Chapter, was accused, and falsely, by a certain woman, of having plighted troth[2] with her in youth upon oath, as she pretended. The clerk, however, being summoned, denied it altogether, although freely confessing that when he was young and lustful he had committed common

[1] Bywell, on the North Tyne, consists of two parishes, Bywell–St. Andrew's and Bywell–St. Peter's, the churches being close together and locally known as the White church and the Black church respectively.

[2] *Praestita.*

fornication with her. But he was deemed by all his acquaintances so worthy of credit that he could by no means assent to the falsehood. Therefore a day was assigned for the woman to prove her charge; while the Episcopal judge, as well as the Dean and the rest, urged the clerk not to conceal the truth from them, and they themselves would provide means of escaping [the consequences]. He, on the contrary, became ever more immoveable, declaring and swearing that the affair was not otherwise [than he had stated]. At last, after many precautions and delays, the woman was brought up with the witnesses for her, and the duties of episcopal judge in this part of Lancashire were committed to a certain rural vicar who had formerly been Dean. And because he hesitated to accept the oath offered, believing it to be an afterthought, he publicly requested all present that they would unite in repeating before God the Lord's Prayer, so that He should grant them on that day that they should not proceed with an unjust cause. At this moment the woman, kneeling down, stretched out her hand to the book, when suddenly she fell upon the bosom of the said vicar, as if composing herself to sleep. But the vicar, thinking that she was trying to cajole MS. fo. 194b
him by such wanton behaviour (for she was beautifully adorned), said: 'Get up! why do you lie down thus? Finish what you have begun.' But when she gave no sign of feeling or movement, he raised her in his hands, and showed to all [present] that she was dead. He who told me this had it from the lips of the vicar who held the chapter.

In this year the Welsh again brought upon themselves misfortune, provoking afresh a royal expedition against themselves;

and David himself, author of the mischief, was taken and slain (as you will find in the ninth chapter).[1]

At this time on the vigil of S. John the Baptist,[2] William of Wykeham, Archbishop of York, came to Durham for a visitation, where he suffered an undignified repulse, not only from the monks but from the laity also, so that he thought he must appeal to arms. Which insult God beheld from on high, and, albeit he is slow to vengeance, yet he afterwards vindicated [himself] through Antony,[3] who afterwards visited them severely enough.

In the same year, on All Souls Day, the body of Thomas, first Lord of Multon, was moved.[4]

In the same year John Peckham, Archbishop of Canterbury, attacked vigorously the preaching friars[5] upon the unity of form.

At the octave of the Epiphany,[6] Antony Bek, King's Clerk, was consecrated Bishop of Durham in presence of my lord the King and the Queen and almost all the nobility of the land, not without great searching[7] of conscience as to what kind [of person] should be appointed Christ's vicar and suffragan of His church.

A.D. 1286.

On the following day, with the utmost rejoicing, they translated the relics of Archbishop S. William[8] enclosed in a costly

[1] See page 34 *antea*. [2] 23rd June. [3] Antony Bek, Bishop of Durham.

[4] *Translatum. Corpus domini Thomæ de Multona primi.* The title *dominus* is ambiguous; sometimes it means a feudal lord, sometimes, merely an honorary prefix to a cleric's name.

[5] *Prædicaciter* in Stevenson's text is probably a misreading for *prædicatores.* Peckham supported the doctrine of unity of form of Christ's body in the Eucharist, and was actively promulgating it at this time.

[6] 13th January. [7] *Singultus.*

[8] William Fitzherbert, Archbishop of York, d. 1154, canonised in 1227.

DURHAM CATHEDRAL

FROM THE RIVER WEAR

shrine, who when living was profligate for a time, but turned himself resolutely to righteousness.

About the same time, as he himself informed me, there lived at Rome a certain Minorite Friar of English birth, who, in travelling round the places of the saints, arrived one day after dinner at a house of virgins consecrated to God, erected in honour of S. Agnes. After he had inspected the church thereof, he found an old cardinal sitting with his [clergy] behind the high altar; who, the boards fixed to the back of the altar having been removed, was contemplating, for the strengthening of his faith, the body of the martyr without a taint of corruption consecrated to God; because this [cardinal] was perfectly faithful to God. When he had bedewed his face plentifully with tears, he uncovered the virgin [martyr's] countenance, which was hidden under a black veil, and beheld, with all [the others], the youthful features as it were of one sleeping, showing no hollows except at the point of the nose, and also the shoulders and fingers as flexible as they may be seen in a man lately dead and not long passed away. In addition, the arms and the body, which was not larger than that of a girl of twelve years old, were clothed with a tunic of some unknown white material, so fine [in texture] that none who beheld it could doubt that it was the raiment brought to her from heaven by angels.[1] But if any one should be at the pains to collect the records of early times, he will find that there were then completed one thousand years from the time of her martyrdom. These things therefore I have described

[1] The reference is to the miraculous robe which was brought to Agnes by angels when she was exposed naked in a brothel.

in order that the reader may note by what a distance God separates the incorruptible sons of corruption from the sons of iniquity.

In the same year John Romanus returned consecrated by the Roman court.[1]

In the same year King Edward of England sailed across to Gascony.

Nicholas the Fourth was created Pope after Honorius, and sat for four years, one month and twenty days. He
A.D. 1287.
was formerly called Jerome, being a Minorite Friar and Minister General of the Order, [and] Cardinal of La Sabina. As Head of the Church he displayed such humility as to discharge the guards[2] which his predecessors had for the protection of their persons, and caused jesters' bladders to be carried before him. So sincere a friend also was he of poverty that he entirely abandoned the suits of wealthy persons to his colleagues, and specially reserved for himself the suits of the poor. He granted privileges very seldom, and even these were insignificant; but he was most earnest in raising funds for an expedition to the Holy Land, wherefore he decreed that a sexennial tithe should be collected in every parish church for that purpose.

Because of the fame of this [Pope's] justice, the aforesaid Lord Archbishop of York hastened to his Court to lay before him the case of his church, and on the journey was struck down by fever at *Pountenei* and died, feeling that the thing in his life which he chiefly regretted was that he had received and consecrated an unworthy [Prior of]

[1] As Archbishop of York, 1285.

[2] *Clavarios.*

Durham.[1] It is affirmed by very many persons that the truth of his life manifests itself in miracles at the place where he lies, and it is said to possess special benefit for fever patients.

My lady Eleanor, mother Queen of England, now, for Christ's sake, despised the withering flower of this world wherein she had formerly delighted, and on the feast of the Assumption[2] was made a nun at Amesbury, where she had already dedicated her own daughter to God. For love of her my lord the King, her son, increased the wealth of that house with large rents.

In the same year Risamaraduc, one of the most noble men of Wales, began hostilities against royalists, and especially the English. Wherefore my lord the King of England expended 15,050 pounds of silver upon infantry alone, besides the expenses of the nobles. He [Risamaraduc] was ultimately captured and drawn at York.

At this time the wall of Castle Droslan fell and crushed Sir William de Michens and the Baron of Stafford.

In the same year a certain esquire named Robert Chamberlain,[3] with his accomplices, set on fire the booths of tradesmen at S. Botulph's,[4] and, as the fire spread, he burnt down a great part of the town and the church of the Preaching Friars; and while the tradesmen exerted themselves to put out the fire so as to save their goods, they were slain by the said esquire and his people, and their goods were plundered.

[1] Alluding to his controversy with Antony Bek over the subjection of Durham to the see of York

[2] 15th August.

[3] Or Chambers, sc. *Camerarius*.

[4] Boston.

There was such abundance of crops in England this year that a quarter of wheat was sold in some places for twenty pence, in others for sixteen and [in others] for twelve.

In the same year the Carmelite Friars changed their habit at Lincoln on the day of the Exaltation of the Holy Cross.[1]

MS. fo. 195 Sir John de Vesci died and was buried at Alnwick.

In the same year there abode with us William Greenrig, who used to eat neither flesh nor fish; about whom H. said:

> 'You may not seek the monkish dress to wear,
> Who cannot feed yourself on common fare?'[2]

Also about a certain malefactor, H.:

> 'For the sinner who fears not the keys of St. Peter,
> Than death at the stake what reward can be meeter?'[3]

On the vigil of the Lord's Ascension[4] the church of Gisburn in Cleveland was burnt by an unfortunate accident. A.D. 1288. For the plumber to whom was committed the duty of repairing the roof of the church had been employed in making good some defects about the bell tower. He had carelessly put a fire which he had for heating his tools near the timbers of the church, and when he went down to the lower buildings of the monastery had taken no heed to the danger. As the monks, having performed their solemn litanies, were returning through

[1] 14th September.

[2] *Vivere sub veste non quaeras canonicali,*
Commune more qui nequis, hortor, ali.

[3] *Qui se dant sceleri, claves Petrique vereri*
Nolunt, terreri debent de morte rogi.

In these couplets H.'s prosody is even more shaky than usual, at least according to classical standards.

[4] 5th May.

the fields and houses, fire broke out suddenly in the upper part of the tower, and as there was no remedy at hand, only a few valuables were got out and many thousand marks' worth was burnt.

There happened also something else to enhance the honour of S. Francis, which at that time had not become sufficiently well-known to the northern part of the English province.[1] A certain burgess in the town of Newcastle, who is alive at this day, Alexander Furbur [by name], contracted such a severe hot dropsy that he was given up by the physicians, and, from the swelling of his body, presented the appearance of a great tun, while his legs were beyond the compass of any leggings. This man, constrained between dread of praying and love of his children,[2] being ill-prepared to meet death, brought himself round to seek God's pardon and the help of the saints. By advice of his friends he caused himself to be measured[3] with various saints upon whose assistance his hope more fully relied. And whereas he felt relief from the power of none of them, he made a vow to S. Francis that he would personally visit his tomb, if through his help he should recover the health he desired. In that very moment, therefore, he was affected by a flow of water so continuous that it never ceased running for

[1] Of Franciscans. The 'English province' was early divided into two parts, one being Scotland, the other England.—*Monumenta Franciscana R.S.* i. 32-3.

[2] *Inter timorem precaminum et amorem pignorum.*

[3] *Mensurari*: a common form of invoking a saint's help. A string with which the saint's body had been measured was passed round the forehead of the sick person (see Camden Society's *Rishanger*, p. 152). Other explanation occurs in a late edition of Ducange, to the effect that a candle of the height of the sick person was placed in the saint's shrine.

the rest of that day and the whole of the following night, so that it sufficed to fill a very large tub. Hence the skin of his body became so loose through loss of flesh that, to the neighbours who gathered to view him he would stretch out his skin like a garment, and it seemed as if he could make himself leggings about his shins out of his own hide. Having thus recovered some degree of strength, straightway he set out upon a journey piously to fulfil his vow, and shewed forth the praises of God's saint in presence of many persons, returning home happy and healthy, having many witnesses, including myself, to this event.

On the other hand, I will relate something that may instruct posterity how great is the difference between God's service and worldly vanity. There lived at that time in the diocese of Glasgow a young cleric, strong and handsome, and beneficed out of the patrimony of Christ; but, as is to be deplored, more concerned in mind about getting into the company of rich men than about the cure of souls. He who neglects his own [soul], despises or vilifies that of another. And so this vain man, called Adam Urri, learned as a layman in lay law and disregarding God's precepts against Ulpian's *Prætorialia*,[1] used to employ the laws for litigation, lawsuits for quibbling, the statutes of the Emperors for pecuniary gain. But when he had become advanced in years and had become notorious for his villainy, and was endeavouring to involve the affairs of a certain poor widow in his toils, the divine mercy arrested him, chastising his body with a sudden infirmity and enlightening his mind so that he should discern more of hidden things and discourse of

[1] Roman law.

another life. For, lying in bed for four days and having made confession, he altered his intention of wronging the widow, foretold the day of his death, vehemently condemned the court of pleaders, and ordered his servant to come quickly to him, adding that just as he himself would go first on the Saturday, so he [the servant] would follow next Monday, just as the event turned out in the end.

At that time King Edward was staying in Gascony, and on a certain day when he and the queen, having met together in a chamber, were sitting conversing upon a couch, a flash of lightning entered a window behind them, and, passing between them, killed two domestics who were standing in their presence, they themselves remaining wholly unhurt. All the rest who were present were amazed on beholding what had happened, discerning that a miracle had not been wanting for the royal safety.

At this time on the fourteenth of the kalends of August,[1] Brother N. de Mor received the canonical habit. The Dominical letter was then C.

In the same year many of those who burnt Botelstane[2] were hanged.

The King of England returned from the lands of Gascony, whither he had gone to put down the sedition among the people of Bordeaux. For, having received there an embassy from Scotland urgently beseeching him that he would deign to assist them in their leaderless condition, and that he would take charge of their realm until they should succeed in getting a prince regularly elected, he set out with them to his native land, where he soon heard grave complaints

A.D. 1289.

[1] 19th July.

[2] Boston.

about the corruption of the justiciaries of the province, who, in the king's absence, and blinded by bribes, had betrayed the justice of their country. Moreover, there were in collusion with them,[1] enfeoffed knights or beneficed clergy, whose misdeeds, when detected, brought much treasure into the royal store, that the Solomon's precept should be observed, who says in the twenty-second of Proverbs: 'He who oppresseth the poor to increase his own wealth, shall himself give to a richer man and come to want.' Those, then, that are greedy of fame and rob the poor, when they are adjudged punishment for the deeds they have done, lose also what they appeared justly to possess. This happened manifestly to these [persons], although I am unable to state the fine [inflicted upon] all of them, yet I know that one of them, a rector of Holy Church, paid to the king upwards of thirty pieces[2] of silver and as many carucates of land.

MS. fo. 195b Concerning the Jews, I will relate an instance of their injustice occurring at this time, which may be of no small service to posterity against the crime of perjury and fraud.[3] In upper Lindsey, then, there is a priory, in the place called Marchby, occupying long and broad pastures for feeding stock, not altogether by exclusive right, but sharing with their neighbours a common liberty by gift of the patrons. But whereas avarice, [which is] in the minds of all men of the present day, endeavours to make all common [lands] private property, the aforesaid

[1] Or 'frequently'; *communiter*.

[2] *Bigatus* is a synonym for the Roman *denarius* = 8½*d.*; but the term *bigatas* evidently represents a far larger amount here.

[3] *Pervasionis*.

monastery brought an action in London to the prejudice of all their neighbours, the suit having been suborned and the judges bribed. But as they [the commoners] defended their cause at great legal expense, the matter was at length submitted to the verdict of twelve. But they [the jury] casting aside all reverence for God and the truth, and perpetrating fraud for the sake of favour, adjudged the ground to be freehold of the said monastery, and they [the monks] caused a great part of the land to be ploughed in token of seisin. But, on the other hand, God did not allow His name to be usurped with impunity, and he sowed the furrows of unrighteousness with the infamy of the act. For the twelve jurymen began to be steadily, but gradually, removed from the world, and ever as they were removed they were submitted to a terrible yoke. For during about two years afterwards there appeared in that country a fiery plough, glowing like hot brass, having a most foul fiend as driver, who drove the dead men, harnessed in that manner, to the ground where he had incited them to guile when living. Many persons beheld these wretches clearly, committed to the plough like oxen, always at the hour of noon, and this, I imagine, was done because it is at such an hour men most assiduously press litigation[1] before the judges. Those coming to behold the spectacle were warned to be careful for their safety; nor did they know[2] for whom were reserved those yokes which they perceived to be empty. Howbeit, after these years Alan of Hotoft, the spiritual advocate of the said prior in this suit, and the contriver of the fraud which it is not expedient to explain in detail, was seen plainly before [men's]

[1] *Prætoria negotia.* [2] *Innotescebant.*

eyes after his death driving and guiding the said plough; and repeatedly addressing many of them, he explained to them the reason for that punishment, and implored urgently that the judgment which had been pronounced might be revoked, if in compassion they proposed to mitigate the punishment of these [persons]. Although all this was made public throughout the province, yet was I unwilling to believe it easily, until I heard particulars of the truth from the lips of a certain nobleman, who lived not more than three miles from the place in question.

At this same date King Edward gave his daughter, the Lady Joan of Acre, in marriage to Gilbert Earl of Gloucester, with great celebration, that the bond of love should be more strongly knit. Also in the same year the king gave his second daughter Margaret to John, son and heir of the Duke of Brabant.

In the same year John Romayn was created Archbishop of York, a man of mean birth but sufficiently distinguished in science; in fact he was an eminent authority in dialectics and theology.[1]

The clipping of coins which was detected at this time rendered the new coinage necessary, which is now current; but forasmuch as the Jews were afterwards found to be the perpetrators of clipping both the old coins and the new, besides being authors of all kinds of crime—usury, rapine, sacrilege, theft (which is excessively common among them), and corrupters of the Christian faith—they were all proscribed in accordance with the advice of Parliament, unless they either professed the faith of the Church

[1] Already recorded *ad ann.* 1286, whereas the consecration took place in 1285. This is another indication, were one required, of the chronicle having been compiled from several different sources.

or supported themselves exclusively by manual labour. Besides, there was a day appointed for their clearing out of the realm,[1] so that those [who should be found] within the bounds of England after the day of S. John the Baptist[2] should suffer penalty.

On the feast of S. Bartholomew,[3] Patrick Earl of Dunbar, departed this life at Whittingehame, a man whom we have seen to be addicted to many vices, but who was mercifully forgiven by God on his deathbed. His body rests in the church of Dunbar, lying buried on the northern side.

Also, Duncan Earl of Fife, was cruelly slain on the Saturday preceding the Nativity of the Virgin.[4] He was the chief Guardian of Scotland for the time. As a young man he was cruel and greedy beyond all that we commonly have seen, abstaining from no injustice whereby he could minister to his avarice. And when curses without number had accumulated upon him, and enmities provoked by his deeds had been deservedly roused against him, he was slaughtered on horseback by his own men and kinsfolk as he was travelling along the king's highway to Parliament, and was buried in Cupar Abbey.[5] He had recently married the Lady Joan, daughter of the Count of Gloucester, who being with child at the time of her husband's murder, afterwards bore a son who still lives, bearing his father's name by hereditary right.

[1] *Limitatæ eliminationis.*
[2] 24th June, 1290.
[3] 24th August.
[4] 10th September.
[5] He was murdered at Petpollock, 25th September, 1288, by Sir Patrick Abernethy and Sir Walter Percy, but Sir Hugh Abernethy was the real instigator. Moray of Bothwell took him and Percy. Sir Hugh was imprisoned for life in Douglas Castle, Percy was executed, and Sir Patrick Abernethy escaped to France.

About the same time something marvellous happened in England near Richmond,[1] in a village which is called Dalton.[2] Whereas this place lies close up to the forest, and pasture abounds there for cattle, a certain man of advanced age, John Francis by name, being too careless in his [conduct], had fallen into serious neglect of the faith. For when his neighbours sought the precincts of the church for the sacred office of the Lord's day, and refreshed the spirit of devotion by the sacrament, this brutish man was in the habit of hurrying off to inspect his beasts, turning his back upon the church and traversing hill and dale. So, having wandered into the wilds one Lord's day, he penetrated to a remote spot full of the powers of the air, who were all of small stature like dwarfs, with hideous faces, falsely imitating in the garb of an abbot the sacred vestments of the church, and following one superior to the rest, as though he were invested with sacerdotal authority. They summoned the astonished and deluded layman, insisting that he should hear the Lord's day service. They began with laughter in place of song, and with a wretched murmur
MS. fo. 196 instead of a chant, together with a clever subtlety of a kind to uproot the faith of a layman. At last it came to the time, as it seemed, for the aspersion of water, when the leader went round and besprinkled all his comrades in iniquity as a punishment for their guilt. But coming to the living man last in order to besprinkle him, he assailed the fool, not with spray but with blows, so that to this day he [Francis] knoweth not whether he was struck by drops of water or by stones; but this was afterwards ascertained on the testimony of many persons

[1] In Yorkshire.

[2] In Topcliff parish near Thirsk.

that he was bruised over his whole body by the blows of volleys of stones, so thoroughly was he found to have been pelted by such a hurtful shower. Further, when he beheld these seducing spirits rising bodily as if about to fly away, he seemed to feel a force compelling him to fly away with them as they departed. But by means of grace he recovered himself, and, terrified by his imminent peril, he recalled to memory by degrees as he was able the passion which the Lord endured; and, as often as he began to fly, recalling to memory Christ's passion, he clung to the earth, and, grasping the turf and lying prone on the ground, strengthened his faith until the spirits of iniquity had all departed. And so, when he had reached home, lain down in bed and described the event to friends who visited him, during eight days following he strove to fly, until by truthful confession he set right the infidelity of his mind. For, as he confessed, suddenly and at certain times, when these spirits presented themselves to him in the air, he stretched himself upwards as if he were about to fly, had he not been held down by the main force of his servants.

On the top of other ills, in this year the city of Tripoli in Syria, which was girt about with three walls, was lost by reason of the sins of Christians. The Saracens took possession thereof, together with many tenements of the Templars and Hospitallers, many knights being killed there. I leave to be remembered by posterity two notable things in the course of this affair.

On one of those days, while the citizens, besieged by the enemy, were deliberating how they might escape slaughter, there was present among them a Minorite Friar, an Englishman by birth, well known for his courage. Perceiving that their minds were in panic, he ascended a high place, and, setting forth the word of God, he endeavoured to kindle their hearts with boldness to attack and firmness to endure; but the populace on the other hand, demoralised by despair, greeted him with derision, saying, 'Thou who boldly advisest us to be brave, wilt flee like a dastard when thou beholdest a spear. For see, the enemy have made an assault: they are storming the walls; show what you can do in such a strait, while we look on!'

Fired by faith he straightway seized the greater cross, which is wont to be displayed freely before the people, and, gripping it in his arms, placed it on his shoulder, and going before the armed ranks bade them stoutly follow him though he was unarmed; and he led the way most impetuously to the breach where the enemy had broken in. But the purblind Gentiles, beholding a ragged man carrying a crossed beam against them, contemptuously cut him down. First they struck off his left arm, which notwithstanding he quickly changed the cross to the other shoulder, [whereupon] they cut off his remaining arm, and throwing his body to the ground, trampled it to pieces under the hoofs of their horses. Thus did he who had vowed to bear the cross of Christ, who thirsted after the cross in his pilgrimage, and preached the cross in time of siege, earn a triumph through the cross in martyrdom. Many of the faithful, inspired by his example, and preferring to die bravely rather than cravenly, went out voluntarily against the enemy, and, committing to the Lord the issue of the matter, were either slain or taken, becoming a sacrifice for Christ.

Now there was in that city a convent of nuns, into which, as into other places, the enemy forced their way, carrying off everything they found there, [and] either killing or violating God's handmaidens. But there was a matron of the nuns, charming in person, still more distinguished by faith and bearing, who, when captured, fell by lot to the share of a certain Emir;[1] and because of her beauty, and in the hope that she would change her religion, she was kept alive. And when that Gentile, attracted by her beauty, meditated betrothing to himself the bride of Christ, and to this end reiterated kisses and embraces, this wise virgin called to mind that carnal love was brief and brittle; and in order to beguile the attention of her lover, and that she might escape through martyrdom to her true spouse, she sweetly said to the lover—'If I am to have you as my dear husband, I wish to secure you against the peril of death. I know the words of a potent charm of power, which, if you will learn from me and repeat faithfully when in difficulty, you will be preserved from all harm.'

The ignorant man approved of the proposal, desiring eagerly to be instructed by her skill; whereupon Luceta, for that was the virgin's name, replied: 'That you may test for certain the virtue of the charm I spoke of, I will begin to chant before you the sacred words; and you, having drawn your sword, will attempt, if you can, to cut my throat.' When he heard this, he shuddered, declaring that he would on no account do such a thing. In reply, she said: 'Yes, but you can safely do it, if you love me, and thereby you will have proof of my teaching.' Therefore, impelled by the tenderness of his love,

[1] *Cujusdam admirandi.*

for he did not wish to displease her, he obeyed her by drawing his sword, and when she, bending her head, began to repeat in a low voice—'Ave Maria!' he struck his sword into her neck, cutting off her head and throwing her body to the ground. Thus was Luceta, a daughter of the light, joined to the ministry of the heavenly lights and to the brightness of the eternal light to which she had devoted herself. Thereupon, in consequence, this barbarian would fain have stabbed himself for grief, when he beheld his love so cheated and what cruelty he had wrought. One who well knew the virgin's face and conversation afterwards consigned her to the tomb, MS. fo. 196b [namely,] my Lord Hugh, Bishop of Biblis,[1] of the Order of Minorite Friars, whose episcopal see and city were destroyed in that devastation, and we beheld the worthy bishop himself remaining two years in England under favour of King Edward. These things have I briefly noted about Tripoli as I received them.

As to the rest, the friar above-mentioned, who has encouraged many others to martyrdom by his example, had been for a considerable time warden of a monastery in Oxford. Being distressed once by the scarcity of food among the brethren, when the service of vespers was being offered one [evening] before the image of the cross he commended the sons[2] under his charge to the Father of Mercies. In that very night there appeared to a countryman of that district in his sleep a terrible apparition, reproving him thus with piercing words for his hardness: 'Thou foolish and stingy man! thou never ceasest to be vigilant in piling up thy heaps of pence, and carest not to

[1] *Episcopus Biblinensis.* [2] *Filios, i.e.* the friars.

afford help to my servants who are vigilant in prayer in that place [and are] in want. Arise quickly, on peril of your head, and see that they receive relief according to my commands!'

The country farmer rose without delay, and taking his way through the dark shades of night, he stood at dawn knocking at the gate of the friars. When the janitor, not without amazement, asked what he wanted, he stated that he wished to speak with the master of the place. The other, supposing him to be a master of the schools, replied: 'I dare not knock at his private door[1] so early in the morning, when he is applying himself to study what he has to read.' But the layman said: 'I demand [to see] him who has authority of ruling in this house.' When [the warden] was brought to him, he [the farmer] begged him civilly that he would deign to show him the church and the altars. When he entered he began straightway to behave like a scrutator in going round, muttering to himself. 'It is not thou,' quoth he, 'nor thou.' Coming at last before the crucifix, to which the warden committed him [the farmer] and his. 'Of a truth,' exclaimed the man, 'thou art he who hast appeared to me this night and shown me what I ought to do!' The meaning of the above-mentioned revelation being thus made manifest—'If there is anything,' said he turning to the warden, 'which I can do to assist thy Mother, make it known to me at once.' 'Surely,' replied the other, 'we have a payment of ten marks due to creditors in the town, if you deign, sir, to come to our help in this.' 'Gladly,' exclaimed the farmer, 'will I pay the whole at once.' The friars, wondering at the countryman's spirit, praised God as their provider.

[1] *Ostiolum.*

The Bishop of Biblis afore-mentioned, a person of honourable life and a man skilled in many things, imparted in conversation many edifying things while he lived in our province. He used to say that he had known a German knight who, having entered the Holy Land upon a pilgrimage, forasmuch as he was ignorant of the position of the holy places where the Saviour of the world went about working out our salvation in the heart of the land, sent for a native of that country and took him into his following for hire; from whom he extracted an oath that he should serve him faithfully and conduct him in his search for the sacred footsteps of Christ round all the places wherein, on the authority of the Holy Gospel, human devotion might show forth any praise of the Lord's work. The bargain having been struck, the servant fulfilled it without guile, the knight setting forward with a light heart. Examining here and there the venerable memorials of the acts of Christ, they arrived after many days, according to historical order, to the place of the Lord's ascension, where his footsteps still remain impressed upon the dust.[1] Then did the servant claim to be discharged of his oath, saying: 'See, my lord, hitherto I have pointed out to your pious desire the stations of Christ upon earth; what remaineth beyond I cannot do, seeing that here he took flight into heaven.' When he heard this the knight burst into tears, with groaning of the heart, and prostrated himself on the ground, placing his mouth in the dust that he might obtain hope from the Eternal Love. Rising erect at length and gazing to heaven with streaming eyes: 'O God,' said he, 'Thou didst undergo in this land a pilgrimage of labour and

[1] Mandeville (*ob.* 1372) states that in his time the imprint of the left foot still remained on the stone.

sorrow for my salvation, and I, coming hither out of love for Thee, have followed the ways of Thy holy journey up to this place; even as I believe that Thou didst here leave the world and go to the Father, so command that here my soul may be received into peace.' Thus saying, he paid the debt of nature and went to rest in Christ.

The aforesaid bishop related another thing, how that between the place of Olivet (where the Lord replied to the chiding Jews: 'If these should hold their peace, the very stones will cry out') and the gate of Jerusalem (which he entered for his passion, seated upon an ass), you could not lift a pebble and break it without finding within it the likeness of a human tongue, that, as is evident, the Creator's word may be fulfilled.

It pleases me to add in this place what ought to have found a convenient place in the beginning of this eighth part, forasmuch as it happened at that time, although I did not receive timely notice of this matter. Now there lived in the city of Milan a celebrated man named Francis, abounding in riches, intent upon usury, and, which is worst of all things, contumaciously disdaining to pay tithes to God and the Church. The rector of the parish, taking no notice for a while in hopes of amendment, at length became so incensed by this [conduct] that he pronounced sentence [of excommunication] against him, and demanded without delay papal letters confirmatory of the published sentence. But while the rebel was biting his lips and uttering threats, one of these days, he invited the parson of the church, half in spite and half in jest, to dine with him. The other declined this, unless he would comply with the commands of the Church. 'Suspend the sword of sentence for the nonce,'

said he [Francis], 'and come, so that I may be able to confer reasonably with you.' When they had sat down to a splendid banquet, having the servants in attendance to wait upon them,
MS. fo. 197 the man of wavering faith said: 'Sir rector, why should I care for the vexation of your sentence, seeing that I possess all that you behold, and soundness of heart to book? But if you would compel me to believe that your malediction can avail to do me hurt, curse that white bread placed before you, that I may see what virtue may be in your authority.' Whereupon, while the man of the Church was disquieted in conscience as being unworthy because of his own character, and the other as a reprobate insisted, lest the faith should suffer reproach, he stretched forth his hand, trusting in the goodness of God, and said boldly, 'On behalf of Almighty God and by authority of the most high Pontiff, I place thee, oh bread, prepared for the use of that rebel, under the ban of anathema!' No sooner was this spoken than the bread displayed a smoky hue and the cracks of staleness. When the impenitent[1] man saw this, he exclaimed in terror: 'Since you have shown sufficiently what you can effect by cursing, I now beg that you will show me what power you have in absolving.' Then the ecclesiastic, made more confident through the grace granted to him, by the same power restored the bread to its original appearance. The layman, in consequence, immediately feeling sorrow and devotion said: 'How long is it, sir father, that I have defrauded God and the Church, yea, and my own soul also, of what was due in tithes?'—'. . . . .'[2] said the other. 'Then,' said he [Francis], 'I offer satisfaction

[1] *Imperitus* in Stevenson's text, probably a misreading for *impenitens*.

[2] Blank in original.

for my rebellion; moreover I entreat for solemn absolution in presence of the clergy, and I now endow the church over which you preside with an annual rent of twenty marks.' This said, they both rise from table and hasten to the parish church; and the bells being rung,[1] clergy and people hurry in, and, when the occasion has been explained, the priors of the Church perform the desired absolution. At that very hour, certain clerics, who afterwards informed me of the circumstances, travelling from Scotland to Bologna, entered the city. Dismounting from their horses they hastened thither[2] still fasting, to witness and marvel [at the event].

In the same year died Alan de Mora, about Eastertide, and Sir John of Galloway, formerly Prior of Lanercost.[3]

In the same year died Dervorgilla[4] de Balliol, about whom H. said:

> Thy peace, oh King of Kings! may we implore
> For noble Dervorguilla, now no more?
> Give her among the sacred seers a place,
> Uniting Martha's faith with Mary's grace.
> This stone protects her and her husband's heart,
> So closely knit not even death could part.[5]

These verses are inscribed upon her tomb. In the same year

[1] *Personatis campanis.*

[2] To the church.

[3] Resigned with a pension 1283, *ob.* 1289.

[4] Daughter and co-heiress of Alan, Lord of Galloway, married John de Balliol the Elder, and was mother of John Balliol, King of Scots. She built Sweetheart Abbey (*Abbacia Dulcis Cordis*) in her husband's memory, causing his heart to be embalmed and placed in a 'cophyne' of ebony and silver which she kept constantly beside her. When she died in 1290 it was buried beside her according to her instructions.

[5] *In Dervorvilla moritur sensata Sibilla,*
Cum Marthaque pia contemplativa Maria.
Da Dervorvillæ requie, Rex summe, potiri
Quam tegit iste lapis cor pariterque viri.

[1293] died John of Kirkby. In the twenty-first year of the king's reign, about the feast of S. Michael,[1] the king's daughter, Eleanor, was given in marriage to Henry, Comte de Bar, by whom he had a son, Edward, and a daughter whom Earl John de Warenne took to wife.

In the same year there was granted to King Edward of England a half of their goods by the clergy, a sixth by the citizens, and a tenth part by the rest of the people as a subsidy for his war in Gascony.

In this year there was a great scarcity of victual in England, and the suffering poor were dying of hunger.

In the twenty-fourth year of this king's reign (1296), his daughter Elizabeth was married to John, son of the Count of Holland, at whose death Humphrey de Bohun, Earl of Hereford, married her.

At the same time Pope Boniface bestowed the archbishopric of Dublin upon William de Hopume, giving him indulgence to be consecrated by any Catholic bishop wheresoever he chose. This William was Provincial Prior of the Order of Friars-Preachers and a Master in Theology; he was jocund in speech, mild in conversation, sincerely religious, and acceptable in the eyes of all men. Having travelled with the king to Flanders, he there received the rite of consecration from my Lord Antony of Durham, by whose mediation on the part of the English and the Duke of Brittany's on the part of the French, a truce was arranged between the kings.

[The chronology of these later paragraphs has been dislocated in compilation.]

[1] 29th September.

LANERCOST

There happened on Christmas day something to which I give a place here by way of a joke, and for the sake of an old saw that gamblers and loose livers always come to poverty. Now there was in the parish of Well, in the district of Richmond,[1] a careful, but profligate cleric, A.D. 1290. proctor for the rector. He kept unlawful company with the pretty daughter of a certain widow in the village, keeping her privately in the house of the absent parson, seeing that there was nobody who could restrain him from doing so. But when his bed was set in the great upper chamber of the mansion, his master's steward arrived unexpectedly, coming to this northern region to collect the rents of the churches, whereof, being at once ecclesiastic and King's chaplain, he had too many. The proctor, being obliged to make way for the steward, set about moving his bed; but, for the life of him, he could not think where to hide his bedfellow that she might not be seen. He placed her, therefore, in a secret, strong and vaulted, but narrow, cell under the entrance to the upper chamber, where he used to keep the rents and valuables of the church, because of the security of the place. The girl, when she beheld around her plenty of cash, nor could expect in any other way to provide a competency for herself, thrust into her bosom a bag containing ten marks, and pretending that she required to withdraw,[2] requested the proctor, whom she called privily, to allow her to go out. He, suspecting no deceit, allowed this daughter of guile to depart; and on the morrow when he was obliged promptly to render account and acquit himself of what he had received, he found himself

[1] In Yorkshire. [2] *Simulata ventris necessitate.*

cheated by his whore, in consequence whereof he lost his appointment.

On the festival of S. Agnes an illustrious woman, the Lady Dervorguilla, ended her long life, relict of Sir John de Balliol, a woman eminent for her wealth and possessions both in England and Scotland, but much more so for goodness of heart, for she succeeded as daughter and heir of the illustrious Alan, sometime Lord of Galloway. She died at a great age at Castle Barnard, and was buried at Sweetheart in Galloway,[1] a Cistercian monastery which she herself built and endowed.

At the following Easter it happened in the city of Paris that, although the holy decrees of God's church declare that Christians
MS. fo. 197b shall not consort with Jews nor do them service, a certain woman, a daughter of Eve [and] handmaid to some Jews, being about to go to church on the holy day of the Lord's resurrection, adorned herself specially for the honour of God. Her master saw her and, perceiving her purpose, said—'Dost thou intend to go to church after the manner of Christians and take part in the vain ceremonies of your superstition?' As she did not deny it, he came nearer to her, commended her kindly, and freely promised to reward her if she would consent to keep the Lord's body, which she was to receive, uneaten until she returned home, so that she might show him what it was that the Church worshipped. The wretched woman agreed, being as flexible as a reed; and while she was attending the service, the enemy of Christ caused a multitude of Jews to be assembled, and, having revealed to them the impiety he intended, caused

[1] *Duquer*, i.e. *Doux coeur* or *Dulcis cordis*, so named by her because her husband's heart was there enshrined.

them all to await the return of the foolish woman. He ordered the upper table to be cleared and spread with a better cloth, and, when the mother of sacrilege arrived, he bade her place what she carried upon the white linen. When she obeyed the will of the wicked man, he, as if performing a legal ceremony, drew out a knife in sight of them all, and, exclaiming—'Behold what Christians call their God, and which we crucified!' struck what had the appearance of bread so violently that he thumped his arm on the table. Immediately there burst forth jets of blood, staining the table, the cloth, the hand, the knife and the garments of the bystanders, the flow of gore being more copious than from a human wound All of them fled, terrified by the incident and seeking to hide themselves for fear of death, leaving the author of the crime alone with his household. He, after the manner of men, suspected some trick, and tried to wash himself with water; but directly the blood touched anything, it made it, not only bloody, but soaked in blood; as with the table linen, so with the knife. At last, thinking to hide in a deep well the crime he had attempted, with wicked hands he plunged the Lord's Body, which makes the guardian angels tremble, into the abyss. But in vain, for it continued indestructible, floating on the surface of the water, which was now turned into blood, and causing the spring which had been flowing at the bottom, to fill the whole well to the very top. The gore increased its flow, turning all things that it reached into blood. The news having gone abroad, the wicked fellow was apprehended and, having been tried by the clergy, was remitted to the royal authority.[1] Each of them suffered

[1] That is to the secular arm for punishment.

judgment, for the woman was burnt to death. Friar W. Herbert, however, an eyewitness, tells another story, saying that the woman repented, went to the bishop, related the fact and was saved; but the Jew was drawn, hanged and burnt because he refused to believe.

After these things, at the beginning of winter, King Edward proposed to sojourn in the northern parts of England, so that he might more readily communicate with the council of the Scots, and that his presence might strengthen the weaker parts of the frontiers of his realm. Setting forth, therefore, for this purpose with the Queen-Consort, his children and the court, and arriving near Lincoln, on the festival of the holy apostles Simon and Jude,[1] his wife departed this life. Her mournful obsequies caused the King to return speedily to London, where [her remains] received a place of sepulture in Westminster, with great ceremony and a notable assembly of nobles.

In this year the meek S. Francis revived the memorable truth of his acts of old, in order to spread the knowledge of himself in England. For there were living together about three miles from Oxford a young and well-born couple, in the fifth year after they had entered the marriage bond; and as they were without offspring, they deplored themselves as if already half dead, despairing of an heir to succeed them. But the lady, yearning with desire for offspring, and laying the absence thereof to account of her transgressions, forthwith, impelled by faith, sought the sacrament of confession in Oxford, and laid open her life to one of the Order of Minorites. And when with tears

[1] 28th October. The Queen did not die till 28th November, which date is correctly given in the duplicate entry on page 60.

she deplored her barren state and explained the love her husband bore her, the confessor, moved by piety and calling to mind the acts of the holy father, advised her to commend herself to S. Francis by a vow, and thereby, as he firmly believed, her desire would not be disappointed. The woman agreed immediately, and vowed that for the rest of her life she would abstain from all food except bread and water on the vigil of the saint, if through his merits she should obtain the wished-for fruit of her womb. She did according to her vow in the first year, and conceived, and before the return of the saint's festival she was delivered safely of two male twins, and thenceforward suffered no more from her former trouble.

For variety of matter may here be told what happened about this date in Cunninghame, a district of Scotland, which may frighten publicans and be a check upon tipplers. There was then, and still survives (albeit a changed man) a certain countryman in the said district, William by name, a man possessed of means, but inclined to stuff his belly with more than he ought. In truth, how slothful gluttony renders a working man! This one was in the habit of sneaking away from his own cottage, and in another village, as he could not have it at home, he would spend the means of other men in carousals[1] and drink, until he was checked by the divine hand in the following manner.

He was sitting alone by the hearth in the house of a certain publican, gulping down rather than drinking the beer he had bought, all the inmates of that house being busy in outdoor occupations, when there appeared to the fool an exceedingly

[1] *Symbolis.*

hideous likeness of a spirit of the air seated opposite him, with a foul body, ghostly countenance, fiery eyes and of terrific dimensions. The disciple of Bacchus shuddered at the sight, but being bolder through drink, which makes even the unwarlike pugnacious, accosted him with an enquiry whose satellite he might be, or what business he had to be there. The other haughtily disregarding these questions, asked with a laugh who was the bold fellow who did not recognise him as the owner of a MS. fo. 198 house in that place, who for thirty years past had held the foremost place among the topers of that same tavern. 'And that I may not deceive you,' said he, 'come and see what I have stowed up from the gluttony of spendthrifts.' The other crossed the hearth without delay and beheld beside the spirit of deceit an open vessel crammed with abominations so filthy, that they almost drove the foolish fellow crazy. 'These which you see,' said the minister of evil,' 'I have collected from the vomit of thy companions in your revels.' Having his conscience thus awakened, although, as Solomon said, he had not felt the rod, and forewarned of the impending danger, William voluntarily made a vow to the Lord that he would never in any circumstances taste malt liquor again for the rest of his life, which [vow] he keeps inviolable at this day to the wonder of all his former acquaintance. He bears witness to all men of what he saw with his own eyes, and he told what is stated above to two trustworthy and religious men, with whom I am well acquainted.

The solemn obsequies of the Queen having been performed, whereat John Archbishop of York was present, between whom and the Bishop of Durham the King had endeavoured without success to establish peace, the Archbishop, having sought and with difficulty obtained licence, crossed the channel on the festival of All Saints[1] to go to Rome, and did so accordingly, and was honourably received by the leading men of the city and their retainers. Here he pled for the liberty and ancien rights of his church in the presence of the Pope; but how far he succeeded is not yet fully known.

Eleanor, Queen of England, died on the 4th of the Kalends of December,[2] at Harby. Her entrails were interred in the mother church of Lincoln on the fourth of the nones of December,[3] and on the fourth of the ides of December,[4] her body was buried at Westminster, and on the day before the ides[5] her heart was buried at the [church of] the Preaching Friars of London; whereupon Henry de Burg wrote [as follows].

O reader pause and pray: 'Dear Christ, allow
No ill to vex her who is laid below!'
How brief's the human span this Queen bears witness;
Pray for her soul, and mend thine own unfitness.
Nor birth nor worth nor wealth nor strength availeth
To ward off death, which over all prevaileth.
Mourn not too long: thou canst not by much weeping
Bring back her soul who in this tomb lies sleeping;
But pray that she abide with Christ in glory,
While here below her virtues live in story.
Long live the King, and prosper in achievement!
Would'st thou record the year of his bereavement?
Write once a thousand and a hundred thrice,
Add them, and from the total take five twice.
Also the month and day thou must remember,
Queen Alianora died on fifth November.[6]

[1] 1st November. [2] 28th November. [3] 2nd December.
[4] 10th December. [5] 12th December. [6] Wrong; it was the 28th.

Pope Nicholas the Fourth died on Easter Eve[1] after he had sat for four years and one month; and the Church A.D. 1291. was without a head for three years and more; wherefore all was revoked that the Archbishop (who was returning home) had obtained by his presence at the Curia during two diets.

It happened also by God's permission on the same Easter Eve that Acre, a city of Galilee, which for so long had alone withstood by supernal protection the fury of the infidels, was taken and utterly destroyed, owing undoubtedly to the corrupt life of its citizens which wrought the ruin of the papal troops and also to the false and craven faith of the spiritual fathers, as the result of this affair clearly proves. All this [tends], as is believed, to the desolation of the Church in future and also to aggravate the ascendency of the infidels, because it [Acre] was the last domicile of the Catholic Church in Asia, the sanctuary for all pilgrims and the chief market for merchants. Now whereas this city was a mercantile emporium as much for Christians as for Saracens, the traffic being by ships on one side and by beasts of burden on the other, whereof these people stood in no little want, and as access and return was secured by a truce, the knights whom the Pope commanded to remain there until the coming of the crusaders,[2] used to behave cruelly to the Saracen traders, either by seizing their goods without payment or treating their persons with indignity, transgressing the law of kindness as if in zeal for the Christian law. When

[1] 22nd April.

[2] On 14th October, 1290, King Edward announced his intention to set upon another crusade, and received from Pope Nicholas IV. six years' tithes from England, Scotland, Ireland and Wales (*Fædera*).

this was reported to the Sultan he civilly demanded of the Priors that, for the protection of the city, they would refrain from molesting his people and that they would hand over the wrong-doers to himself; or, if they preferred it, that they would execute justice upon these men according to their own law.[1] When this proposal had been made thrice to them,[2] and they continued to put the matter off, fearing, perhaps, to inflict punishment on the foreigners, there was sent at first a strong body of armed men, either to avenge the breaking of the truce or to execute the malefactors who should be surrendered to them. And when they laid siege to the city, not more than 15,000 men made a sortie against 100,000 of the enemy, and at the first onset cut down many of them, forced them to fly from the walls for about three mile, and took captive about five thousand of the rearmost fugitives. They performed this exploit before Palm Sunday.[3] The enemy, therefore, having had a taste of this bravery, increased their army so that it amounted to 300,000 light troops, investing the city once more and shooting so hotly against it that, as one who was there informed me, you might see the little arrows which they call 'locusts' flying in the air thicker than snowflakes. Those, then, who were in command upon the walls, perceiving that they could not hold the town for long against so many foes, determined by common counsel to make confession and receive the communion, penitently imploring help for their arms from the Lord, and that all should sally forth on the day of our common redemption, with ranks arrayed and

1 An unusual example of fair criticism of the Paynim, by a Christian clerical writer.

2 The Priors of the Templars and Hospitallers.

3 15th April.

the prisoners set in the van, and adventure their lives for the Author of life. And when they had so resolved with undaunted
MS. fo. 198b hearts and kindled faith, they sent to the Patriarch, who was in the place, that they might accomplish under his authority and with his blessing the purpose which they had begun. He, broken in spirit and depending on the advice of perfidious persons, replied that none should attempt this, nor open any of the city gates under pain of excommunication. Thus it came about that those who were outside, rendered more daring by what had happened, redoubled their bitter insults; until, when the city had been taken, their patriarch and pastor—indeed their very idol—was the first to take flight with the other nobles and owners of great wealth; and it is said that those defended themselves longest who had no desire on earth but to have justice and poverty. About a thousand of the religious were slain in the city with the common people, incalculable treasure was plundered, and so many arms of different kinds and such lots of jewels were divided as spoil as exceeded all the booty that the Saracens had won hitherto. Whereat they may greatly marvel who know that God had not changed, but had been alienated by transgression; for He had promised that his servants should possess every place upon which they set foot; and yet He utterly deprived the worshippers of Christ of that land whereon he set his holy footsteps and gave it to the persecutors of the Church.

At that time King Edward, travelling to the northern districts for reasons above described, celebrated the Lord's Pasque[1] at Newcastle. For the glory of his renown, throughout the whole of his journey, he expended vast sums in oblations in monasteries,

[1] 22nd April.

immense and unheard of charities in the streets; so much so that many persons of means, attracted by so liberal a distribution, blushed not to pose as paupers, although in the law courts they were at pains to show that they were others than paupers.

And when he had observed the Holy Pentecost[1] at Berwick, having after the festival of Holy Trinity[2] clearly shown from many and different chronicles, both of Scotland and England, what rights he and his predecessors possessed in Scotland, he was acknowledged Lord Paramount of all Scotland by unanimous consent of the nobles,[3] homage being done to him by all, and the sign manual of all being confirmed by their seals. The homage of the nobles was done in these words:

'Forasmuch as we have all come to the faith of the noble Prince, Sir Edward King of England, we promise for ourselves and our heirs, so far as that is within our power, that we shall be loyal and serve you loyally against all men who may live and die; and that so soon as we know of anything to the detriment of the king or his heirs, we shall oppose it to the best of our power. To this we bind ourselves and our heirs, which we have sworn upon the Holy Gospels. Moreover, we have done fealty to our Lord the aforesaid King in these words, each one for himself: "I will be faithful and loyal, and bear faith and loyalty to King Edward of England and his heirs, with life and limb and earthly honour against all men who may live and die."'[4]

He held this saisin peaceably until the creation of King John [Balliol], and he appointed his constables in all the castles and lands belonging to the King of Scotland.

He received there the news of the death of the queen, his mother, who died on the festival of S. John the Baptist.[5]

[1] 10th June. [2] 17th June. [3] Norham, 5th June [Rymer's *Fœdera*].

[4] Given by the chronicles in what purports to be the original Norman French: but it is incomplete and incorrect. The date was 13th June, 1291.

[5] 24th June.

From the day of her conversion[1] until her death, besides other liberal charities, she caused five pounds of silver to be bestowed upon the poor every Friday of the week, for the furtherance of her prayers and in adoration of the wounds of Christ. Forasmuch, therefore, as the king desired to be present at all the stages of her obsequies, her body was solemnly prepared and embalmed with spices, the funeral being deferred until the Assumption of the glorious Virgin.[2] But when her body was committed to the earth with much pomp, King Edward, with his own hand, gave his mother's heart, enshrined in gold, to her near relative, the Minister-General of the Minorite Friars for the time being in the Provinces, with these words :

'I commit to thee, as the nearest in blood to my mother, the dearest treasure I have ; and do thou lay it up honourably with thy brethren in London, whom she herself loved most of all in the world.'

At the festival of S. Michael[3] there was such rain over the whole of England and such floods as caused great trouble not only to farmers, but especially to travellers, because of the miriness and wetness of the roads. In many places also the lightning and thunder were extraordinary, whereof I shall here note an instance, known to not a few, and related to me by one who was there and saw.

There is a country village called Staveley, near Chesterfield, containing a stately parish church, wherein, while the priests were performing the service on the first Sunday after the feast

[1] She died a nun at Amesbury, in Wiltshire.

[2] 15th August. [3] 29th September.

of Angels suddenly, about the first hour of the day, the air became thick and dark, and by a single stroke of lightning much damage was caused all at once. For the lightning, entering from the east part of the choir by a window towards the north, defiled everything it touched along the northern wall with a black smoke, splitting the stones and loosening the joints of the couples. It killed one priest and injured the other in such manner that he lived afterwards as a cripple for not more than two years. Turning south at the end of the chancel, it blackened all the right side of the image of the glorious Virgin over the altar, and did to death a certain cleric who was kneeling in prayer at the right end [of the altar], having there performed his mass, so suddenly that it turned that part of his body which was nearest the wall from head to foot, together with his garments, into something like pitch, the rest of him remaining entire. Thence crossing westward to the bell-tower, which, with its roof, was all of stone, it shattered the cross-beams with a loud crash, and easily swept away the stone dowel with its great iron spike. Such mysteries as these deserve to be shrewdly investigated at leisure and to be gravely considered.

In the same year King Edward the Fourth, son of Henry the Third, in the course of investigating upon whom the kingdom of Scotland should devolve by hereditary right, decreed that any one who claimed the aforesaid kingdom by hereditary right, should set forth his case so that he should have justice. The pleadings between them took place before the responsible deputies of the kingdoms of England and Scotland. MS. fo. 199

Concerning a certain Earl of Chester named Ranulph : this earl had a certain sister named Matilda, who had been married to David, the King of Scotland's brother.[1] This Matilda had by her lord David one son, who was called John, and three daughters—Margaret, the eldest, Isobel, the second, and Ada, the third and youngest.[2] Margaret afterwards was married to Alan, Earl of Galloway,[3] who, by the aforesaid Margaret, begat one daughter, who was called Dervorguilla, afterwards married to Sir John de Balliol, whose son was Sir John de Balliol, who claimed and obtained the kingdom of Scotland, because his maternal grandmother was the eldest daughter of King David,[4] who left no male surviving issue.

Isabella, the second daughter[4] of King David, was given in marriage to a certain Earl of Carrick, who was called Robert de Brus,[5] who also claimed the kingdom of Scotland in right of his wife, who was the second daughter of King David.

Ada, third and youngest daughter of the aforesaid king, was given in marriage to Henry de Hastings, father of John de Hastings, who claimed the kingdom in right of his mother.

But the aforesaid King Edward, having been informed of this, caused forty responsible persons to be elected for both realms—to wit, England and Scotland, twenty for one and twenty for the other, and directed them to examine the aforesaid question and other papers bearing on it, and to decide

[1] David, Earl of Huntingdon (1143-1219), third son of Prince Henry, second son of David I., King of Scots.

[2] She had three sons and four daughters.

[3] He was not an earl (*comes*), but a lord (*dominus*).

[4] Really the grand-daughter.

[5] He was not Earl of Carrick, but fifth Lord of Annandale. It was Robert de Brus, seventh Lord of Annandale, who became Earl of Carrick in right of his wife.

which of the aforesaid [competitors] had the better right to the kingdom of Scotland; and, that they might do this more thoroughly and assuredly, he gave them time for deliberation from the feast of blessed John the Baptist[1] until the feast of S. Michael.[2] When they reached that date, they determined that Sir John de Balliol had the better title to the kingdom of Scotland, and that it fell to him by right. When he heard this, my lord Edward, by common consent of the nobles and of the majority of the deputies, conferred the kingdom of Scotland upon Sir John de Balliol, who did homage.

In the same year Eleanor, formerly Queen of England and mother of King Edward, died, a nun, at Amesbury, and was there honourably interred. Her heart was buried in London on the feast day of S. Andrew[3] and birthday of the said Eleanor; on which day all the archbishops, bishops, abbots and other dignitaries of the church, earls and many others were assembled.

In the same year, after Easter, Edward, King of England, held a Parliament at Norham, in the nineteenth year of his reign, concerning the affairs of the realm of Scotland, where the suzerainty of Scotland was adjudged to him and unanimously conceded by all the magnates of the aforesaid realm elected for this matter and closely examined upon oath, having touched the sacred gospels.

> The land that groaned so long without a king
> May now a joyful restoration sing;
> The folk whom anarchy did once oppress
> Do now an honourable prince possess,
> Able and anxious to redress all wrongs.
> Scotia, distraught by lawlessness too long,
> Is now, by English Edward's guidance, strong.

[1] 24th June. [2] 29th September. [3] 30th November.

Strong and at peace; each chief hath sheathed the sword,
Which he had drawn against his neighbour lord.
Let Scotia prosper, while, from o'er the border,
King Edward shields the cause of law and order.

In the same year, on the kalends of March,[1] died my lord Ralph of good memory, sometime [Bishop] of Carlisle; and the see being vacant Master John of Nassington[2] was sent to Carlisle, etc.

In the same year a provincial council was held at York by command of the Pope, concerning the recovery of the Holy Land and the union of the Templars and Hospitallers.

Item, in the same year there was granted by my lord Nicholas, the Pope to Edward the Fourth, King of England, a tithe to be levied for six years upon all the goods temporal and ecclesiastical of all religious persons and upon all the spiritual goods of all the clergy, according to actual value [ascertained] upon oath throughout all England.

A.D. 1292.

When the lawful inheritance of the kingdom of Scotland had devolved, after many pleadings and mature discussions, to Sir John de Balliol in preference to the rest of the competitors for the honour of governing the people of Scotland, on the appointed day, to wit that of S. Andrew the Apostle,[3] he was raised to the kingly seat at Scone, with the applause of a multitude of people assembled, the King of England's attorneys also taking part, and he set out for England to make personal acknowledgement of the honour he had received and perform the homage of fealty.

At this time Ralph, Bishop of Carlisle, departed this life at Linstock.[4] For being greatly fatigued by a long journey which

[1] 1st March.
[2] In Northamptonshire.
[3] 30th November.
[4] In the parish of Stanwix, Cumberland.

he made in deep snow, returning from the parliament of London,[1] he bled himself [on arriving] in the aforesaid episcopate, and when he was liberally refreshing his body, he desired to sleep. In his slumber the vein burst, and before he could be attended to he took leave of human affairs, deluged in blood and deprived of speech.

Also on the festival of the Purification[2] my lord John of Peckham, Archbishop of Canterbury, died, who from the time of his consecration had abstained from eating meat, would have none but coarse garments and bed-clothes, surpassed all his associates and the ministers of his chapel in vigils and prayers, so that often he would light the lamps and candles with his own hands, and would not disdain other menial offices. Master Robert of Winchelsea, Archdeacon of East Anglia and doctor of theology, was elected in his place, whose consecration was delayed because the Apostolical See was vacant. Also on the Sunday within the octave of the Ascension of our Lord, which, in that year, fell on the third of the kalends of June,[3] the city of Carlisle was burnt, so that the loss of the bishop was followed by the desolation of the people in this manner. Just as it is declared in Holy Writ that the ruin of the people was caused by evil priests, which the Saviour confirmed by the cleansing of the temple, and as the aforesaid see [of Carlisle] was weakened by many vices, so that, as holy Job made observation, the heavens should reveal the iniquity of the people and the earth should rise up against them, [so] God caused a disturbance of the air, of the sea and of fire during the space of one day and MS. fo. 199[b]

[1] Held on the morrow of the Epiphany, 1292. [2] 2nd February.

[3] This is the 30th May, but the real date of that Sunday was 18th May. Hemingburgh gives S. Dunstan's day, 19th May, as the date of the fire.

night, and, what is more, there was an exercise of human malice. For such a furious wind arose as destroyed all vegetation, and either overthrew travellers afoot or on horseback or drove them easily out of their right course. There was also such a tremendous inroad of an unusually high tide as to overflow the ancient landmarks of the country [in a degree] beyond all memory of old people, overwhelming beasts pasturing along its shores and destroying the sown crops. Satan even caused the son of a certain man [1] to set fire to his father's house outside the town at the west end of the cathedral church, and this, escaping notice at first, soon spread over the whole town, and, what is more, it speedily consumed the neighbouring hamlets to a distance of two miles beyond the walls, and afterwards the streets of the city, with the churches and collegiate buildings, none being able to save any but very few houses. The fire, indeed, was so intense and devouring that it consumed the very stones and burnt flourishing orchards to the ground, destroyed animals of all kinds; and, which was even more deplorable, it burnt very many human beings of different ages and both sexes. I myself saw birds flying about half burnt in their attempt to escape.

The valuable contents of warehouses and treasuries were wasted there; but, which was more striking than the rest, the price of the timbers, glazing and stalls [of the cathedral] which a brigand rather than a high priest [2] had extorted from the purses of stipendiary priests, earning thereby ill-will and malediction; so that the flames devoured the sepulchre of that wicked extortioner, but the

[1] The son is said to have done so in revenge for being disinherited.

[2] *Prædo non præsul*, referring to Bishop Rafe de Ireton. For the offence given by his exactions see under the year 1280.

bounds of his predecessor, Robert de Chalix, remained uninjured in every part.[1]

In the same year Pope Nicholas the Fourth died on Holy Thursday.[2]

In the same year Rismaraduc, one of the nobles of Wales, a traitor to the King of England, was judicially drawn at York on the morrow of the Holy Trinity,[3] and was hanged for three days and nights at Knaresmire.

The kings of Scotland are bound to make submission to their overlord, the King of England and his heirs, as is proved from the time of King Edward named the Elder, and can still be learnt from deeds and papal bulls.

Charter of William, King of Scotland.

'In a charter made by William King of Scotland to John King of England it is set forth that William King of Scotland granted to his dearest lord John, King of England, that he [John] should arrange a marriage for Alexander his [William's] son wherever he wished, as for his liege man, so long as he [Alexander] was not disparage thereby.[4] Item, that whatsoever might happen to John, the said King William and his son Alexander, should keep faith and loyalty to his [John's] son Henry, as to their liege lord, against all mortals, and shall help him to hold the kingdom for him according to their powers, saving always the allegiance whereby they are bound to King John. Given in the thirteenth [year] of the reign of King John.'[5]

Among the papal bulls for the kings of England it is found that Pope Honorius the Third calls the King of England lord of the King of Scotland, who was waging war wickedly against his lord himself, and is therefore placed under the bond of excommunication.

[1] Hemingburgh states that the incendiary was taken and hanged.

[2] 3rd April. Fleury gives the date as Good Friday.

[3] 2nd June.

[4] *I.e.* that the marriage should befit his rank.

[5] *Fœdera*, A.D. 1212.

'Item: Gregory the Ninth saith that long ago a friendly compact was made between Henry the Second, grandfather, and John, father, of Henry King of England on the one part and William King of Scotland on the other, whereby the said William and Alexander, son of the aforesaid King of Scots, made allegiance and homage to the grandsire, the father and the same king, binding their successors, the earls and barons of Scotland, to perform the same to the kings of England themselves; and, should the terms of the compact not be observed, [then] the earls and barons of Scotland should adhere to the kings of England.[1]

'Item: Gregory writes to the Archbishop of York and the Bishop of Carlisle to admonish and persuade the King of Scotland to keep to the aforesaid amicable compact.[2]

'Item: Gregory writes to the King of Scotland, addressing him as liege-man of the King of England, [desiring him] to keep his oath of allegiance and expressing surprise that he is not keeping it by spending more in honour of the King of England.'[3]

On the day of S. George the Martyr,[4] my lord John of Halton was elected Bishop of Carlisle.

Verses on the Burning of Carlisle.

'Twas in the jocund month of May
That fair Carlisle in ashes lay.
Ah, wretched city! hard's thy fate,
Swept by the flames from gate to gate.
Of stately buildings none, alack!
Remain, except the Friar's Black.
Organ and bells and tuneful choir
But serve to mourn this dreadful fire.
May'st thou yet see a brighter morrow!
Christ hear our prayer and ease our sorrow.

In the same year, on the morrow of All Souls,[5] the Itinerant Justiciaries sat in Carlisle; to wit, Sir Hugh de Cressingham, Sir William de Ormesby, and the others associated with them.

[1] 25th September, 1237 (*Fœdera*).
[2] 4th January, 1235 (*Fœdera*).
[3] 27th April, 1231; 4th January, 1235.
[4] 23rd April.
[5] 3rd November.

Christ's holiness renewed in his servant S. Anthony, confessor and doctor, the accustomed miracles, whereof I was informed by the letter of an Anglican friar of the same convent, who was present and beheld them, and whose letter I here insert in its order.[1] A.D. 1293.

'One of the friars of the Minorite order, by birth a Parmesan, by name Bernardinus, of good enough family, young and strong, healthy and active a fortnight after Easter, was suddenly deprived of voice, sight and speech, and suffered such difficulty in breathing as only to blow out the smallest candle with difficulty. His parents and brethren decided to send him, thus crippled, as speedily as might be for the advice of the doctors of Lombardy. However, after being thus disabled for three days and having hastily begun his journey, he recovered his sight, although the use of his MS. tongue and power of breathing showed not the least improve- fo. 200 ment. The most celebrated medical men failing either to detect the cause of the illness or to apply a remedy (albeit they tried cautery in various ways), sent him away without any hope [of recovery]. But as the memorial services of S. Anthony were being held in the neighbourhood, the invalid, no doubt divinely inspired, obtained by signs and nods license from his minister to go with the rest of the friars of his province to Padua, where the saint reposeth. Arriving there on the fourth day before the festival should be celebrated on the Sabbath, the friars of the convent were profoundly affected, weeping to behold such a fine young fellow as dumb as a statue. On the morrow

[1] S. Anthony of Padua lived 1000 years after S. Anthony, the founder of monasticism, and died in 1231.

the sufferer devoutly repaired to the place of the shrine,[1] wherein the saint is set, when it happened that the Most High glorified his saint, so that about evening of the same day there came upon the invalid as he prayed there a certain commotion of his entrails, not without excruciating pain. Overcome by this, he left the shrine and vomited something filthy and, as it were, sulphurous. Feeling thereafter that he could breathe [freely], but that he had not yet recovered the use of his tongue, he took some tablets and gave them to a friar whom he met, after writing on them that he believed he would be able, through help of the Holy Father, to read the epistle on the morrow. Then hastening again to the shrine, accompanied by three friars, after waiting a little while he recovered the use of his tongue. Immediately a number of friars collected, who, when they beheld what had been done, with streaming eyes united in praising the Lord and [His] saint. Then there was a gathering of the villagers, in whose presence he who had been healed, standing in a high place in front of the shrine, began in a loud voice [to chant the] *Salve regina*, etc. When the antiphone of the blessed S. Anthony had been solemnly sung, the minister took up the subject and preached a sermon, making known the circumstances of the miracle.

'But when the report of the miracle spread abroad, some people, through their shortsighted infirmity, threw doubts upon the divine goodness, declaring that there had been no miracle but [only] an imposture by the friars, since he who had been cured was a stranger. Wherefore, lest the bounty of the divine condescension should be brought into contempt, a second manifestation

[1] *Archa.*

followed, which, in proof of good faith, was attested by the formal oaths of clergy, of magistrates and of knights, and also by the evidence of six parsons.

'Well, at dawn of the vigil of the festival [there came] a certain lay brother of the nuns of the monastery of the Order of S. Bernard, who had been a lay brother at Padua for five-and-thirty years, or thereby, and was deaf and dumb from his birth, and, which is more remarkable, was wholly destitute of a tongue, besides being ignorant of every form of speech. Only by means of eyesight and signs and nods he lived with the others, being employed as a baker. Beholding the crowd of people assembling from all parts, as is the custom, in honour of the saint, he could obtain no leave from the abbess to repair to the saint's shrine, although he earnestly besought it. Then, when he had sorrowfully composed himself to sleep, about midnight there came to him, as he declared, a Minorite friar, stout, of lofty stature and of middle age, who wakened him by touching him and said: "Dost thou desire to be cured? Rise and go to the shrine."

'He arose at once and struck a light, [but] when he looked for him who had appeared to him, he could not find him. Taking for granted that it was another lay brother of his monastery, he hastened faithfully to fulfil the saint's command; but, on arriving at the church, he was unable to get in, because, being entirely filled with the women performing the vigil of the saint, it was closed under an armed guard, as is the custom every year. Being forced of necessity to remain outside, he entered at the first stroke of dawn, and did not leave the shrine until the solemn mass was finished. Then he went out to breakfast with the friars, as the clergy, priests and especially the Regulars, wherever they may have come from, usually do.

'The meal being over, he returned to the shrine, around which there remained a constant throng; and, when the service of Nones was finished, at the rest hour he began to sweat copiously and to suffer severe pains, so that he seemed about to faint. Then he felt in his head, between his ears, a great cleaving and violent dragging at his ears, and suddenly he began to speak, although he had never learnt [to do so]. There was such a multitude of men there, and the gathering increased so much, because the healed man was well known to everybody, that, although the doors were strong, they were scarcely fit to withstand the violence of the worshippers, so that the whole place was filled with shoutings within and without, and *oripilationem*[1] was brought upon the slanderers of the preceding miracle. There was among them a certain youth named Cambius, of the Roman province, but a native of Bologna, who had been sent by his minister to consult the Bolognese doctors about a rupture from which he suffered terribly. This youth, taking account of the grace bestowed upon others and glowing again with fervid faith, when he neither was able nor dared to join the women collected in the crypt, being prevented both by modesty and by the crush, followed the example of the woman with the bloody flux. He touched the stones of the shrine with his hand, which he thrust into his bosom and touched the seat of his trouble. He then felt the parts which had fallen out to be replaced in their proper position by following his hand, and the rupture to be comfortably healed.

'In the same city there was a little two-year-old boy named

[1] Meaning doubtful.

Thomas, son of one of our fellow-townsmen, who had been carelessly left by his mother near a *mascellum*[1] half full of water. Falling into the water, head and body [were immersed] to the waist, with his feet in the air, the boy was drowned. The mother, after she had attended to one of her husband's shoes, recollected the boy, and when she had looked everywhere for him, found him at last in the water, as cold and stiff as a log. Horror-struck, she was not sparing in screams; the neighbours were roused and hurried in from all parts, and the wretched woman showed them the body of the dead boy. The [boy's] father or grandfather, employed at that time within the walls of our church and in the saint's service, made hasty arrangements with some friars for the funeral. Now when the spectacle[2] was over, after having been on view until dusk, some of the neighbours advised the parents to have recourse with confidence to the favour of SS. Francis and Antony. The grandfather then vowed to give the boy's weight in corn, and to keep the vigils of the said saints fasting, and to travel in person to the dispensation of S. Francis, if the boy should be restored to life. No sooner had the vow been uttered, than suddenly the boy began to vomit a great quantity of water, and was restored to life and health.' MS. fo. 200b

These things [are recorded] without hope of reward for the glory of the saints and the edification of posterity.

In this year war broke out at Dieppe in Neustria,[3] when the citizens of that place inhumanly attacked A.D. 1293.

[1] Literally 'a shambles.'

[2] ? Of the boy's corpse.

[3] An archaic term, indicating the ancient Frankish realm between Meuse and Loire, roughly corresponding with modern Normandy.

our people of the Cinque Ports[1] with slaughter and rapine at the instance of an agitator, nay and what is more, [they were] encouraged by the ambition of their prince, to wit Charles, brother of the King of France, who had conceived hatred for our people, because he could not supplant his own brother in that kingdom, whom it was King Edward's policy to support in this district. So, in order that he might make more evident the venom which he had conceived, he subjected pilgrims and scholars to many afflictions, even putting some poor people to death on the gallows and hanging beside them live dogs to which he likened them.[2] And when these hostilities had grown to such a pitch that the Cinque Ports people attacked the inhabitants of Dieppe with sword and fire the King [of France] issued an order in council that all scholars from our side of the sea, Scots as well as English, should clear out of France. The same [edict] closed Paris to burgesses coming from beyond the sea, but this was not carried into effect. He even dared, bad Christian that he was, to consult a soothsayer as to what harm might happen from the ill will now engendered against England; and when the soothsayer replied that nothing could prevail against that kingdom so long as it was under the protection of a Lady of great majesty and a noble ecclesiastic, it is said that he put him to death by way of fee. No wise man may entertain a doubt that the diabolic art indicated in metaphor[3] that Lady who, according to John of Damascus, is

[1] *Portuenses.*

[2] This insult is charged against the Norman seamen in a contemporary state paper. In the margin is sketched a gallows whereon hang some Englishmen, alternated with dogs.

[3] *Per antinomiam.*

ruler of all things, being Mother of the Creator. In whose honour I insert here something which happened at that time, which I received on the oath of a religious man in the parish of Aysgarth near Richmond.

A certain countryman of blameless life worshipped the blessed Mother of God with devout mind, and was for seven years or more under the spiritual guidance of the aforesaid person. Certain fellows, banded together and burning with cupidity, robbed him of three oxgangs of his farm,[1] thinking that he was helpless in his own defence. Deeply distressed by his misfortune, he prayed devoutly to his protectress, and brought an action at York against the evildoers. Having obtained little success there because the palms [of the court] had been well greased,[2] and preferring to die rather than be beaten, he took his case to be pled in London. Arriving there with much difficulty and with scant means, he laid his weary limbs to rest in an empty and cold house at the end of a street on this side of London, incessantly and with tears imploring the Queen of Mercy, that she would deign to have compassion upon him in his just cause, vowing that thenceforward he would always distribute a yearly allowance of wheat among the poor in her honour at the feast of the Purification, which was then at hand. And when sleep had wholly deserted him because of the emptiness of his stomach, the anxiety of his mind and the narrowness of his bed, the Holy Mother of God appeared, as he often used to swear, to the disconsolate wretch, shining with dazzling brilliancy and attended by two companions. She was encompassed by marvellous lights, intellectual he used to

[1] *Tres bovatas* = 39 acres.

[2] *Propter manus inunctas.*

call them, without doubt the angelical powers; for as such they were revealed to the simple rustic, as they stood around the Queen of Virgins.

Addressing the countryman—'Thou hast put thy trust in me,' said she, 'and behold, to-morrow through my aid, thy land shall be restored to thee. Moreover thou shalt return home whole and unhindered, so that thou shalt not even bruise thy foot with travelling.'

All that the Mother of the Word of God promised was fulfilled straightway; and one night, after he had returned home, the Mother of Consolation deigned once more to appear to him as he was quietly sleeping. 'In like manner,' said she, 'as thou seest that I have performed what I promised, and quickly attended to thy prayer, so do thou firmly believe me ready to attend to all those who invoke me with sincere affection.' This statement is in accord with what the saints have declared about the Mother of Mercy, in whom [the Saviour], coming from on high, rested bodily during nine months in the bowels of mercy for our salvation.

But I will add yet another [instance] bearing upon this matter, which happened to take place some thirty years ago or more.

A few years ago there was in London a certain vicar of the church of Dalmeny, Sir James [by name], who used to discourse to many persons what he had experienced of the Blessed Virgin. In his youth, as he said, he was a scholar of Cambridge, sharing board and bed with a comely English youth who was called William Wilde, because he was not only playful and tuneful, but also too much given to wantonness.[1]

[1] An interesting example of a surname originating in a personal trait.

He [James] used to worship the glorious Virgin in a devout spirit, attending her office, exercising himself at her services in songs and prayers, and, as he trusted that she would obtain pardon for him, calling her, in the usual phrase, the Mother of Mercy.

Now one night, as he was reposing beside his comrade aforesaid, he seemed to be hurried off towards the east by two malignant monsters who were about to cast him into a vast fire which he saw before him. Looking back, however, he beheld a company of the blessed coming like priests in exceedingly white raiment and with shining faces, one of whom cried in a loud voice: 'Bring him back whom you are carrying away, that he may be examined. It is not justice that one who has not been sentenced by the judge should suffer punishment.' Returning then with his enemies, he MS. fo. 201
[James] was taken in charge by the senate of saints, and was brought trembling before a handsome and dignified man of lofty stature, whom he understood to be a protector from his tormentors, who were vociferously accusing him. Then, after one of the adversaries had declaimed from a long roll, covered with black characters, setting forth all his [James's] misdeeds, however many, in an exact manner, the just judge asked him whether he wished to say anything in his defence. James, through remorse of conscience, made no answer at all, whereupon the malicious persecutor exclaimed: 'Just judge, do not take from us him whom thou perceivest to be rightly our prisoner?' But the Creator of man turning graciously towards the prostrate [James] said: 'Look around carefully and see whether among my attendants there be one who may

be willing to offer intercession for thee.' He, casting his eyes over the whole host, which, as he said, seemed to consist only of male beings, could not see her whom he most earnestly longed for, the Mother of Mercy. Straightway the dire sentence was pronounced, and he was being violently dragged away to cruel torments, when in the background he beheld again a choir of virgins, brightly shining and rejoicing with gladsome praise, of whom the Mistress, more refulgent than the rest, commanded the party that was leaving to halt. When he beheld her he humbly invoked the Queen of Mercy, imploring that she would deign to pity him in such dire extremity, reminding her of the hope, devotion and labour he had given to her service. 'Thou hast incurred a sentence,' quoth the Mother of Clemency to him, 'which cannot be revoked. What would'st thou that I should do for thee?' 'O Lady,' said he, 'if more may not be done, help me in this that I may be given the libel of the accusation against me.' The Empress of Heaven, assenting immediately, laid hold of the adversary, and, seizing from him the document, restored it to the hands of the petitioner, saying, 'It is now necessary that thou delete what is written.'

In all this he [James] moved his body so uneasily—trembling, sweating and muttering—as to awaken and cause no little terror to the comrade beside whom he lay, who failed to rouse him from his dreadful moaning either by poking him or shouting at him, until, the aforesaid vision having come to an end, he [James], like one returning from a great distance, began to ask his comrade where he was or whence he had come. At length, when his comrade told him how he had been behaving in his sleep, James then and there described to him in turn all that he had seen, exhibiting in his fist as testimony the very roll which the Virgin had seized from the demon, though he would never show to anybody what was written therein. Also he started immediately at daybreak on the morrow and, confessing himself with tears, obliterated all that Satan had written. Thenceforward he practised such extreme penitence by denying his flesh all indulgence and keeping fasts, that the austerity of his life caused religious men to blush.

Now, whereas virtue shines clearer by contrast with vice, it may be permitted to put in writing what I know to have happened nine years ago. In the west of England, about twelve miles from Bristol, there dwelt in the country town of Wells (a church which is divided into portions for secular canons) a certain prebendary, whose life I know not how to describe otherwise than by means of an observation by S. Augustine, who said that he who lived well could not die amiss. When God in His good pleasure had numbered his days, He permitted him to be grievously afflicted, and later on, as the disease increased, He sent some Minorite friars to be at hand for his assistance. They, indeed, having been informed beforehand by rumour about the invalid, met on their journey a messenger who explained his master's condition to them. When they arrived at his house and ascended to the attic where he lay in order to comfort him, the sick man declined or hesitated to take the medicine they had brought, desiring them to go down to the hall and refresh their bodies with food, seeing that they must be fatigued. Also he kept with him, as his whole household, a boy to assist him and do his bidding, and, when the others had begun their meal, he bade this boy bring him out of the open chest which stood opposite [his bed] a silver bowl which he would find within, full of silver and gold. When this was brought to him and placed in his lap, he stared at it with startled and fixed gaze, and, thrusting in his hand, attempted, as if smitten with mania, to thrust the yellow metal into his mouth, biting and sucking it as if it had an exquisite flavour. Then the simple lad beside him rushed in horror down to the hall, crying for help because his master, like a lunatic, would not stop devouring coins. The friars, running up in haste, found the whole chamber swept and the corpse of the defunct thrown on the bare ground, stripped naked and darker than lead. Moreover it bristled from head to heel with coins stuck in it, just as cooks stick lard into all parts of meat for roasting when they wish to make it more toothsome. This event took place in the year when Alexander King of Scotland departed this life, and was told to our congregation by a friar who belonged at that time to the convent of Bristol. And so was fulfilled in this wretch the saying of the holy Job in the twentieth chapter, 'he shall vomit the riches he has devoured, and God shall draw them out of his belly,' *et cetera*.

There happened in this year [1293] a great scarcity of victual, so much so that in many places a quarter of wheat was sold for thirty shillings.

At the same time Gilbert Earl of Gloucester, who had married King Edward's daughter, the Lady Joan of Acre (so called because she was brought to light in that place when her father was a pilgrim in the Holy Land), having had a son by her, immediately made over the whole of his English property to the royal hands in such manner that he [the King] should endow his infant grandson out of his bounty, while the earl undertook the office of guardian till the end of his life.

Early in the morning of Saturday next before the feast of S. Margaret virgin,[1] as I was travelling with my scrip, we beheld in the east a huge cloud blacker than coal, in the midst whereof we saw the lashes of an immense eye darting fierce lightning into the west; whence I understood that Satan's darts would come from over the sea. Sure enough on the Sunday following,[2] there began and continued throughout the night over the whole of the west part of the diocese of York, thunder and lightning so prodigious that the dazzling flashes followed each other without intermission, making, as it were, one continuous sunlight. Not only men were terrified and cried aloud, but even some domestic animals—horses for certain. In some places houses were burnt or thrown down, and demons were heard yelling in the air. MS. fo. 201[b]

On the feast of All Saints, Henry of Galloway, a bishop beloved of God, departed this life; to whom succeeded Master Thomas of Daltoun, who was consecrated at Ripon on the feast of the Assumption of the most blessed Virgin.

Also on Sunday following the feast of S. Martin[3] the daughter of Robert Earl of Carrick was married to Magnus King of Norway.[4]

[1] 11th July. [2] 12th July. [3] 15th November.

[4] Isobel, eldest daughter of Robert Earl of Carrick, and sister of King Robert I., married Eric (not Magnus) King of Norway, whose first wife was Princess Margaret of Scotland. It has been commonly alleged that Isobel married first Sir Thomas Randolph, Great Chamberlain to Alexander III., and she bore to him Thomas Randolph, afterwards Earl of Moray. But, as Sir James Balfour Paul has pointed out, she cannot have been old enough to be the mother of Randolph, who witnessed John Balliol's fealty to King Edward in 1292. The Rev. J. Anderson suggests that Randolph's mother was a daughter of the Earl of

In the same year there was intestine naval war between the English and the French at Saint-Mathieu in part of Brittany, where the French lost two hundred and fourteen vessels and six thousand and sixty men;[1] but on the English side only three men perished.

Item, Friar John of Peckham, Archbishop of Canterbury died, and holy Robert of Winchelsea was elected to the Archbishopric of Canterbury.

Item, the Comte de Bar was married to Eleanor, daughter of King Edward.[2]

On the Saturday before Palm Sunday, which in that year
A.D. 1294. fell on the fourth of the Ides of April,[3] there took place in Lothian an event most marvellous, enough in itself to warn wise persons that it is evil spirits that stir up tempests, and also to teach the ignorant that, according to the teaching of the saint, in every act and at every step thy hand should make the sign of the cross.[4]

Verily, on that day, when crowds gathered in the town of Haddington from various districts to attend the market, a young fellow with an equally young wife came thither with his neighbours from a distance of six miles[5] to buy some necessaries. But there occurred such a dense fog and driving snow as struck

Carrick by a former marriage. See the *Scots Peerage* sub vocibus Moray and Carrick.

[1] This somewhat startling disparity of numbers is confused in Stevenson's edition by a misplaced comma. *Franci ducentas naves amiserunt, et quatuordecim et sex millia hominum et sexaginta.* The comma should be placed after *quatuordecim.*

[2] She was the widow of Alphonso, King of Aragon.

[3] April 10. [4] Tertullian, *de Corona militari*, c. iii. [5] *Ad sex miliaria distans.*

with dismay the countenances of all who beheld it. Having done their business [the couple] were returning home about mid-day, and the wife, who was a hale and hearty [young woman], riding on the horse behind her husband's saddle. On arriving at a rivulet about half a mile from their house in the town of Lazenby,[1] she persuaded her husband to let her alight from the horse and follow on foot, while he went forward to the house and ordered a fire to be kindled against the cold. He consented, out of love for his wife; and no sooner was she left alone than suddenly she encountered by the side of the stream an evil spirit, of a pale countenance, but presenting the appearance of a girl scarce seven years old. This [creature], seizing the woman by the left hand with a hand like a horse's hoof, tore the flesh off her arm and flung her, terrified, into the water; then, as she struggled to rise, it dealt her such a gash between the shoulders that a man's fist might easily be thrust into the wound, and as it cruelly handled [the woman], who resisted with all her might, it made some parts of her body black and blue, and other parts deadly pale, tearing off the flesh, as was said, and as those who saw and touched her have testified to me.

The husband, wondering why she tarried, galloped back [to her], and, finding his wife almost in a swoon, placed her on the horse and took her home. Strengthened through confession and by extreme unction, she showed to all who visited her the humour[2] and extravasated blood, and departed this life on the second week day following.

[1] *Villa de Laysynbi*—not identified.

[2] *Seriem*, in Stevenson's edition; perhaps a misreading for *serum*; but perhaps *seriem*, *i.e.* a relation of the facts.

About the same time, King Edward, having been summoned to present himself in person before the French, caused suitable arrangements to be made at Amboise for his reception; but, on receiving letters from privy friends warning him to beware of being made prisoner, and not to cross the sea, he abandoned his intention; and on the feast of the Lord's Ascension,[1] contrary to every form of justice, he was deprived of all his lands and holdings beyond the sea, as being liable to forfeiture. Also, the King of France[2] issued interdict against the King of England's brother, the Lord Edmund, who had married Queen Mary,[3] relict of the King of Navarre, that he should not cross the frontiers of the French. Moreover, he tyrannously withheld from the said Queen Mary,[4] mother of his own wife and royal consort, the terce which belonged to her as her portion of the kingdom of Navarre, unless she would consent to desert her husband (as he in vain expected her to do), and consent to live in foreign parts.[5] But Gascony, wholly escheated by this proceeding, was consigned for custody and defence to the haughty Charles, brother of the King, about whom it has not yet become known how he succeeded. From this time began the interdict of entry to travellers, and of the purchase of wool and hides from England, and much inconvenience in consequence. Then the Cluniac monks were banished from our borders, and in one day at the same hour, throughout the whole province, an inventory was made and vouched for of the treasures, as well in the houses of the clergy as in the churches—cathedral, urban and rural.

[1] 27th May.

[2] Philip IV., *le Bel.*

[3] Her name was not Mary, but Blanche.

[4] That is, Blanche.

[5] That is, foreign from England.

LANERCOST

The Lord Edmund had three sons by that lady Queen[1]—the eldest being Thomas Earl of Lancaster,[2] the second Henry Earl of Leicester,[3] and a third who remained in France with his sister.

In this year, Friar John of Darlington, of the Order of Preachers, confessor of the late King Henry, was appointed collector of tithes in the realm of England by papal authority. It was by his learning and industry that the great Concordances, which are called Anglican, were published. The same was afterwards made Archbishop of Dublin by papal appointment. In the same year (1294) the miserable Welsh, formerly almost done for, rebelled for a third time, having made Madoc, the bastard son of the last Llewellyn, their prince. Having destroyed three castles, they betook themselves to Snowdon, numbering, as is reported, about eighteen thousand. King Edward marched against them; although he could speedily have brought them to subjection by force, yet, forasmuch as they never dared to meet him in the open, he prudently weakened their resistance by gradually occupying Anglesey and other lands, which he was able to lay waste within the space of one month.

On the commemoration day of S. Paul,[5] Celestinus the Fifth was created Pope, who, albeit illiterate, was the priest and confessor of his predecessor. Before his election, he had acquired a false reputation for sanctity, because, being grieved for the death of the [late] Pope, he had devised and sought after religion for himself. But, having been created [Pope], he had no intention MS. fo. 202

[1] Edmund, fourth son of Henry III., married secondly Blanche, Queen-dowager of Navarre.

[2] Beheaded in 1322.

[3] Succeeded his brother as Earl of Lancaster.

[4] John, Lord of Beaufort, *d.s.p.*

[5] 30th June.

of acting by the advice of his college, wherefore he betook himself from Rome to Naples. Here he added ten to the number of cardinals, and began many innovations. In his time the Sicilians deposed Charles because of his tyranny, but not before the Pope, with certain cardinals at Naples, when they failed to conciliate James of Aragon, fulminated a terrible sentence against him and the Sicilians who supported him.[1]

Then, after the feast of S. Peter ad Vincula[2] there happened a sudden stupendous flood in the river of Scotland called Teviot, prognosticating future events at hand, such as we have witnessed before our eyes. For the waters of the Teviot suddenly waxed without much rain, overflowing bridges and lofty rocks, sweeping away the mill below Roxburgh Castle and others, besides everything else that was in their way. Also, the flood broke down the bridge of Berwick, and threw down a tower, even overthrowing all the piers of masonry, and many of the people who were crossing [the bridge] were washed away to sea.

Also on the feast day of S. Matthew the Apostle there was held in London a council of the clergy and a parliament of the people, when the ecclesiastics granted to the king a moiety of their revenues as subsidy for his expedition, and the laity [granted] the third penny of their goods.

Item, the Welsh rose and did much damage. On hearing of this, Edward King of England, unwilling to imbrue his hands

[1] The French Pope Urban IV. bestowed Sicily in 1264 upon Charles, Count of Anjou. The massacre of the French, known as the Sicilian Vespers, took place in 1282, and it was Frederick, not James, of Aragon, who was crowned king of Trinacria in 1296. But as Pope Celestine V. resigned in the year of his election 1294, the chronicler has confused the dates.

[2] 1st August (Lammas).

with blood, commanded his forces not to injure any of them from Septuagesima[1] till Easter,[2] and then again to the following feast of S. Lawrence.[3] Their prince having been betrayed and taken, the whole of Wales was restored to its allegiance; for the king imprisoned about five hundred of their nobles, who were given as hostages, in various castles of England.

At the feast of All Saints[4] despatches were received by King Edward from Sir John de St John and Sir John de Bretagne, and the other nobles who had sailed with them for the defence of Gascony, announcing that they had fared successfully, having inflicted defeats on the enemy and captured fortresses wherein they were able to protect themselves.

About the same time, many ships, in numbering two hundred and four score, which had been sent by the King of Spain to the coast of France, were driven by the violence of storms into various parts of England. These were splendidly equipped for war, and heavily freighted with arms, gold, wax, bitumen, timber, and poles. The men of the Cinque Ports having attacked them at great risk to themselves, made a great booty of the lot.

Also on the said festival there departed this life one who was illustrious in name, but not in character, Bovo de Clare; not, as is said, very 'clear' in his death or reputation,[5] inasmuch as he held innumerable churches and misgoverned those which Christ had committed to his trust, for he was careless in his office of guardian, disdaining the cure of souls, wasting the revenues of the churches, and having so little regard for the Bride of Christ as [to be indifferent] whether the Church should receive

[1] 30th January. [2] 3rd April. [3] 10th August. [4] 1st November.

[5] 'Clear'—that is 'illustrious': the play is on the word *clarus*.

enough from her own revenues [to keep] the necessary vestments whole and clean. This might be proved by many flagrant instances, whereof I will record one as an example.

In the famous church of Symunburne, over which he presided, on Easter Day I saw pleated withies, smeared with fresh cow-dung, in place of the panel over the high altar, and this, although the church is rated at seventy marks! Moreover, so wasteful and wanton was he, that he sent to the dowager Queen of France for her jewellery, a lady's coach of matchless workmanship—body and wheels being wholly wrought in ivory, and all the fittings that should have been ironwork were made of silver, down to the smallest nail, the housings, down to the smallest cord by which it was drawn, being of gold and silk. The cost, it is said, amounted to three pounds sterling, but the scandal to a thousand thousand.

At the festival of S. Lucia,[1] Pope Celestinus called together the college of cardinals, and, with the unanimous assent of all, decreed and ordained that it should be lawful for any pope or cardinal to renounce his dignity should he wish to do so. Immediately after this declaration he resigned the pontifical dignity in their presence. Then Charles[2] caused to be read the Gregorian constitution *de inclusione*,[3] and caused a house to be prepared for each of the cardinals, allowing only ten feet [of space] and one servant [apiece]. But, in compliance with the constitution, he waited ten days for three new cardinals who had not yet arrived; and, when these were present on Christmas eve, he shut them all in. Then they all committed their authority in the creation of a new pope to the said Celestine in this wise—that he should nominate four

[1] 13th December.

[2] Charles of Anjou, King of Naples.

[3] Prescribing the manner of the conclave.

of the cardinals, who, acting for all the rest, should elect the new pope, and that they [the other cardinals] should acknowledge him as elected by themselves to the supreme pontificate. He [Celestine] agreed, and nominated Benedict de Gaytan with three others, who unanimously chose Benedict. A native of Anagni, now known as Boniface the Eighth, he was ordained on the morrow of the Circumcision,[1] and ordered his predecessor to be arraigned on a charge of heresy. The latter fled in fear to Sicily.

On the vigil of Christmas a few Englishmen, allied with the natives and with some of the King of Aragon's men, recovered by force of arms a great part of the land of Gascony, and on the day of the Circumcision[2] Bayonne was restored to their possession, whereupon the English sent to the King of England as a complimentary offering fifty ship-loads of wine.

In the same year on the day before the Ides of February,[3] Thomas, second of Multon, died, being at the time Lord of Holbeach.

Item, on S. Dunstan's day[4] died that most noble lady of pious memory, Dame Matilda of Multon, Lady of Gilsland, mother of the aforesaid Thomas.

The Lord Robert de Brus, a noble baron of England as well as of Scotland, heir of Annandale, departed from this world, aged and full of days. He was of handsome A.D. 1295. appearance, a gifted speaker, remarkable for his influence, and, what is more important, most devoted to God and the clergy. He passed away on Cæna Domini.[5] It was his custom to entertain and feast more liberally than all the other courtiers, and was

[1] 2nd January, 1295. [2] 1st January, 1295. [3] 12th February, 1295.
[4] 19th May. [5] 12th May.

most hospitable to all his guests, nor used the pilgrim to remain outside his gates, for his door was open to the wayfarer. He rests with his ancestors at Gisburne in England, but it was in Annan that he yielded up his spirit to the angels, the chief town of that district, which lost the dignity of a borough through the curse of a just man, in the following way. Some time ago[1] there
MS. fo. 202b lived in Ireland a certain bishop and monk of the Cistercian Order, a holy man named Malachi, who, at the command of the Captain-General of the Order, hastened to that place[2] where also he died and rests in peace, remaining famous by his tokens.[3] When he died the holy Bernard, who was present, preached with tears an exceedingly mournful sermon, which I have often seen.[4]

Now this bishop, beloved of God, when he had crossed over from the north of Ireland and, travelling on foot through Galloway with two of his fellow-clerics, arrived at Annan, enquired of the inhabitants who would deign to receive him to hospitality. When they declared that an illustrious man, lord of that district, who was there at the time, would willingly undertake that kindness, he humbly besought some dinner, which was liberally provided for him. And when the servants enquired of him, seeing that he had been travelling, whether they should anticipate the dinner hour or await the master's table, he begged that he might have dinner at once.

Accordingly, a table having been dressed for him on the north side of the hall, he sat down with his two companions to refresh himself; and, as the servants were discussing the death of a

[1] About the middle of the 12th century. [2] Clairvaux.

[3] Or 'images' (*signis*). [4] It is preserved among S. Bernard's works.

certain robber that had been taken, who was then awaiting the sentence of justice, the baron entered the hall, and bade his feasting guests welcome.

Then the gentle bishop, relying entirely upon the courteousness of the noble, said—'As a pilgrim, I crave a boon from your excellency, [namely] that, as sentence of death has not hitherto polluted any place where I was present, let the life of this culprit, if he has committed an offence, be given to me.'[1]

The noble host agreed, not amiably, but deceitfully, and according to the wisdom of this age, which is folly before God, privily ordered that the malefactor should suffer death. When he had been hanged, and the bishop had finished his meal, the baron came in to his dinner; and when the bishop had returned thanks both to God and to his host, he said—'I pronounce the blessing of God upon this hall, and upon this table, and upon all who shall eat thereat hereafter.'

But, as he was passing through the town, he beheld by the wayside the thief hanging on the gallows. Then, sorrowing in spirit, he pronounced a heavy sentence, first on the lord of the place and his offspring, and next upon the town; which the course of events confirmed; for soon afterwards the rich man died in torment, three of his heirs in succession perished in the flower of their age, some before they had been five years in possession, others before they had been three.

When the said Robert [de Brus] was informed of this, he hastened to present himself in person before the holy man beseeching pardon and commending himself to him, and thence-

[1] Early Christian bishops had the privilege of remitting sentence of death on criminals.

forth paid him a visit every three years. Also, when in his last days he returned from a pilgrimage in the Holy Land,[1] where he had been with my lord Edward, he turned aside to Clairvaux and made his peace for ever with the saint, providing a perpetual rent, out of which provision there are maintained upon the saint's tomb three silver lamps with their lights; and thus, through his deeds of piety he [de Brus] alone has been buried at a good old age.[2]

Six days before Palm Sunday,[3] came Charles, brother of the King of France, to Rioms, whither part of the English had retreated. Now, he came about midnight with 6000 horse and innumerable foot against 400 horse and 7000 foot; and after he had attacked the city, which was stoutly defended, for fifteen days, they[4] sallied forth on the advice of a certain old man, gave battle to the enemy and, selling their lives dearly, perished. And thus twelve English barons were taken prisoners, one of them being a traitor; of whom hereafter.

In the same year the Scots elected twelve peers, by whose counsel the kingdom should be governed.

Where no man due obedience feigns
To laws of half a dozen reigns,
The people suffer grievous pains.

The Scots craftily sent envoys to the King of France [conspiring] against their lord, King Edward of England—to wit, the bishops William of S. Andrews and Matthew of Dunkeld, and the knights John de Soulis and Ingelram de Umfraville, to

[1] In 1273.

[2] Mr. George Neilson has dealt fully with this interesting legend and its confirmation in *Scots Lore*, pp. 124-130.

[3] 21st March.

[4] The English.

treat with that king and kingdom against the English king and kingdom. The aforesaid envoys took with them a procurator, endeavouring to bring about war. So after the report had reached the ears of my lord the King of England, he was very angry (and no wonder!), and sent repeatedly to the King of Scotland, commanding him to attend his parliament in accordance with his legal obligation both for the kingdom of Scotland and for other lands owned by him within the English realm. But he [John Balliol] utterly refused to attend, and, which was worse, began assembling a large army to withstand the King of England.

On Monday in Passion week,[1] Sir John Comyn of Buchan invaded England with an army of Scots, burning houses, slaughtering men and driving off cattle, and on the two following days they violently assaulted the city of Carlisle; but, failing in their attempt, they retired on the third day. Hearing of this the King of England sent an expedition against the Scots at Berwick, and in Easter week, to wit on the third of the kalends of April,[2] that city was taken by the king, its castle also on the same day, and about seven thousand men were put to the sword.

On the octave of the Apostles Peter and Paul,[3] the magnates, prelates and other nobles of the kingdom of Scotland having assembled, a solemn parliament was held at Stirling, where by common assent it was decreed that their king could do no act by himself, and that he should have twelve peers, after the manner of the French, and these they then and there elected and constituted. There they pronounced forfeiture of his paternal heritage upon Robert de Brus the younger, who had fled to

[1] 26th March, 1296. [2] 30th March, 1296. [3] 6th July.

England, because he would not do homage to them. Also they forfeited his son in the earldom of Carrick, wherein he had been infeft, because he adhered to his father. They insultingly refused audience to my lord the Earl of Warenne, father-in-law of the King of Scotland, and to the other envoys of my lord the King of England; nor would they even allow so great a man, albeit a kinsman of their own king, to enter the castle.

Also they then decided upon active rebellion and to repudiate the homage done to King Edward, devising how they should enter into a treaty with the King of France so that they should harass England between them, he with his fleet by sea, and they by land, and thus, as they believed, should overcome her.[1]

Upon this God began to make many revelations to his servants, whereof we perceived the truth in the following year. For at break of day on the sixth of the kalends of August,[2] the whole firmament seemed to a certain cleric in Lothian to be overcast with clouds, the wind blowing from the north-east; and presently
MS. fo. 203 he perceived red shields coming from the same quarter, charged with the arms of the King of England, which, keeping together, united at the top and joined at the sides, covered the whole expanse of the sky with their multitude. Now while he was marvelling at this with anxious countenance and confused thoughts, he saw in a little while a white and beautiful person appear in the very same region, seated upon an ass's colt, who, approaching exceedingly swiftly and appearing quite nude, displayed the tokens of our salvation on his extremities and side, dropping blood. When the other perceived this, he worshipped on bended knees, and so the vision vanished.

[1] The treaty is printed in Rymer's *Fœdera*, ii. 695.

[2] 27th July.

In confirmation of this I will record another vision which a simple citizen of Haddington beheld about the same time. In this wise: he saw, as he stated, a raging fire, coming from the southern quarter of the firmament, suddenly precipitate itself upon Berwick, where it miserably consumed all things. Afterwards, travelling through the centre of Lothian and devastating everything till it came to an arm of the sea. When it reached that, it ascended again to the sky and returned to the south by the same way it came.

In this year the only son and heir of Sir William de Vesci, a comely youth, was taken from the light of this world between Easter and Pentecost; upon whose death the boy's tutor, a certain knight of Scotland, Sir Philip de Lyndesey, son of Sir John, fell into sore melancholy, and, following the melancholy, contracted a mysterious malady, took to his bed at Beverley, and, being miserably racked by the violence of fever for eight days, entirely lost the power of speech, took no notice of those who visited him, and seemed to be bereft of his bodily senses. Yet he took food daily like a maniac from those who put it before him, lying down again after receiving it, and remaining as if asleep. Saint Cuthbert the bishop, commiserating his affliction, appeared plainly to him as he lay on the eighth day and accused him of neglect, saying—'Thou hast deserved the illness which thou hast contracted, for the place which was assigned to me by thine ancestors, and the hermitage which I inhabited of old (the chapel of Innippauym[1]

[1] Not identified. Perhaps on the Headshaw Burn in Lauderdale, where is Channelkirk, near Holy Water Cleuch and St. Cuthbert's Well. Here the saint, still bearing his Irish name Mulloch, served as a shepherd lad and saw visions, before he was received by Prior Boisil at Old Melrose, and submitted to the tonsure.

situated on thy land) thou hast allowed to fall into neglect, and from a habitation of holy men to become a stable for brute beasts. But let thy errors of the past be forgiven thee ; when thou hast recovered health be thou careful to repair the ruins of my place and to cleanse its defilement.'

Then he [Lyndesey] immediately recovered his speech, and, before anything else, returned thanks to the saint and craved pardon for his lack of diligence. While he lived safe and sound, he often testified to listeners what he had seen.

At this time also there befel a great calamity to the students of Oxford, so much so that many of them died suddenly, and in a single day sixteen corpses or more were carried into one church.

Something equally horrible and marvellous happened then in the West of Scotland, in Clydesdale, about four miles from Paisley, in the house of a certain knight, Sir Duncan de Insula,[1] which may serve to strike terror into sinners and foreshow the appearance of the damned in the day of the last resurrection. Now there was a certain fellow wearing the garments of holy religion who lived wickedly and died most wretchedly, being bound by sentence of excommunication on account of certain acts of sacrilege committed in his own monastery. Long after his body had been buried, it vexed many in the same monastery by appearing plainly in the shade of night. This child of darkness proceeded to the house of the said knight in order to disturb the faith of simple persons and terrify them by molesting them in broad daylight, or, more probably, by a secret decree of God, that he might indicate by such token those who were implicated in his misdoing. Having then assumed a bodily shape

[1] Delisle.

(whether natural or aerial is uncertain, but it was hideous, gross and tangible) he used to appear at noon-day in the dress of a black monk and settle on the highest parts of the dwellings or store houses.

And when men either shot at him with arrows or thrust him through with forks, straightway whatever was driven into that damned substance was burnt to ashes in less time than it takes to tell it. Also he so savagely felled and battered those who attempted to struggle with him as well-nigh to shatter all their joints.

Now the knight's eldest son, an esquire of full age, was especially troublesome to him in this kind of fighting; and one evening, when the father was sitting with the household round the hearth, this malignant creature came in their midst, throwing them into confusion with missiles and blows. All the rest having taken to their heels, the esquire attacked him single-handed; but, most sad to say, he was found on the morrow slain by the creature. Wherefore, if it be true that a demon has no power over anybody except one who leads the life of a hog, it is easy to understand why that young man came to such an end.[1]

On the festival of the Nativity of the Glorious Virgin[2] the King of France gave orders to a numerous fleet which had been equipped that it should sail with all speed to burn up England; but through the divine protection and the care of

[1] It is not so easy to understand how Christianity retained its ascendancy among reasonable beings, when its doctrines were enforced by such gross and unscrupulous falsehoods as those with which this chronicle abounds.

[2] 8th September.

the Queen of Mercy (to whose succour, as is recorded above, the island is committed) the fleet was so severely buffeted by gales in a sudden tempest that it only regained the shores of France with the greatest difficulty. And when two cardinals had crossed to England as mediators of peace, and had obtained assurance from the King of France[1] that his people would do no injury to the English in the meantime, he [the King of France] was not afraid to break faith, and, cruelly venting his anger upon those who had escaped shipwreck, by his brother's advice put many of them to death. Then he re-issued his command, forced the rest of them to sea again, warning them with threats on no account to return unless they brought with them to Paris the glorious relics of S. Thomas, archbishop and martyr. Then they set out once more upon the waves of the sea, which they seemed to cover with their multitude; nevertheless, none of them all ventured to land upon the coast of England, except only the crews of two galleys, according to what one told me who was there and with his eyes saw what happened. The first of these [galleys], more strongly manned than the rest, surprised the town of Dover and easily overcame it with sword and fire, but in the end derived no advantage from their success, for the inhabitants gathered out of the villages and took possession of the shore, killing them all to the number of 220, and divided the spoil among themselves. The other [galley] also landed at Hythe, having on board nine score armed men with steel caps; these the men of the Cinque Ports attacked with two vessels only and put them all to death in less time than it would take to bake a single biscuit.

[1] *Rex Galliarum*, usually referred to as *Rex Franciæ*.

And whereas it is declared in holy writ that evil counsel shall fall upon him who deviseth it, just so there took place at that very time a fraudulent conspiracy among the princes of France. For he who, as has been described,[1] contrived that twelve barons, his comrades, should be taken by guile, was now plotting against the person of the King of England himself and his kingdom. This deceitful spy, assuredly sent by the King of France, came to England feigning to be an escaped prisoner, and, in order to hide his bitter malice, pretended that he was willing to lay bare to our people the designs of the French. Accordingly, having been admitted to the parliament of London, and after he had investigated the secret affairs of the country, he took two servants and hastened to the coast, intending to cross over. But one of these servants, detesting the wickedness of his master, happening to meet a member of the [royal] household, revealed to him the malicious intentions of the traitor. 'Go,' said he, 'and tell the king without delay that we are hurrying away to cross over, in order to betray England.' MS. fo. 203b

This man delivered the message; the villain was overtaken and arrested, and, having been brought back, confessed his treachery, and, as a just reward, was drawn and hanged.

Now this man was a knight, by name Thomas de Turberville, whom the Lord troubled at that time, because he endeavoured to bring trouble upon England.[2]

[1] See the account of the fall of Rioms, p. 278 *supra*.

[2] The chronicler delights in puns which do not bear translation into English: '*Thomas de* Turbe*vile, quem ex*turb*avit Dominus . . . quoniam nisus est* turb*ationem inducere Angliæ.*' Various documents relating to the spy Turberville are printed in the appendix to Stevenson's edition of *The Lanercost Chronicle* (pp. 481-487), including a letter from Turberville to the Provost of Paris, which was intercepted.

After this, on the sixth of the Nones of October,[1] Master Robert of Winchelsea, doctor of sacred theology, who before his creation had been Archdeacon of Canterbury, but now was Archbishop of the same see, returning home with the cardinals from Rome, was received to his diocese honourably by the king, and was enthroned with great pomp in the presence of many nobles.

In like manner, as we know that it is truly written, that evil priests are the cause of the people's ruin, so the ruin of the realm of Scotland had its source within the bosom of her own church; because, whereas they who ought to have led them [the Scots] misled them, they became a snare and stumbling-block of iniquity to them, and brought them all to ruin. For with one consent both those who discharged the office of prelate and those who were preachers, corrupted the ears and minds of nobles and commons, by advice and exhortation, both publicly and secretly, stirring them to enmity against that king and nation who had so effectually delivered them; declaring falsely that it was far more justifiable to attack them than the Saracens. Certain mercenary [priests] also, not really pastors, pretending to be dealers in wool, had crossed over to the country of the French at the preceding feast of S. Lawrence,[2] commissioned by their people to disclose this nefarious plot to the king [of France]. These were the Bishops of S. Andrews and Dunkeld, who, according to the prophetic saying, 'delighted the king by their wickedness and princes by their fraud.' For, not long afterwards, they succeeded

Turberville paid for his treachery on the gallows. His case is dealt with also by Hemingburgh, Walsingham, and in *Flores Historiarum*.

[1] 2nd October.

[2] 10th August, 1294.

in making them believe their falsehoods, and sent letters by their servants announcing that the King of France was most favourably inclined towards them, and that a huge fleet was setting sail with a large force of men, and with arms, horses and provender. In corroboration whereof the Bishop of S. Andrews sent in advance to Berwick many new and valuable arms, and also most sumptuous pontifical vestments, all which we know were seized and taken by the Bishop of Durham's sailors in the very mouth of that port.

Also, to confirm what was said by the holy Job—'the vain man is puffed up by pride, and thinketh himself to be born as free as a wild ass's colt,' this foolish people, yielding credence to these rumours, turned fiercely upon all the English found within their borders, without regard to age or sex, station or order. For the authority of the Church, which was very oppressive, decreed that those rectors and vicars of churches who were of English origin should be ousted and expelled from the country by a given date; also the stipendiary priests were suspended and were sentenced to expulsion with their clerical compatriots. Moreover, the royal authority ejected monks from their monasteries, and unseated those who were in high office; it even forced laymen out of their own houses, confiscating under royal sasine or taxing the goods found therein. Also the biting tongues of certain evil men, who either could not or dared not do injury by force, composed ballads stuffed with insults and filth, to the blasphemy of our illustrious prince and the dishonour of his race; which, though they be not recorded here, yet will they never be blotted from the memory of posterity; for by their aforesaid insolence and oppression they meant nothing less than this—that just as the cry of the children of Israel in Egypt reached the Most High, and he saw their affliction and came down to set them free, so would it now come to pass in these our days. That which the revelations described above portend, was also made clear in an open vision manifested at Berwick to the eye of sense before Christmas following. For verily as some little children were hurrying off together to school in that same city to be taught their letters, at break of day, as is usual in the winter season, they beheld with their natural eyes (as they afterwards assured many persons) beyond the castle, Christ extended upon the likeness of a cross, bleeding from his wounds, and with his face turned towards houses of the city. Time coming was soon to show whatsoever chastisement that [vision] indicated.

Also on the night of All Saints[1] the Holy Lord of the Saints destroyed and cast away the ships of the perjured French, under guise of helping them, so as he might show that their expedition was against himself and his people; and this in the following way. For, as the perfidious French (who, as is aforesaid, had suffered reverse already), devised among themselves that, on such a solemn anniversary, neither those dwelling on the coast of the English sea, nor the men of the Cinque Ports would care to miss the church services, they adopted another foolish project, after the example of proud Nichanor, who commanded the troops to arm and the king's business to be transacted on the Sabbath day. And so, preparing in the dead of night to cross the deep sea, while they avoided human observation they incurred divine judgment; for, intending to make a descent upon an unsus-

[1] 1st November.

pecting people, suddenly they discovered these were safe in the protection of the saints. A fearful storm sprang up from the hand of the Lord, which immediately deranged and scattered them, sending every one on board of those nine score ships to the bottom of the sea, so that not one survived to tell the tale to his children.

King Edward was warned by these and other events that he was threatened with war in front and rear; and when both the parliament of the nobles of Scotland and the council of prelates were to assemble in Edinburgh, he, endeavouring to win the goodwill of these ingrates, demanded through an emissary that they would hand over to him shortly four of their castles overlooking the frontier of the realm, to wit, Berwick, Roxburgh, Jedworth and Edinburgh, for the protection of the natives against invasion by foreigners. This they MS. fo. 204 refused unanimously and obstinately, just as they had refused all previous demands, declaring that they were in no need of any aid.

The Cardinals also, who had spent all their means in their long journey requested of the clergy of Scotland through emissaries a moderate grant of money, which should hardly exceed one farthing[1] from each of the churches to be taxed. But in refusing the assistance demanded, they [the Scots clergy] made this reply, that these Pillars of the Church had not crossed land and sea in the service of the Church, but in that of King Edward's realm. And whereas we know that it is written that wickedness proceedeth from the wicked, they did all these things in order to achieve their hateful design by tokens, since they

[1] *Assem unam.*

could not do so by arms, imagining that the dominion of King Edward could be extinguished by them. To whom applies that saying of S. Gregory—While they loosed the shoe-string they tied a knot. Indeed it turned out for them as it did for Zedekiah, according to Ezekiel, who saith—'But he rebelled against him in sending his ambassadors into Egypt that he might give him horses and much people. Shall he prosper? Shall he escape that doeth such things? Or shall he break the covenant and be delivered?'

Gilbert, the great Earl of Gloucester, died after the festival of S. Lucia,[1] a man prudent in council, puissant in arms and most spirited in defence of his rights. For when the aforesaid King required of [him] and all his tenants to show by what warrant each one held possession, Gloucester, drawing his sword in presence of the King and nobles in London, delivered this reply:—'Behold my warrant! by which right thou, oh King, holdest from conquest by thine ancestors two feet of English soil; and I possess the third foot from my forefathers.' Thus the curiosity of the inquirer was repelled.[2]

Now, in order to take up the thread of the narrative I have begun, the knights and esquires who had been associated with the bishops with the above-mentioned mission to France, returned on the festival of SS. Vincentius and Anastatius[3] disappointed and with nothing to report; while those horned ones remained behind,[4] after the fashion of many modern dignitaries, who,

[1] 13th December.

[2] This writ of *Quo warranto* was issued in October, 1274, and caused much discontent by its inquisitorial character. The story attributed to Gloucester in the text is told elsewhere of the Earl of Warenne.

[3] 22nd January.

[4] *Cornutis illis retro residentibus*, a contemptuous allusion to the mitred bishops.

either out of craven fear for their own skins or sensual indulgence of their own bellies become, not feeders *of* the flock but feeders *on* them.

Indeed there was pressing need for these Scots to return home, seeing that they found victuals to be very dear in France and were sensible of shortage of cash in their own purses; nor could they after their arrival [in France] find any creditor from whom they could borrow, nor was there given them even one ship wherein they could make the return voyage. When therefore these needy persons met with certain easterling mariners[1] preparing to sail for Scotland and found that the agent of some Edinburgh burgess was about to consign his merchandise to the said skippers, they obtained by favour (seeing that they had not the money) a passage for themselves and their people, promising to pay the fares so soon as they should be landed in Scotland. Thus did the Lord confound those who fled to the Chaldeans (that is to the ferocious people, whence the Franks obtained their name)[2] who boasted about their ships, so that those who purposed to invade the coast of England with an innumerable fleet might count themselves lucky in obtaining a single pinnace of their own. Moreover, when they landed at Berwick, they showed this favour to their fellow-countryman, whose merchant-factor they had in their company, that all his merchandise was seized, to the value of nine score of marks or more. But they brought this news from France, that the King of Norway had been dead for some time, leaving no heir of his body, and that his brother, who had been Count before that, had taken the daughter of the

[1] *Marinariis de orientali patria*, i.e. from the Baltic.

[2] The etymology of 'Frank' is suggested as = *ferox*.

Count of Clermont as wife and consort at the instance of the nobles.[1]

Deluded by these follies, they sought still other safety in falsehood. For, according to theological testimony,[2] 'vain hope is the snare of the foolish man and ignorant fellows rely on dreams;' although these men heard that the Pope was mediating for peace between the French and English, they pretended and even announced in their own country that the King of France had declared that he would not agree to peace unless under a treaty embracing the Scots as well as his own people: whereas in truth, when the peers were assembled at Cambronne on Quadragesima Sunday,[3] there was nobody present who put in a single word for them [the Scots], according to what was told me with his own lips by a certain noble, who attended there daily on behalf of the King of England; nay, he heard many persons execrating that very nation as deceitful and ungrateful for the benefits they had received from King Edward.[4]

In consequence of dreams of this nature, all bailiffs received orders at the beginning of Lent[5] that they should seize for the use of the King of Scotland all goods belonging to the English

[1] Eric II. (father of the Maid of Norway, who succeeded Alexander III. as Queen of Scots) did not die till 1299, when he was succeeded by his brother Haco V.

[2] *Teste theodocto*, a hybrid word for which I know of no authority.

[3] 20th February.

[4] All this is purely partisan fiction. On 23rd October 1295 the Scottish plenipotentiaries concluded a treaty of offensive and defensive alliance with the King of France, each country binding itself not to make peace with England unless the other were included (*Fœdera*). When truce between England and France was struck in October 1297, Scotland was not included.

[5] 16th February.

throughout the realm wheresoever they might be found, and that they should store them in the castles and other safe places; also that all these men[1] were to be bound by a fresh oath to hold fast and stand firm with the people of the country in every emergency. They considered that such an oath would be binding; declaring, on the other hand, most preposterously that their own oath to King Edward had been made under compulsion, and therefore might be broken under compulsion.

Accordingly a wapinschaw was held and account being made of those who were capable of military service, all who had power, wealth, arms and strength were warned to be ready to assemble at Caldenley[2] on the Sunday in Passion Week.[3]

Herein thou mayest clearly perceive that what the sage wrote was exactly fulfilled—'The universe will fight for him against the madmen.' For, as if the elements were taking vengeance upon the enemies of the truth, there is no doubt that, from that time forth, snow, rain and easterly winds from the district where their army [was] began to prevail to such a degree that others dwelling in the towns and in timbered houses[4] were smitten with alarm, so that half-naked men could only avoid the severity of the cold under rocks and cliffs, thickets and trees. And like as they had broken their plighted faith, so in turn they carried sword and fire into the English borders in Passion Week,[5] MS.
whereby the others [the English] in retaliation attacked Lothian fo. 204[b]
by sea on the vigil of Palm Sunday,[6] burnt the seaside towns and

[1] *I.e.* Englishmen.

[2] ? Caddonford on the Tweed.

[3] 27th March.

[4] *Domibus laqueatis.*

[5] 27th March—2nd April.

[6] 26th March. According to these dates, the English seem to have been the aggressors.

inflicted great damage upon them. Thou mightest see on the holy day of Good Friday and the vigil of Easter the presage of that double carnage which took place twice afterwards on a Friday; for a cloud, undoubtedly of wrath, overshadowed Lothian, so thick, so wet and so evil-smelling that it concealed everything at a distance of ten paces from the view of those passing through it. This having changed in the evening to a tearing wind and drenching rain throughout the night and the following day, made the roads so bad for travellers as to weary people looking out o' window.

It was reported at this time that John, Archbishop of York, had died in distant parts, in whose place Henry of Newark, dean of that church, was elected.

At the same time we received news that in Easter week[1] there had been a most terrible conflict in Gascony. For the French from one side and the citizens of Bordeaux from the other attacked the English, and while many were slain, and many were wounded, our people kept the upper hand so well that the enemy turned tail, and, besides those taken prisoners, thirty principal nobles[2] were done to death and interred in the place of the Friars Minor. Moreover the fleet of the Cinque Ports which had been sent out there, returned home in its full number and with all well. Part of the said city [Bordeaux] was taken by our people on that occasion, to wit, the outer wall, the army being commanded by my lord Edmund, brother of King Edward, with the Earl of Lincoln and others, who, it is said, would have finished the business then

[1] 3rd—9th April.

[2] *Nobiles signiferi*: literally 'standard bearers,' but here probably the allusion is to their pennons or banners.

and there, had not arrears of pay forced them to disband the army. When King Edward, who was then at Stirling, was informed of these things, he directed that plenty of both corn and money should be sent to them. In consequence we beheld on the festival of the Nativity of S. John[1] envoys coming from Gascony, both clerics and very many secular knights, to announce that the English had occupied the whole country and were all safe and sound.

Here endeth the eighth book and the ninth beginneth.

Applying now our mind as well as our pen to the ninth division of this work, which, both in order to avoid being tedious and because of the beginning of a new period, requires A.D. 1296.
a new book to be begun, we bear in mind first and foremost this most wise precept of the most holy Gregory, who saith—'The power of the wicked is as the flower of the grass, because their carnal glory fadeth while yet it flourisheth, and while they boast of it among themselves suddenly it is brought to an utter end.' That this befel the Scots[2] in the year of our Lord MCCXCVJ (which, by the way, was leap year) is shown by their manifest arrogance. Notwithstanding that in past ages they have always been subject to the English sceptre (although they often rebelled and spurned the prince assigned to them, and also many times did not only exclude Saxons from the King's Council and service but also expelled them from the land, as the above quoted chronicles testify), they now relapsed into callous hatred, and, after the expulsion of all the courtiers whom my lord John, their King, had

[1] 24th June.

[2] *Albanactis*, latinised form of the Gaelic *Albannach*.

brought with him, they committed a fresh crime by preventing him, who was the head of the people, from performing any act of state or from going wherever he wished, confining him like a fugitive under guard night and day, so that he was not allowed to attend a conference [1] to which he was summoned by King Edward, nor could he make known to him [Edward] his good will. Moreover, trusting vainly, as aforesaid, to allies and arms, they constrained the King and his children to stay at home and to take the field for war; and for this reason, seizing corn and cattle and other provender in all quarters, they repaired their castles, fortified Berwick, the principal seaport and town of the kingdom, and brought foreign auxiliaries thither, paying no heed to the divine wrath which was impending over them, whereby they were collected as sheep for the slaughter and were consecrated at Easter for the day of massacre.

At last, when they ought to have learnt to fear God through the disaster of their prince [2] so lately deceased, whom God smote dreadfully for all their sakes, and afterwards gave the nation itself ten years for repentance, which they misused in their pride, adding daily worse and worse transgression, no remedy remained but that declared by the wise man—'destruction must needs overtake those who practise tyranny.' Whereof I, a sinner, who write these facts, received by the Lord's revelation the following token.

Now shortly before the impending misfortune, after mass on the Lord's day, as I was composing my limbs to rest and courting

[1] King John attended King Edward's Parliament in May, 1294, but refused a summons to attend Edward in his expedition to Gascony (29th June).

[2] Alexander III.

sleep with closed eyelids, I beheld a winged man [clothed] all in white whom I recognised at once as an angel, holding a drawn sword in his right hand, proceeding from one end of the house to the other, and brandishing the sword in a menacing manner against the book-cases of the library, where the books of the friars were stored, indicating by this gesture that which afterwards I saw with my eyes, [namely,] the nefarious pillaging, incredibly swift, of the books, vestments and materials of the friars. Thus the life of just men often suffers injury for the punishment of transgressors, and by the affliction of the former the latter are purified.

But before we investigate the course of history whereon we have embarked, in the same leap year,[1] on the festival of S. Matthew the Apostle,[2] the Apostolic and just man Pope Boniface, being in the second year of his pontificate, issued the letter decretal—*Ad perpetuam rei memoriam*, etc.—reproving the insatiable and rapacious cupidity of princes ever intent upon extorting property from the Church, and threatening laymen who should transgress with severe excommunication and interdict. He subjected all ecclesiastics impartially to deposition and deprivation who should dare to bestow upon princes any gift, subsidy, loan or tax upon the revenues of the church without the consent of the apostolic see. Also on the fourth of the kalends of April[3] in the same year he issued another edict—*Ad perpetuam rei memoriam*—most salutary for souls, directing generally and without distinction that all ecclesiastics whatsoever, charged with the cure of souls, should reside regularly as pastors in their [respective]

[1] *In eodem die bisextili*, probably a slip for *anno*.

[2] 21st September. [3] 29th March.

offices and localities; adding this punishment for delinquents, that whosoever was found to absent himself for a whole month from the church assigned to him, should be deprived of his benefice.

Just as the Scripture uttered by God declareth that 'upon the evildoer shall fall his own device, nor shall he know
MS. fo. 205 whence it cometh upon him,' so that illustrious man Robert de Ros, the owner of much land, thinking to secure prosperity, broke faith and joined the King of England's enemies, betraying his secrets to them and promising them support. When this was found out, the King solemnly observed the thanksgiving services on Easter day[1] at his castle of Wark, and tried to persuade the head men of Berwick to surrender, promising them safety in their persons, security for their possessions, reform of their laws and liberties, pardon for their offences, so that, had they considered their own safety, they would not have slighted the proffered grace. But they, on the contrary, being blinded by their sins, became more scornful, and, while he waited for three days, they gave no reply to so liberal an offer; so that when he came to them on the fourth day, addressing them personally in a friendly manner, they redoubled their insults. For some of them, setting themselves on the heights, bared their breeches and reviled the king and his people; others fiercely attacked the fleet which lay in the harbour awaiting the king's orders and slew some of the sailors. Their women folk, also, bringing fire and straw, endeavoured to burn the ships. The stubbornness of these misguided people being thus manifest, the troops were brought into action, the pride of these traitors was

[1] 25th March, 1297.

humbled almost without the use of force and the city was occupied by the enemy. Much booty was seized, and no fewer than fifteen thousand of both sexes perished, some by the sword, others by fire, in the space of a day and a half, and the survivors, including even little children, were sent into perpetual exile. Nevertheless this most clement prince exhibited towards the dead that mercy which he had proffered to the living; for I myself beheld an immense number of men told off to bury the bodies of the fallen, all of whom, even those who began to work at the eleventh hour, were to receive as wages a penny a piece at the King's expense.

These events took place on the third of the kalends of April, being the Friday in Easter holy week, a penalty exacted by God corresponding to the crime. For it was on the Friday in Passion week that a detachment of the Scottish army made their first incursion into England, devastating with slaughter and fire some country villages and the monastery of Carham; yet these very citizens, perjured and hardened in evil-doing, feared not to receive at Easter the communion of perfect love in fraternal hatred to their own perdition. Whence it may be assumed as proved that 'day unto day uttereth speech'—that is, punishment, and 'night unto night'—that is, the penal scourge upon wickedness, indicates knowledge of sin. Besides, as Chrysostom bears witness [although] wickedness is sometimes overcome by reason, it is never so checked in those who sin by deliberate intent and not through ignorance. Thus these madmen added fresh insolence to their folly, and on the sixth of the Ides of April[2] invaded the bounds of England in two columns, and ravaged different districts

[1] 30th March. [2] 8th April.

thereof; the men of Galloway, led by the Earl of Buchan [went] through Cumberland, the whole band of young knights and fighting men[1] forcing their way through Redesdale. In this raid they surpassed in cruelty all the fury of the heathen; when they could not catch the strong and young people who took flight, they imbrued their arms, hitherto unfleshed, with the blood of infirm people, old women, women in child-bed, and even children two or three years old, proving themselves apt scholars in atrocity, in so much so that they raised aloft little span-long children pierced on pikes, to expire thus and fly away to the heavens. They burnt consecrated churches; both in the sanctuary and elsewhere they violated women dedicated to God, as well as married women and girls, either murdering them or robbing them after gratifying their lust. Also they herded together a crowd of little scholars in the schools of Hexham, and, having blocked the doors, set fire to that pile [so] fair [in the sight] of God. Three monasteries of holy collegiates were destroyed by them—Lanercost, of the Canons Regular; and Hexham of the same order, and [that] of the nuns of Lambley[2]; of all these the devastation can by no means be attributed to the valour of warriors, but to the dastardly conduct of thieves, who attacked a weaker community where they would not be likely to meet with any resistance.

Forasmuch as it is God alone who can bring the best out of the worst, I shall here relate two matters for the sake of edification, because perfidious persons desire under the cloak of Christianity, to be esteemed like righteous ones, not in reality, but in appearance. This may be easily proved about these [Scots];

[1] *Tota virtus tyronum et juvenum.*

[2] Lambley-upon-Tyne, a convent of Benedictine Nuns near Haltwhistle.

HEXHAM ABBEY CHURCH

EAST END

for whereas they knew that they had acted most wickedly towards the aforesaid nuns, at the last they sought out a priest who should celebrate mass for them. He, induced, as I suppose, more by fear than any other motive, performed the sacred office as far as the Confectio, but when he was about to handle and consecrate the bread, suddenly it vanished. Wishing to conceal his shame, he took another host intending to consecrate it, but it disappeared between the fingers which held it. All those present, beholding the priest's temerity rebuked and understanding the vengeance of God, fled from the place conscious of their guilt.

Again, in the church of Hexham, which was built by that illustrious bishop of the Lord, S. Wilfrid, there were placed of old several shrines, enclosing relics of the holy fathers, whereof the holy Beda describes the merits and effects in *De Gestis Anglorum*. That very church, carved with Roman work, was dedicated by the ministry of S. Wilfrid[1] to the honour of S. Andrew, the meekest of the Apostles and the spiritual patron of the Scots. And although both the dignity of the saints and respect for the pious friars ought to have been a defence against the irreverent, yet these madmen aforesaid neither had any regard for these things nor felt any dread of all-seeing God, but with barbarous ferocity committed the consecrated buildings to the flames, plundering the church property stored therein, even violating the women in that very place and afterwards butchering them, sparing neither age, rank nor sex. At last they reached such a pitch of iniquity as to fling contemptuously into the flames

[1] Son of a Northumbrian thegn; Bishop of York, died A.D. 709. It was Wilfrid's successor, Bishop Acca, who according to Beda, collected the relics of the saints and their legends.

the relics of the saints preserved in shrines, tearing off them the gold or silver plates and gems. Also, roaring with laughter, they cut the head off the image of S. Andrew, a conspicuous figure, declaring he must leave that place and return to his own soil to be trodden under foot.

About the same time a voice was heard in the high heavens by trustworthy ears, calling thrice for vengeance upon the unrighteous nation. How this reached the divine ears will be made clear by the misfortunes which were shortly to befal that people. For as these cowardly fellows were hastening home, impelled by divine vengeance they adopted a further counsel of foolishness, whereby in separate columns one part of their
MS. fo. 205b army occupied the narrow pass into Lothian, the other, the passes bordering on Teviotdale, so as to threaten the march of an English force should it attempt to pass beyond them, when they would attack it upon both flanks. In accordance with this plan, on the eleventh of the kalends of May[1] the Earl of Mar and others came before Dunbar with the chosen candidates for knighthood, intending to have that fortress as a base. After they had plundered the neighbourhood and burnt the town, they laid siege to the castle. Now as there was no proper garrison in the place, the countess, with her slender household and the earl's brother, defended it for two days. But the enemy, pretending that the earl was a traitor through his having joined the cause of the King of England in order to keep faith, persuaded the lady to surrender honourably; and so, at dawn of the fourth day[2] they entered the castle,[3] having as commander a man renowned in war and expert in arms, Sir Richard Siward. And when they

[1] 21st April. [2] 25th April. [3] *Municipium.*

had crowded in, like sheep into a pen, straightway they were beleaguered before evening by land and sea, as though God had assembled them as a sacrifice for their enemies. When it was known that they were besieged, summons was issued to all parts of Scotland for an early muster to relieve the besieged and a day was fixed at the beginning of May for hostilities in the field. Nor was it only the secular arm [that was raised] but also the ecclesiastical arm drew a poisoned sword, ordering, under pain of suspension, that all in charge of parishes should on every Lord's day in the presence of the people fulminate solemn denunciation of the Prince of England and the Bishop of Durham, the clergy chanting *Deus laudem ne tã.* Thereafter many ordained priests are known to have taken part in the war, not only by exhortation, but also by wielding arms.

Howbeit, forasmuch as the truth ever remains invincible, although the uneasy conscience will always imagine dire events, when they perceived the flower of their youth and the main part of their army confined within the walls, they determined to put an end to the siege by a sudden assault and so to unite the relieved garrison with their own forces. Therefore on the fifth of the kalends of May,[1] at the ninth hour of Friday (which thus a second time proved unlucky for them) when the Earl of Warenne and barely a fifth part of the King's army were preparing to go to bed, they showed themselves boldly on the brow of a steep hill, provoking their enemy to combat. And although their columns were in close order and strong in numbers, before it was possible to come to close quarters [with them], they broke up and scattered more swiftly than smoke, the fiercest of them being

[1] 27th April.

first in flight. Yet their foot-soldiers would have stood firm had not the knights showed their heels so readily; and because victory consisteth not in the multitude of a host, but cometh from Heaven, thou mayest discern in that conflict what the Lord promised to his chosen people—'They come,' said He, 'against thee by one way, and they flee in ten ways.'

In this manner there were slain not less than ten thousand rebels, and several tonsured [priests] were found among the dead; yet upon the English side, not one man fell, except a single foolhardy knight. It is evident that the Supreme Truth, who said that He had come into the world to set a man against his own father, decided the issue of this combat, which was waged against the truth; for there you might see in the same people a son bearing arms against his father, and a brother putting his neighbour to the sword.

After this, justice was directed against the besieged. For they had lighted on the tower of the castle a signal beacon, informing the relieving force when they might surprise [the enemy] and at what moment they should deliver the assault. Therefore some [of the English] having been set to work with a will to dig mines, others to throw up earthworks from which they could forcibly breach the castle wall, the garrison fell into a panic, and straightway surrendered on the morrow to the royal will. There were captured there and sent into captivity in divers parts of England, among the nobility, four earls—Mar, Menteith, Atholl and Ross, besides six score and fourteen others, among whom there were several barons, twenty knights, and eighty esquires. Also, three hundred foot-soldiers were taken there whom the King had no wish to detain, but set them free after receiving their parole;

also he granted them safe conduct to whatever place outside the neighbourhood of the camps they would go to, which greatly contributed to the credit of his clemency, even from the lips of his enemies.

At this agitating time the Lord Bishop of Durham caused to be seized all the lands which Sir John de Balliol held of the fee of S. Cuthbert; and upon these lands at Castle Barnard he caused a prisoner of the same John [aged] eighty-eight, to be brought out of filth, had him shaved, gave him a change of clothing and set him at liberty, besides restoring to him the lands of which he had been deprived. All these things go to prove the Christian mercy of the English, who despite the response of ill-disposed people, returned good for evil gratuitously.

In the same year Pope Boniface made a decree and caused it to be promulgated, that anniversary services[1] should be celebrated throughout the universal Church of Christ on the feast of every apostle and evangelist and also of the four doctors. Also he issued another decree against dogs returning to their vomit, that none of the Preaching or Minorite friars, nor of the Hermits of S. Augustine, nor yet of any of the Mendicant friars, should furnish any assistance to any election, postulation, provision, or call at his own instance in any contest for any promotion beyond the ministry of his own Order. And especially, if the Masters, Ministers or Priors of their General Orders or of their inferior prelates should proceed by license or assent without spiritual sanction of the Papal See, he [Pope Boniface] pronounceth such action to be null and void, whether [it be done] knowingly or ignorantly, no matter by whom it may have been accepted. On

[1] *Duplicia.*

account of this, as I suppose, one of the clergy, humorous enough but vastly indignant, composed the facetious verses inserted below, and privily affixed them to the door of his Holiness the Pope's chamber. And these are the verses:

> Once known as Benedict, we Boniface invoke;
> Both names are seemly, may they be the cloak
> Of thy good works in piety and blessing,
> Rightly thy conduct in St. Peter's chair expressing.
> But if with wrongs and curses thou afflict us,
> We'll call thee Malefac and Maledictus![1]

On the feast of S. Barnabas the Apostle[2] there happened a memorable instance of the untrustworthiness of the Welsh.

A.D. 1296.

While my lord King Edward was besieging with a great army the lofty castle of Edinburgh, huge machines for casting stones having been set all round it, and after he had

MS. fo. 206

violently battered the castle buildings for the space of three days and nights with the discharge of seven score and eighteen stones, on the eve of the festival named, he chose a certain Welshman, his swiftest runner, whom he reckoned most trustworthy, committed to him many letters and, having provided him with money, ordered him to make his way to London with the utmost dispatch. This man was named Lewyn (as befitted his fate[3]), which in English is pronounced Lefwyn. Now, going straight to the tavern, he spent in gluttony all that he had

[1] *Papa Bonifacius modo, sed quondam Benedictus,*
Nomina bina bona, tibi sit decorus amictus.
Ex re nomen habe—benedic, benefac, benedictus;
Aut hæc perverte—maledic, malefac, maledictus.

[2] 11th June.

[3] There is here some play on the name which is not apparent to modern wits.

received for travelling expenses. Early on the morning of the vigil, being Sunday,[1] he made himself a laughing-stock to the English by ordering his comrade to carry his shield before him, declaring that he was not going to leave the place before he had made an assault upon the garrison of the castle. Presenting himself, therefore, with a balista before the gates, he cried upon the wall guard to let down a rope to him, so that, having been admitted in that manner, he might reveal to them all the secrets of their enemy. The constable of the castle, as he informed me, was taking the air when this rascal intruder was brought before him, holding out in his hand the case with the royal letters.

'Behold, my lord,' said he, 'the secrets of the King of England; examine them and see. Give me also part of the wall to defend, and see whether I know how to shoot with a balista.'

But when the others would have opened the letters, their commander forbade them to do so, and straightway, standing on a high place, called loudly to men passing that they were to make known in the king's court that one of their deserters had proposed to those within [the castle] that they should perpetrate a deceit, to which he [the constable] absolutely declined to consent for honour's sake.

Sir John le Despenser attended at once to this announcement, and to him the traitor was lowered[2] on a rope, with the letters intact, and the manner of his [Lewyn's] capture was explained to the king when he got out of bed. Now that

[1] *Mane diei festi*—literally 'early on the feast day,' but as S. Barnabas's day fell on a Monday in that year, we must read 'Early on the morning of the vigil.'

[2] *Demittimur* in Stevenson's edition, probably a clerical error for *demittitur*.

prince greatly delighted in honesty. 'I gratefully declare to God,' quoth he, 'that the fidelity of that honourable man has overcome me. Give orders that henceforth no man attempt to inflict injury upon the besieged, and that no machine cast a stone against them.'

Thus the king's wrath was soothed, for he had previously vowed that they should all be put to death. So sleep came to the eyelids of those who had watched for three days, many of them having vowed that, for security, they would so continue while alive. On the morrow, by the royal indulgence, the besieged sent messengers to King John [Balliol] who was staying at Forfar, explaining their condition and demanding assistance. But he [John] being unable to relieve them, gave leave to each man to provide for his own safety.

But let me not be silent about the punishment of the aforesaid traitor, Lewyn. He was taken, tried, drawn and hanged on a regular gibbet constructed for his crime. This tale I have inserted here in order that wise men may avoid the friendship of deceivers.

Pending the report of the messengers, King Edward raised the siege and marched with a small force to Stirling, where he found the castle evacuated for fear of him, the keys hanging above the open doors, and the prisoners imploring his mercy, whom he immediately ordered to be set at liberty. And so, in the king's absence, after fifteen days siege, the Maidens' Castle[1] was surrendered into the hands of Sir John le Despenser, a place whereof it is nowhere recorded in the most ancient annals that it had ever been captured before, owing to its height and strength.

[1] *Castrum Puellarum*, one of the names for Edinburgh.

LANERCOST

It was called Edwynesburgh of old after its founder, King Edwyn, who, it is said, placed his seven daughters therein for safety.

Now when it had been laid down by the Scots to their king [John] that he was neither to offer battle nor accept peace, but that he should keep in hiding by constant flight, King Edward, on the other hand, strengthened his resolve that neither the ocean should bear him [John] away, nor the hills and woods hide him. Rather than that, having him surrounded by land and sea at Kincardine, he compelled him to come to Montrose, subject to King Edward's will and judgment. There he renounced his kingly right, and, having experience of dishonest counsellors, submitted to the perpetual loss both of his royal honour in Scotland and of his paternal estates in England. For, having been sent to London with his only son, he led an honourable, but retired life, satisfied with the funds allotted to him from the king's exchequer. By divine ordinance these things were accomplished on the morrow of the translation of S. Thomas the Martyr,[1] in retribution for the crime of Hugh de Morville, from whom that witless creature[2] [John] was descended; for just as he [Morville] put S. Thomas to death, so thereafter there was not one of his posterity who was not deprived either of his personal dignity or of his landed property.

Also on the same day[3] fell the anniversary of my lord, Alexander,[4] formerly King of Scotland, who descended from the other daughter of the illustrious Earl David, besides whom there proceeded from that sister no legitimate progeny

[1] 8th July. [2] *Acephalus.* [3] 8th July.
[4] *i.e.* Alexander II., who died 8th July, 1249.

of the royal seed to her King Edward,[1] who alone after William the Bastard became monarch of the whole island. It is clear that this succession to Scotland [came] not so much by right of conquest or forfeiture as by nearness of blood to S. Margaret whose daughter, Matilda, Henry the elder, King of England, married [and became] heir, as is shown by what is written above.

On the same day as the abdication King Edward gave a splendid banquet to the nobles and commons; but inasmuch as in this life sorrow is mingled with rejoicing, the king received on that day news of the death in Gascony of his brother, my lord Edmund, a valiant knight and noble, who was genial and merry, generous and pious. It is said that his death was brought about by want of means, because he had with him a large body of mercenaries and but little ready money. He left two surviving youths, Thomas and Henry, his sons by the Queen of Navarre; of whom the elder took in marriage with her entire inheritance the only daughter of my lord Henry, Earl of Lincoln, who then possessed the earldoms of Lancaster and Ferrers in right of his father, and those of Lincoln and Salisbury in right of
MS. fo. 206b his wife.

About the same time there came an astonishing and unprecedented flood in the Seine at Paris, probably a presage of things to come, such as is described above as having happened in the

[1] *Qui ex altera germana filia descendit David illustris comitis, ultra quem non processit ex illa sorore legitima soboles regalis seminis regi suo Edwardo.* It seems impossible to make sense from this passage. Probably something has dropped out or become garbled. 'The illustrious Earl David' might either be King David I., who was Earl of Northumberland, and reigned in Cumbria and Strathclyde till he succeeded his brother, Alexander I., or King David's third son, who was Earl of Huntingdon.

Tweed.[1] For of a sudden, while men were not expecting it, and were taking their ease in bed, the floods came and the winds blew and threw down both the bridges of the city in deep water with all upon them, which consisted of the choicer houses, superior merchandise and brothels of the costlier class; and, just as in the Apocalypse, all this wealth was ruined in a single hour, together with its pleasures and luxury, so that the saying of Jeremiah may be most aptly applied to them, that the iniquity of the people of Paris was greater than the sin of the people of Sodom, which was overwhelmed in a moment, nor could they avail to protect it.[2]

It is quite certain that this people had given such offence to the Lord that they suffered punishment, not only for their own transgression, but because of the corruption of their nation, the consequence of whose pride is to undermine obedient faith throughout the world. Having the appearance of piety, they deny the power thereof; they make a mockery of the sacraments; they blaspheme with sneers the Word of Life made flesh by a virgin mother; they boast of their iniquity more openly than did Sodom; and, as said by the Apostle Jude, they defile the flesh, they spurn authority, and they blaspheme majesty.[3] These things did the Virgin of virgins, as I consider, intend to avenge terribly—she who, dwelling between the river banks of that city, has wrought so many signs of salvation for that people, especially in quenching the fires of hell, wherein no one worthy of her protection remains abandoned beyond the ninth day.

[1] P. 108 *ante*.

[2] History repeated itself in the inundation of Paris during the winter 1909-10.

[3] The severity of the chronicler's censure may be traced to its source in the friendly relations between France and Scotland.

THE CHRONICLE OF

In honour of the Glorious Virgin I will relate what took place at an earlier time, in the tenth year of King Edward's reign ; at least it was then made manifest, but not yet completed by the actual events. Now, that turbulent and distracted nation, I mean the Welsh, thinking to wreak their long-standing spite upon the English, ever incur severer penalty for their wickedness. Thus when led by a certain David, they were endeavouring to kindle mischief in the realm of King Edward, and to turn his friendliness into hostility, that energetic prince [Edward] mustered a force and, marching against the enemy at Worcester, commended himself and his troops, with many oblations and consecrations, to the keeping of the Glorious Virgin. Immediately the Queen of Virtues granted the petition of the suppliant, and, appearing one night to a cleric named John, of the Church of S. Mary of Shrewsbury, as he was sleeping, with her own hand laid upon his bosom a closed letter fastened with a seal. Also she commanded him—'Rise early, and carry for me the letter I have given thee to King Edward who is quartered at Worcester. Thou mayst be sure he will not withhold from thee a suitable reward.'

On awaking he actually found the letter exactly according to the vision. He remembered the mission commanded to him, but bethought him of his own humble degree and hesitated to take the journey.

The command was repeated to him and a reward was added. He had a beloved comrade (a certain cleric J——, named de Houton, who, being still alive in the Minorite Order, constantly describes the course of this incident) to whom he said :—

'I beg that you will bear me company as far as Worcester, for I have some business to attend to at the king's court.'

But, whereas he never mentioned the sacred declaration of the Blessed Virgin, his friend refused his request, not being aware what reason there was for it. The Virgin, footstool of the Holy Trinity, appeared for the third time to her sluggish servant, reproached him for disobedience, and as a punishment for his neglect foretold that his death would be soon and sudden. Terrified at this, he made his will, appointed executors, charging them to forward the heavenly letter with the utmost haste, and then expired suddenly.

Nobody could be found who would dare to present himself to the king's notice except an insignificant tailor; who, however, was graciously received by the king, and did not retire with empty hands. But when the king, by the hearth in his chamber, had mastered the contents of the letter, he knelt thrice, kissing the ground and returning thanks to the Glorious Virgin. 'And where,' cried he, 'is that cleric who brought this dispatch, and whom the Virgin's word commends to me?'

The substitute having informed him that the messenger was dead, the king was much grieved. As to what the Queen of Glory promised to him, he was not fully informed, except this, that then and ever after he should successfully prevail over his enemies; and from that day to this he has observed a solemn fast on bread and water every Saturday, through love of his protectress. Moreover, he began to build in London a costly and sumptuous church in praise of the same Mother of God, which is not yet finished.

But let me return to my theme. After the abdication of John de Balliol, as has been described, King Edward caused it to be announced that, throughout his progress, no man should plunder or burn, and further, that a fair price should be paid for all necessary supplies. He marched forward into Mar to the merchant town of Aberdeen, where some cunning messengers of the King of the French, detained in some port, were taken and brought into the king's presence, having many duplicate letters addressed to the King of Scots as well as to his nobles. Although he [King Edward] would have paid them out for their guile, he restrained those who would do violence to these men, and, having restored to them the letters which had been discovered, he sent them by rapid stages to the neighbourhood of London, that they might see and converse with the king of whom they were in search, and telling him what they had found, might return by another way to the country whence they came.

With kingly courage, he [King Edward] pressed forward into the region of the unstable inhabitants of Moray, whither you will not find in the ancient records that any one had penetrated since Arthur. His purpose was to explore with scattered troops the hills and woods and steep crags which the natives are accustomed to count on as strongholds. With what piety and frugality he performed all these things, let his pardons, condescensions, bounties and festivals testify. Having brought all that land into subjection he returned to Berwick on the octave of the Assumption [1] where the homage of the people of Alban [2] was repeated to my lord the King of England and his son and successor ; also it was renewed again by a charter with all the seals of the nobles, which remains confirmed by a solemn oath made in touching two
MS. fo. 207 pieces of the Lord's cross. But that ceremony of swearing, not

[1] 22nd August. [2] *i.e.* Scotland.

being imbued by the faith of those who performed it, was worthless to them, as their open acts made manifest in the following year.

Now something very pleasing to our people took place through the aid of the Glorious Virgin on the day after the Assumption.[1] After the men of the Cinque Ports had conveyed some knights and foot-soldiers bound for Gascony, they encountered on the high sea three hundred vessels bound from Spain to France with much valuable cargo. Our people, who had but four score vessels, attacked them and put them all to flight, capturing out of that fleet eight and twenty ships and three galleys. In one of the galleys they found sixty score hogsheads of wine. In celebration, therefore, of that victory accorded them by God, they forwarded part of the wine to the knights campaigning in Gascony, bringing the rest to London for consecration, whereof my informant drank some, a man of truthful conversation and learned in religion. Events of this kind ought to be plainly described to those who delight in vanities, and, having no experience of heavenly matters, lightly esteem intercourse with the higher powers. For few may be found in our age who deserve to share the sweetness of divine revelation, not because of God's parsimony, but because of the sluggishness of the spiritual sense.

Now in this year there happened to a certain holy virgin, long consecrated to the life of an anchorite, a revelation which ought not to be passed over in silence. In the district of Shrewsbury, about six miles from the town, there dwelleth that holy woman, Emma by name, who is accustomed to receive visits from holy men; and at the festival of S. Francis[2] (which is observed

[1] 16th August. [2] 16th July.

rather on account of the merit of the saint than of the Order itself, whose dress she weareth), on the vigil of the saint she admitted two friars of that order to hospitality. At midnight, the hour when the friars are accustomed to sing praises to God, the holy woman rose from her bed, remembering in her pious heart that on such a feast day a similar obligation lay upon her who had become a recluse, and how much honour was shown to the saint throughout the divers regions of the world. Kindled in spirit by these [thoughts], she called her handmaid and told her to bring a lamp for the morning praise. The lamp having been brought and placed twice upon the altar of the oratory, a sudden gust extinguished it, so that not a spark of light remained. Now the patron of that church is the Herald of Christ and more than a prophet,[1] to whom the recluse was bound by more than common love, and, as will be shown presently, had experienced much intimacy with the friend of Christ. Therefore, while she was wondering why her lamp should be extinguished, she beheld a ray of heavenly light coming through the window of his oratory, which was next the church, which, surpassing the radiance of the sun, beautified with a heavenly lustre the features of her maidens, who lay in a distant part of the house, notwithstanding that the maidens themselves were weeping because of the abundance of the celestial illumination. The Prior[1] came in that he might bear witness about the light, so that all men might believe through him. The lamp was burning, shedding light and reassuring the astonished woman. 'Behold,' said he, 'thou wilt presently have a mass.' That saint, as often as he appeared to this handmaid of Christ, held in his hand a roll as a token and badge of his office,

[1] S. John the Baptist.

wherein was contained in order the holy gospel of God—'In the beginning was the Word.'

After the declaration of the Baptist there followed immediately such a transcendent radiance as would rather have stunned than stimulated human senses, had they not been sustained by grace; in which [radiance] appeared, with a wonderful fragrance, the Mother of Eternal Light, environed by a brilliant tabernacle, in token, as I suppose, that He who created her would find rest in her tabernacle; and four of the Minorite Order bore her company in her propitious advent, of whom the chief was S. Antony, an illustrious preacher of the Word, and with him were three others, natives of England, famed either by their lives or by their wisdom.

The Queen of the World took her place, as was proper, over the holy altar of the choir; the others prepared themselves to perform the mass. Then S. Antony led off in vestments ot indescribable [richness], and the others sang with such marvellous sweetness and thrilling melody, that many blameless persons in a distant part of the town wondered at the harmony, not knowing whence it came.

Now the introitus of the mass was this, pronounced in a loud voice—'Thou art the King of Glory, O Christ!' and what follows, as far as—*Te ergo quis famulis* and *subveni quos pretioso*, et cætera. The woman remembered that this was thrice repeated, but the collect and epistle and the other parts of the mass she could not so well recollect. And when she asked what were the names of these persons, and inquired of the holy Baptist why S. Francis was not present, she received this answer—'Upon this his festival he himself has to intercede with God for numerous persons who are invoking him as a new saint, therefore he was unable to come on this occasion.'

At the time of preparing the sacred mystery in the aforesaid mass, S. Antony elevated the Host with great dignity and honour, whereat the holy Virgin[1] prostrated herself with the others devoutly and low. At the close of the office, the Queen of Mercy descended gently to the sister,[2] and comforted her with heavenly converse and confidences, besides touching her beads[3] with her blessed hand. But whereas those who die in the sweet odour of Christ may be reckoned unhappy above all others, while some ignorant persons may cavil at the divine revelations accorded to this humble woman, to show what a slander this is against the Lord, the forerunner of Christ said as he departed: 'Inquire of those who sneer at divine benefactions whether the Evil Spirit can perform such sacred mysteries, and rouse the friars who are slumbering here, to whose senses thou mayest exhibit the light wherewith we have purified this dwelling.'

The holy woman immediately performed his bidding, and from the third cockcrow almost until the morning light they [the friars] beheld with their eyes the whole interior of the church illumined with celestial radiance. One of them, desiring to know the source of this light, looked through the window of the church, and saw what seemed to be a burning torch before the image of the blessed Baptist, who was the herald of Eternal Light.

[1] It is not clear whether the reference is to the Mother of God or to Emma herself.

[2] *Ad sponsam.*

[3] *Numeralia devotionis.*

I will relate something else that happened to this holy soul, worth listening to, in manner as I heard it from those to whom she related it. While she was yet very young and a novice in the discipline of Christ, she still sometimes experienced carnal impulses, and was deluded by tricks of the devil; yet she could not be overcome, because she always had the Forerunner of the Lord as a guardian against the wiles of the Deceiver. Accordingly when she lay sick with a pain in her side, it happened that John the Saint of God foretold that the serpent would appear to her in disguise, and he placed in her mouth an exorcism which should dispel the illusion. No sooner had the saint departed, than Satan appeared without delay in the guise of a certain physician, announced his profession and promised a speedy cure. 'But how,' said he, 'can I be certain about the nature of your ailment? Allow me to lay my hand on the seat of your pain.'

MS. fo. 207b

The maiden persisted in declining these and other persuasions, and exclaimed: 'Thou dost not deceive me, oh Lord of Iniquity! wherefore I adjure thee by that sacred saying of the gospel—"the Word became flesh"—that thou inform me who are the men who hinder thee most.'—'The Minorites,' said he. When she asked him the reason he replied—'Because when we strive to fix arrows in the breasts of mortals they either frustrate us entirely by their opposition, or else we hardly hit our mark.' Then said she—'You have darts?'—'Undoubtedly,' quoth he, '[darts] of ignorance, and concupiscence and malice, which we employ against men, so that they may either fail in their actions, or go wholly to the bad, or conceive envy of the righteous.' Then she said—'In virtue of the Word referred to, tell me how much the said proclamation of the gospel hindereth your work.'

Then the Enemy, groaning heavily, replied—'Woe is me that I came here to-day! The Word about which thou inquirest is so puissant that all of us must bow the knee when we hear it, nor are we able afterwards to apply our poison in that place.'

Since mention has been made here of the protection of S. Francis being faithfully invoked, I will allude here to two incidents which took place in Berwick, about three years before the destruction of that town. That same city was formerly so populous and busy that it might well be called a second Alexandria, its wealth being the sea and the waters its defence. In those days the citizens, having become very powerful and devoted to God, used to spend liberally in charity; among other [objects] out of love and reverence they were willing to provide for the Order of S. Francis, and alloted a certain yearly sum of money from the common chest for the honourable celebration of every festival of the blessed Francis, and further for the provision of clothing for the poor friars dwelling in their city, whereby they fulfilled the double object of charity, and of performing devout service to the saint who began life as a trader,[1] expecting that even in the present [life] greater profits from trading would be the result of their costly piety. Nor did their conjecture play them false nor their hope deceive them, seeing how they increased in riches; until, as [the hour of] their expulsion drew nigh, they were persuaded by the suggestion of certain persons of corrupt mind (who became the source of calamity, not only to these citizens, but indeed to their whole country) first to diminish their accustomed charity and then to reduce it by one

[1] *Ex mercatore converso.* S. Francis was the son of an Italian merchant trading with France, whence the son's name, Francesco.

half. But whereas Sir John Gray, knight as well as burgess, who had departed this life many years before, was the promoter of this charity, God warned the populace of their imminent danger in manner following.

In the year preceding the Scottish war there appeared unto Thomas Hugtoun, a younger son of the said knight, the vision of his father, lately deceased, among the bands of holy friars in a certain abode of delight, and similar in carriage and dress to the rest of the Minorites. And, while he recognised the figure of his father but marvelled because of the change in his condition, the following reply was made to his perplexed meditations. 'Thou marvellest, my son, because thou never didst hitherto behold me attired in the dress of the Minorites; yet thou must learn hereby that I am numbered by God among those in whose society I have taken most delight. Go thou, therefore, instead of me to our neighbours in Berwick, and summon them publicly on behalf of God to revive and restore that charitable fund which I had begun to expend in honour of the blessed Father Francis; otherwise, they shall speedily experience, not only the decay of their worldly possessions, but also the dishonour of their bodies.'

Roused from his sleep, Thomas immediately described to his townspeople the revelation made to him, urging them to mend their ways. As they paid no heed to him, events followed in order confirming the vision; for first their trade declined, and then the sword raged among them.

Something else happened testifying to cause and effect and to the honour of the saint. One of these burgesses, deploring the disrespect paid to the saint, offered to provide at his own expense, the things necessary for the saint's festival; which thing he had no sooner undertaken than he was struck with a grievous malady affecting his whole body, pronounced by all the physicians to be incurable. Then the friars having persuaded him to put his trust in the saint and to hope for recovery, he directed that he should immediately have all the limbs of his body measured in honour of the saint, and in less time than it takes to tell it, he sat up healed, complaining of nothing except a headache. 'And no wonder!' exclaimed his wife, smiling, 'for his head is the only part of him we left unmeasured.' The line having been applied again, immediately he was freed from all pain. The same individual, being delivered a second time, is in good health at the present time, while his fellow-citizens were cut in pieces by the sword; and all this through the merits of S. Francis.[1]

On the morrow of the Epiphany[2] the clergy assembled in London to hold council upon the answer to be returned to my lord the king, who had imposed a tax of seven pence upon the personality of laymen, while from the clergy he demanded twelve pence in the form of a subsidy; which was agreed to reluctantly, the clergy declaring that, while they would freely submit to the royal will, they dared not transgress the papal instruction.[3] And thus all the private property and granaries of the Archbishop of Canterbury were confiscated by the king's authority, even to the palfreys reserved for the primate's riding; to all of which this virtuous man patiently submitted. Also, all ecclesiastics were

[1] See under the year 1285 for another instance of the cure by measuring for S. Francis.

[2] 7th January.

[3] *i.e.* the Bull of 29th Feb., 1295-6—*Clericos laicos.* The papal sanction was required for any tax upon the clergy.

deprived of the king's protection, and all their movables given over to the hands of laymen. Yet was this inconsiderate action speedily checked by the hand of God; for there occurred two calamities on the vigil of the Purification,[1] [namely] a defeat of our people in Gascony, where Sir John de Saint-John[2] and very many others of our countrymen were captured; also stores provided for them, and shipped, were sunk in mid-ocean. When this news was published, bringing much matter of grief to king and country, a certain just, grey haired man, drawing conclusion from a similar event, told me what I repeat here. MS. fo. 208

'In the time,' said he, 'of Henry the father of Edward, when something similar had been executed in ecclesiastical affairs throughout the province, on pretext of aid to those who, resisting the affection of beloved wives and children, had long before set out to rescue the Holy Land from the Saracens, it happened that Bishop Robert Grosstête of Lincoln, [a man] beloved of God, was to perform solemn ordinations at Huntingdon during Lent. One of the Minorite Order, who still survives greatly aged at Doncaster, was present there, received ordination, witnessed the course of events, and describes what took place in the following manner.

'After mass was begun,' said he, 'and the bishop was seated on his throne, he who had to read out the names of those who were to be ordained and presented to the bishop, came forward with the roll; and whereas he was very slow in reading out the list, the bishop leaned his head upon the side of the seat, and fell

[1] 1st February.

[2] The King's Lieutenant of Aquitaine. The actual date of his capture was 28th January. He was released after the treaty of l'Aumône in 1299.

asleep. Those, however, who were near him, bearing in mind his fasting and vigils, interpreted the prelate's repose as an omen ; and it was manifest when he awoke how wakeful had been his mind during sleep. For after the clergy had waited wondering for some time longer, he was gently awakened by a certain secretary, and, as he opened his eyes—'Eh, God !' he exclaimed, 'what great evils has this extortion from the Church of God entailed upon the Christians fighting with the Saracens for the rights of God. For in my sleep I beheld the overthrow of the Christian host at Damietta and the plunder of treasure unjustly collected.'

The confirmation of this oracle followed in a few months, when the sad news arrived of the slaughter of my lord J. Longspee and others, whereof thou mayst read above.[1]

Thus spake my informant: it is to be feared what may happen to funds collected by such pillaging. Nevertheless, the king did not abate the tax ; yea, he commanded that inquisition be made, so that in whatsoever place, whether occupied by monks or other persons, should be found hoards of gold or silver, brass, wool, cups, spoons, or other utensils, they should be rendered into royal possession by marks and inventory ; all which was afterwards carried out on the morrow of S. Mark's day.[2]

Holy Writ saith that 'vain are all men in whom is not the wisdom of God'; whereof verily the present times afford proof. For we know that in these days there hath been found a certain

[1] See the Chronicle of the year 1249, where the defeat and capture of S. Louis is recorded. In that passage Longespee is called *illustris comes de Longa Spata*. Excuse for somnolence might have been found in the bishop's advanced age, he being then in his 75th year.

[2] 26th April.

member of that ancient and accursed sect the Ambigenses, named Galfrid, who led astray many from the faith and hope of salvation, as he had learnt from others. For he entered houses and clandestinely taught about destiny and the constellations, disclosing thefts and mischances, so that in the estimation of weak-minded persons he was reputed to be something great, whereas in reality, he was a most nefarious necromancer. Also he took care to dwell and spend his nights apart, and to lie where he could often be heard as it were, giving questions and answers to divers persons. He used to make light of the doctrine of God and to ridicule the sacraments of the church; for it was ascertained that during sixteen years he would neither partake of the Holy Communion nor witness it, nor afterwards when he was mortally sick did he even deign to be confessed. This wretched man's errors having frequently been exposed by Holy Church, he was forced to flee through divers countries and districts, all men driving him forth, even John of Peckham himself, Archbishop of Canterbury, interdicting him from remaining within the bounds of his diocese, until at length he stopped at the monastery of Stone in Staffordshire, being received into hiding rather than to hospitality. After he had spent his execrable life there for a long time, he fell at length into a last illness, and not even then would he cease to cling to the devil who appeared to him, or to say—'Now thinkest thou to have me? or that I will come with thee? nay verily, for I will by no means do so.' But on the day of the Purification of the Blessed Virgin[1] this infamous man was being constrained to leave the world in deadly torment, when two of the Order of Minorites turning aside thither stood beside his bed, urging him beseechingly

[1] 2nd February.

and gently that he would confess, assuring him of the mercy and grace of God ; but he persisted in turning a deaf ear to the counsels of salvation. And when they perceived by his breathing that he must speedily give up the ghost, they cried aloud in his ears, bidding him at least invoke the name of the Lord Jesus for the sake of mercy. They continued their clamour, persisting in shoutings, yet he never fully pronounced that sweet name, but only with his last breath he twice said feebly, 'Miserere!' and so bade farewell to this life.

At the beginning of Lent so great was the scarcity in Rome, that the citizens, knowing that the stores of the church were laid up in the Capitol, broke into the same, and plundered the corn and salt which they found, forcing their way in with such violence that sixty of them were crushed to death, after the manner of the famine of Samaria.[1] And because the Pope appointed a certain senator against their will, with one accord they would have set fire to the papal palace and attacked the Father of the Church, had it not been for the exertions of a certain cardinal, who assuaged their madness and caused the Pope to alter his decision.

On the very day of the Annunciation[2] the council assembled again in London [to decide] what they would give freely to my lord the king. But certain of the prelates without

A.D. 1297.

the knowledge of the archbishop, had pledged themselves to submit to the secular authority, with whom the Abbot of Oseney was implicated. When he had presented himself

MS. fo. 208b and the archbishop had kissed him, he [the archbishop] was informed by the clergy that the abbot, contrary to the will of the church, had seceded from the unity of the clergy. The arch-

[1] ii. Kings vii. 17. [2] 25th March.

bishop therefore called him back and rebuked him, revoking the kiss which he had given him in ignorance. He so terrified the transgressor by the words of just rebuke that, retiring to his lodging in the town, he suffered a failure of the heart; and, while his attendants were preparing a meal, he bade them recite to him the miracles of the Glorious Virgin, and departed this life before taking any food. There seems to be repeated in this man the story of Ananias, who was rebuked by Peter for fraud in respect of money.

Hardly had a period of six months passed since the Scots[1] had bound themselves by the above-mentioned solemn oath of fidelity and subjection to the king of the English, when the reviving malice of that perfidious [race] excited their minds to fresh sedition. For the bishop of the church in Glasgow, whose personal name was Robert Wishart, ever foremost in treason, conspired with the Steward of the realm, named James,[2] for a new piece of insolence, yea, for a new chapter of ruin. Not daring openly to break their pledged faith to the king, they caused a certain bloody man, William Wallace, who had formerly been a chief of brigands in Scotland, to revolt against the king and assemble the people in his support. So about the Nativity of the Glorious Virgin[3] they began to show themselves in rebellion; and when a great army of England was to be assembled against them, the Steward treacherously said to them [the English]—'It is not expedient to set in motion so great a

[1] Albanacti.

[2] Father of Walter Stewart who, by his marriage with Marjory, daughter of Robert I., became progenitor of the Stuart dynasty.

[3] 8th September.

multitude on account of a single rascal; send with me a few picked men, and I will bring him to you dead or alive.'

When this had been done and the greater part of the army had been dismissed, the Steward brought them to the bridge of Stirling, where on the other side of the water the army of Scotland was posted. They [the Scots] allowed as many of the English to cross the bridge as they could hope to overcome, and then, having blocked the bridge,[1] they slaughtered all who had crossed over, among whom perished the Treasurer of England, Hugh de Cressingham, of whose skin William Wallace caused a broad strip to be taken from the head to the heel, to make therewith a baldrick for his sword.[2] The Earl of Warenne escaped with difficulty and with a small following, so hotly did the enemy pursue them. After this the Scots entered Berwick and put to death the few English that they found therein; for the town was then without walls, and might be taken as easily by English or Scots coming in force. The castle of the town, however, was not surrendered on this occasion.

After these events the Scots entered Northumberland in strength, wasting all the land, committing arson, pillage, and murder, and advancing almost as far as the town of Newcastle; from which, however, they turned aside and entered the county of Carlisle. There they did as they had done in Northumberland, destroying everything, then returned into Northumberland to lay waste more completely what they had left at first; and re-entered Scotland on the feast of S. Cecilia, Virgin and Martyr,[3]

[1] *Ponte obturato.*

[2] Other writers say the skin was cut up into horse-girths.

[3] 22nd November.

1296

oscultatus fuisset · edoctus est per clericos quod contra sentenciam ecclesie decimarum a clero vendiderat · renovatum g[illegible] esse conperiit · detestatusque est osculum quod sic intraverat potaverat · tantum autem timore et verbis sue correpcionis tenebris invasit · quod ad proprium in urbe hospicium secedens · lectum doloris intravit · Et dum clientes mensam pararent · ipse sub miranda gloriose virginis ecclesie consortio precepit · et pro suis abiit sinister subito et hac luce decessit · Renovata videtur in isto elatione hystoria · que contigit Petro · eo quod fraudasset de pecunia ¶ Post hec vero infra tempus elapsum extitit a gente sancto suppositorum quo se Albanacti fidelitatem ac obedienciam Regis Anglorum astrinxerant · cum redivivam prioris malicie ad alias versiones ingenium animi · Jam presul ecclesie Glasguensis predictus cognomine dictus Robertus Wyshard semper in prodicione primus · cum senescallo prince terre · nomine Jacobo nouam sibi fictuit quandam conjurationem · nouam prodicionis fomentum foventes Regi fidelitatem manifeste infringere non audentes · quendam virum sanguinum Willelmum Waleis qui prius fuerat in Scocia princeps latronum · contra Regem insurgere fecerunt · et ipsos in eum adiutorium congregare · Circa nativitatem vero domini gloriose se ostendere et rebellare cepit · Contra quos cum congregatus esset magnus exercitus Anglorum · dixit eis senescallus dolose non est necesse tantam multitudinem · dicens pro uno ribaldo · mittatis mecum paucos viros si electos · et ego vobis eum adducam mortuum sine vivum · Quod cum hoc fecissent · et magna parte exercitus recessisset · duxit eos senescallus ad pontem de Strivelyn · ubi et ultra aquam erat exercitus Scotorum congregatus · quando autem de Anglicis transire pontem presumserunt · quot plures se spendebant · et ponte obturato omnes qui transierunt occisi sunt inter quos erat thesaurarius Anglorum Hugo de Kersyngham · de cuius corio ab occipite usque ad talum Willelmus Waleis latam corrigiam sumi fecit et inde sibi fieri cingulum ensis sui · Comes autem Warenne vix cum paucis evasit · qui precedentes eos ante inimicis · Scoti villam Berwici cum victores intraverunt et paucos Anglicos qui invenerunt ibi occiderunt · villa vero tunc non erat murata · et ideo cito capiebatur ad antiquis in fortitudine venientibus nisi a Scotis · castrum tamen ville non fuit redditum illa vice ¶ Post hec Scoti conglobati Northumbriam invaserunt · et omnem provinciam devastantes facientes incendia depredaciones et homicidia · et venerunt fere usque ad villam novi castri · illam autem declinaverunt · et comitatum Karleoli invaserunt · et sic in Northumbriam redeuntes omnia destruentes · et postea in Northumbriam redierunt · que plus omiserant plenius devastando · Et in festo sancte Cecilie virginis ...

in Scociam redierunt · nullum tamen castrum in Anglia vel in Scocia adhuc capere potuerunt ¶ Interea quod defensam autem illi amni paraverunt se comites et Barones Anglie ad plenum quod Scotos in absencia Regis invasuri essent · et venerunt super eos qui tunc se congregantes usque ad castrum Rokesburgh quod tunc obsidebant aliquamdiu licet parum · In adventu cognito Anglicorum statim fugam inierunt ¶ Comites vero prefati intrantes sunt Rokesburgh · et postea usque Berwicum unanimiter diverterunt · et villam illam ceperunt · post recessum vero comitum a Rokesburgh · supervenerunt Scotti de nocte et villam combusserunt · et sic villam de Hadyngton · et alias omnes villas bonas circa mare Scoticanum · ne Anglia recepta cibum in terra invenirent · exercitus vero Anglorum propter defectum victualium ...to compulsi sunt redire in Angliam · et aliis paucis quos pro villa Berewica custodienda reliquerunt · Audientes vero Scotti tam subitum recessum eorum et inspecta post paschatem.

1297

Posuerunt se ad castra Scotorum que ab Anglicis tenebantur totis viribus obsidenda · et propter famem in castris · castra omnia occupaverunt · preter Rokesburgh Edenburgh Strevelyn · et Berwyk · et pauca alia · et cum in reddicione castrorum promisissent ex pacto Anglicis vitam et membra · et Scoti tenerent in terra sua · Willelmus Waleis non tenuit eis fidem ¶ Interim capte sunt treuge inter Regem Francie et Regem Anglie · et rediit Rex in Angliam · et intelligens quod Scoti in absencia sua se erexerunt versus terram collecto exercitu gressus suos direxit · et cum intrasset terram pergens ultra castrum ¶ In festo autem beate Marie Magdalene occurrerunt ei Scoti apud Fawkirk cum toto robore suo · duce eorum Willelmo Waleis supradicto · ordinantes marte more solito in peditibus lancearis quos in primo acie posuerunt · Equites autem armati Anglorum quorum erat magnus pars exercitus circueuntes undique involverunt eos · et fugientibus cito sibi equitibus Scotorum interfecti sunt de lancearis et peditibus stantibus et viriliter agentibus lx. mil. et alios lxxx. mil. et alios c. mil. · nec fuit aliquis nobilis homo ex parte Anglie interfectus nisi magister templariorum cum quinque vel vi armigeris qui nimis velociter et inconsulte processerant cuneum Scotorum · Devictis autem sic finibus Regis et regni · processit exercitus Anglie per unam viam ad mare Scoticanum et rediit per aliam · destruendo ea que Scotti ante dimiserant · hyeme vero ingruente dimisit Rex magnates Anglie redire ad propria · et ipse meet cum paucis marchiam custodivit ad tempus · Sed ante festum decrevit redire ad partes australes · dimissa custodia in marchia prenominata.

¶ Berwik et Dunbar sine curiali capella.
¶ Convenit quod valeant Scottorum prelia bella.
Princeps absque pare cum sic tuus Anglia gaude · ardua temptare sub eo securius aude

without, however, having been able as yet to capture any castle either in England or Scotland.

Now before Lent in that year[1] the earls and barons of England prepared themselves for war against the Scots, in the absence of the king, who was in Gascony, and came upon them unawares at Roxburgh Castle, which they were then besieging with only a weak force. Being informed of the approach of the English, they took to flight at once ; but the earls remained some time at Roxburgh, but afterwards with one accord turned aside to Berwick and took that town. Howbeit, after the earls had left Roxburgh, the Scots came by night and burnt the town, and so they did to the town of Haddington, as well as to nearly all the chief towns on this side of the Scottish sea,[2] so that the English should find no place of refuge in Scotland. Thus the army of England was soon compelled to return to England through lack of provender, except a small force which was left to guard the town of Berwick.

When the Scots heard of the sudden and unexpected retreat of the English after Easter,[3] they set themselves down before the castles of Scotland which were held by the English, to besiege them with all their force, and A.D. 1298. through famine in the castles they obtained possession of them all, except Roxburgh, Edinburgh, Stirling, and Berwick, and a few others ; and when they had promised to the English conditions of life and limb and safe conduct to their own land on surrendering the castles, William Wallace did not keep faith with them.

Meanwhile, truce was made between the King of France and

[1] 1297-8. [2] Firth of Forth. [3] 6th April.

the King of England, and the king returned to England, and finding how the Scots had risen in his absence, he assembled an army and directed his march towards Scotland, and having entered that country, he passed through part thereof.

So on the festival of the blessed Mary Magdalene [1] the Scots gave him battle with all their forces at Falkirk, William Wallace aforesaid being their commander, putting their chief trust, as was their custom, in their foot pikemen, whom they placed in the first line. But the armoured cavalry of England, which formed the greater part of the army, moving round and outflanking them on both sides, routed them, and, all the Scottish cavalry being quickly put to flight, there were slain of the pikemen and infantry, who stood their ground and fought manfully, sixty thousand, according to others eighty thousand, according to others one hundred thousand; [2] nor was there slain on the English side any nobleman except the Master of the Templars, with five or six esquires, who charged the schiltrom of the Scots too hotly and rashly.

Having thus entirely overcome the enemies of our king and kingdom, the army of England marched by one route to the Scottish sea,[3] and returned by another, in order to destroy all that the Scots had spared before. But on the approach of winter the king dismissed the nobles of England to their own estates, and undertook the guard of the March himself with

[1] 22nd July.

[2] Walsingham estimates the loss of the Scots at 60,000, Hemingburgh at 56,000—both preposterous figures, far exceeding the total of Wallace's forces. The only trustworthy data whereby to estimate the English losses is found in the compensation paid by King Edward for 111 horses killed in the action.

[3] Firth of Forth.

a small force for a time. But before Christmas he returned to the south, having disbanded the aforesaid guards upon the March.

VERSES.

Berwick, Dunbar, and Falkirk too
Show all that traitor Scots can do.
England exult! thy Prince is peerless,
Where thee he leadeth, follow fearless.[1]

PRAISE OF THE KING OF ENGLAND.

The noble race of Englishmen most worthy is of praise, MS. fo. 209
By whom the Scottish people have been conquered in all ways.
England exult!

The Frenchmen break their treaties as soon as they are made,
Whereby the hope of Scotsmen has been cheated and betrayed.
England exult!

O disconcerted people! hide yourselves and close your gates,
Lest Edward should espy you and wreak vengeance on your pates.
England exult!

Henceforth the place for vanquished Scots is nearest to the tail
In clash of arms. O England victorious, all hail!
England exult![2]

---

1 VERSUS.

Berwike et Dunbar, nec non Variata Capella,
Monstrant quid valeant Scottorum perfida bella.
Princeps absque pare cum sit tuus, Anglia, gaude;
Ardua temptare sub eo securius aude.

2 COMMENDATIO REGIS ANGLIA.

Nobilis Anglorum gens est dignissima laude,
Per quam Scottorum plebs vincitur—Anglia gaude!
Fœdera Francorum sunt frivola, plænaque fraude,
Per quam Scottorum spes fallitur—Anglia gaude!
Gens confusa pete latebras ac ostia claude,
Edwardus ne te videat rex—Anglia gaude!
In bellis motis pars contigit ultima caudæ
Devictis Scottis—superatrix Anglia gaude!

Of the Impiety of the Scots.

O Scottish race! God's holy shrines have been defiled by thee,
His sacred temples thou hast burnt, O crying shame to see!
Think not that thou for these misdeeds shalt punishment avoid,
For Hexham's famous sanctuary polluted and destroyed.
The pillaged house of Lanercost lies ruined and defaced;
The doers of such sacrilege must cruel vengeance taste.
Let irons, fire, and famine now scourge the wicked race,
With whom henceforth nor fame nor faith nor treaty can have place.
The Scottish nation, basely led, hath fallen in the dust;
In those who forfeit every pledge let no man put his trust.[1]

Of William Wallace.

Welsh William being made a noble,[2]
Straightway the Scots became ignoble.
Treason and slaughter, arson and raid,
By suff'ring and misery must be repaid.[3]

---

[1] De Impietate Scottorum.

Per te fœdata loca sancta Deoque dicata;
Templaque sacrata, sunt, proh dolor! igne cremata.
Esse nequiverunt destructio damnaque multa
Ecclesiæ celebris Haugustaldensis inulta.
Desolata domus de Lanercost mala plura
Passa fuit, fiet de talibus ultio dura.
Ferrum, flamma, fames venient tibi, Scotia, digne,
In qua fama, fides, fœdus periere maligne.
Sub duce degenero gens Scotica degeneravit,
Quæ famam temere, fœdus, quæ fidem violavit.

[2] Wallace is usually honoured by the knightly prefix 'Sir'; but there is no record of his receiving knighthood.

[3] De Willelmo Waleys.

Postquam Willelmus Wallensis nobilitavit,
Nobilitas prorsus Scottorum degeneravit.
Proditio, cædes, incendia, frausque rapinæ
Finiri nequeunt infelici sine fine.

LANERCOST PRIORY CHURCH

FROM DRAWING BY T. HEARNE, F.S.A. 1780

About the feast of the Nativity of the Blessed Mary the King of England married the Lady Margaret, sister of the King of France, whereby the [two] kings became friends.[1] A.D. 1299.

In the same year died Oliver, Bishop of Lincoln, and Henry of Newark, Archbishop of York. Master John of Alderby succeeded Oliver, and Henry of Corbridge, Doctor in Theology [succeeded Henry in the see of York].

About the same time Pope Boniface wrote to the King of England demanding that he should hand over to his custody John de Balliol, whom he was keeping under restraint, and the King complied with the Pope's demand in obedience to the Roman Curia.[2]

In the same year the Pope issued the statute beginning *Super cathedram, et cætera*, to promote concord between the prelates of the Church and the Orders of Preaching and Minorite Friars.

The King prepared an army for an expedition into Scotland, and during that march the Queen was delivered of her first-born son Thomas, in the northern parts about Brotherton, from which town the son there born derived his sobriquet. A.D. 1300. Howbeit the King did nothing remarkable this time against the Scots whose land he entered, because they always fled before him, skulking in moors and woods; wherefore his army was taken back to England.

[1] 8th September.

[2] John de Balliol was committed to the custody of Sir Robert de Burghesh, constable of Dover Castle, who took him to Whitsand and delivered him to the Papal nuncio. (*Fœdera.*)

In the same year William of Gainsborough, an Englishman, was summoned to the Curia, as reader in theology at the palace before the Cardinals; upon whom, after the lapse of two years, the Pope bestowed the bishopric of Worcester.

In the same [year] about the feast of S. John the Baptist,[1] my lord Edward King of England came to Carlisle with the nobles and great men of England. With him came Sir Hugh de Vere, and he stayed a while at Lanercost, and thence the King marched through the district of Galloway as far as the Water of Cree. Also he took the castle of Caerlaverock, which he gave to Sir Robert de Clifferd, and he caused many of those found within the castle to be hanged.

This, the sixth year of Pope Boniface, was the year of Jubilee.

> In Rome each hundredth year is kept as jubilee;
> Indulgences are granted and penitents go free.
> This Boniface approved of and confirmed by his decree.[2]

In the same year as above a formal embassy arrived at the Roman Curia from the King of England: to wit—the Earls of Seland, Lincoln, and Bar,[3] the Bishop of Winchester, Sir Hugh le Spenser, Galfrid de Genevilla and Otto de Grandison, knights; and the Archdeacon of Richmond and John of Berwick, clerics.[4]

[1] 24th June.

[2] *Annus centenus Romæ semper jubilæus;*
Crimina laxantur, cui pœnitet ista donantur;
Hoc declaravit Bonifacius et roboravit.

[3] *Barensis*: which might be from *Bara*, the Latinised form of Dunbar: but there is no record of Sir Patrick 'with the blak berd,' 8th Earl of Dunbar, being employed on this mission, although he was certainly in King Edward's service at this time.

[4] This embassy was sent to counter the Scottish mission earlier in the year. The chronicler's list of names does not exactly correspond with that set

The ambassadors of France were as follows—the Archbishop of Narbonne, the Bishop of Auxerre, the Counts of Saint-Paul and Boulogne, Pierre de Flota, and others.

In the same year was born Thomas of Brotherton, son of King Edward.

[Here follows in the Chronicle the famous letter of Pope Boniface VIII. to Edward I., in which he claims that 'the Kingdom of Scotland hath from ancient time belonged by undoubted right' to the Church of Rome, commands King Edward to desist from any attempt to infringe upon its independence, to release the Bishops of Glasgow and Sodor, and other clerics whom he had imprisoned, and to submit within six months to the Papal judgment all documents and other evidence which he may be able to produce in support of any claim he may have upon the kingdom of Scotland or part thereof.

The spirited reply from King Edward's Parliament of Lincoln, 12th February, 1300-1, indignantly rejecting the Pope's claim to interfere in the temporal affairs of the kingdom, is also transcribed at length in the Chronicle; but, as it is given in *Fœdera* and elsewhere, it is not necessary to repeat it here.]

At the beginning of summer the king assembled an army against the Scots and placed one part of the force under command of my lord Edward, his son by his first wife and Prince of Wales,

forth in King Edward's letter to Pope Boniface (Rymer's *Fœdera*), which included John, Bishop of Winchester; Friar William of Gainsborough; Gerard, Archdeacon of Richmond; John of Berwick, Canon of York; Amadis, Earl of Savoy (Sabaudiæ); Henry de Lacy, Earl of Lincoln; Sir Galfrid de Genevill, Sir Galfrid Russell, Sir Otto de Grandison, Sir Hugh le Despenser, Sir Amaneus, lord of le Breto; Master Reymund, *vasatensem* of Arnald de Rama; and Peter, Canon of Almeric of S. Severin's of Bordeaux.

and under command of divers nobles of England who were in his company, and these entered Scotland on the west; but [the king] kept the other part with himself and entered by

A.D. 1301.

Berwick. The Scots, however, dared not fight with either army, but fled as they had done the previous year. Howbeit they took some fine spoil from the English and did much other mischief; wherefore the king, considering that whatever he gained in Scotland during the summer he would lose in winter, decided to spend the whole winter at Linlithgow and elsewhere in Scotland, and did so. The Scots were brought far nearer subjection by that occupation than they had been before.

In the same year the Queen bore another son named Edmund, and after her purification joined the king in Scotland.

Also in these times fresh dispute took place between the Kings of France and England about the land of Gascony, but at last they came to an agreement after the truce had been renewed several times.

In the same year—

BISHOP BONIFACE, servant of the servants of God, to his venerable brother in Christ the Archbishop of Canterbury, greeting and apostolic benediction. Not without cause do we hold it to be very grave and most contrary to our wishes that prelates of the Church, who are under obligation through the nature of the pastoral office to set an example to others of praiseworthy conduct, presume with damnable audacity to proceed by uneven ways to nefarious actions, and, giving themselves the rein, do not shrink from perpetrating deeds whereby the Divine Majesty is offended, his glory disparaged, their own salvation endangered, and the minds of the faithful are unsettled by a grave scandal.

Wherefore we are actuated by becoming motives and exhort [thee] to consider advisedly how we may apply the speedy remedy of this warning, for the correction or punishment of the excesses of the prelates themselves, as justice requires.

For indeed we have learnt by trustworthy report, which has now many times been brought to our hearing, that Walter de Langton, Bishop of Coventry and Lichfield, forgetful of pastoral integrity, unmindful of his own salvation, careless of good fame, and, as it were, the destroyer of his own honour, has not feared to perpetrate, nor does he cease from committing, deeds as wicked as they are atrocious, and so nefarious that they must either produce disgust with horror in those who hear about them or else cause a loathing of such abomination; wherefore we do not consider it meet either to describe them now in these letters or to relate them by word of mouth. Wherefore, being unwilling, as indeed we ought to be, to wink at such things as offend God and scandalise men if they receive encouragement from the truth, we must proceed by careful consideration to inflict deserved punishment upon these persons, lest they gain strength through lapse of time. In accordance, therefore, with the law as we perceive it and have decided to enforce, we have issued these apostolic scripts, strictly enjoining upon thy fraternity that, in the virtue of obedience, thou shalt without delay cause the said bishop to be summoned under our authority, either by thyself, or by another, or by others, to appear in person before us, within the space of three months, counting from the day of this citation, on pain of deprivation of the pontifical office (which we will that he shall incur *ipso facto* should he prove disobedient in this matter), to submit humbly and effectually to our decrees and precepts and those of the apostolic see upon all and several matters set forth, and upon any others which may happen to be brought forward or objected against him.

Take thou care in thy letters, describing the course of events, to inform us fully and faithfully of the day on which thou receivest these presents, the citation and its form, and whatsoever thou doest in this matter.

Given at the Lateran, on the 8th of the Ides of February,[1] in the sixth year of our pontificate.

The French, desiring unjustly to subdue the Flemings to themselves, invaded that country with an army on several occasions; but the Flemings, boldly encountering on foot the mounted force, inflicted upon them much slaughter and won some marvellous victories, killing notables and A.D. 1302.

[1] 6th February, 1300-01.

nobles of France, to wit, the Counts of Artois, of Eu, of Boulogne, of Albemarle; and lords, to wit, Jacques de Saint-Paul, Godefroie de Brabayne and his son, Jean de Henaud, lord of Teyns, Pierre
S. 211 de Flota and Jean de Bristiach, barons; and many other knights, [with] upwards of 20,000 men, of whom 3,500 were men-at-arms.[1]

About the Ascension of our Lord[2] the King of England came with an army against the Scots; but they dreaded lest he should remain with them not only in summer but in winter;
A.D. 1303. wherefore all the nobles of Scotland were compelled to come before him, and he received them to his peace. He remained in the country until the Nativity of the Glorious Virgin.[3]

In the same year Pope Boniface declared the King of the Teutons[4] to be Emperor; and this he did, as was said, for the

[1] This was the battle of Courtray, 11th July, 1302, memorable as the first occasion when infantry, fighting in the solid formation afterwards adopted by the Scots, successfully withstood the onslaught of armoured cavalry. It caused as much sensation in military circles of the fourteenth century as did the introduction of breech-loading rifles by the Prussians in the war with Austria in 1866.

[2] 16th May.

[3] 8th September.

[4] Albert I., Duke of Austria. 'The Holy Roman Church and the Holy Roman Emperor are one and the same thing in two different aspects. . . . As divine and eternal, the head of Catholicism is the Pope, to whom souls have been entrusted; as human and temporal, the Emperor, commissioned to rule men's bodies and acts' (Bryce's *Holy Roman Empire*). The reference in the text is to a speech made by Pope Boniface on 30th April, 1303, in which he reminded the King of France that, like all other princes, he must consider himself subject to the Roman Emperor. 'Let not the pride of the French rebel which declares that it acknowledgeth no superior. They lie: for by law they are, and ought to be, subject to the King of the Romans and the Emperor.' Boniface had previously declined to recognise Albert I. as Emperor because he had but one eye and was the reverse of good-looking (*est homo monoculus et vultu sordido, non potest esse imperator*): and when Albert's envoys waited upon him in 1299, Boniface exclaimed 'Am I not Pontiff? Is not this the chair of Peter? Am I not able to guard the rights of the empire? I am Cæsar—I am Emperor!'

humiliation of the King of France and the French. But the King of France and the men of his realm, clerics as well as laity, wrote many lengthy complaints against the Pope, and pledged themselves to prove all that they wrote.

But in the meantime the Pope, whom all the world feared as a lion because of his wisdom and courage, was captured and imprisoned by the Colonnas, because he had expelled cardinals who were of their kin from the College of Cardinals and made them incapable of holding any degree or dignity in the Church. In the following October[1] he died, whether by a natural death or, as is more probable, through grief. Within a few days Cardinal Nicholas, of the Order of Preachers, was appointed in his place, and was named Benedict the Eleventh ; and because it appeared to him that the aforesaid statute of Boniface had been issued to the detriment of the aforesaid two Orders, and was too much in favour of prelates, he quashed it and issued a new one, which begins thus—*Inter cunctas*, etc. And he died in the same year on the festival of S. Thomas the Martyr,[2] and was succeeded (though not immediately after his death) by the Archbishop of Bordeaux, who was named Clement the Fifth, from whose time the Roman Curia has been removed to Avignon.

On the festival of S. Hieronymus[3] Thomas of Corbridge died, and William of Greenfield succeeded him in the archbishopric. Shortly before this, to wit, about the Nativity of the Blessed Virgin Mary,[4] the King returned from Scotland to England, having received the Scots to his peace. A.D. 1304.

William Wallace was captured by a certain Scot, to wit, Sir John de Menteith, and was taken to London to the King, and

[1] 1303. [2] 7th July. [3] 30th September. [4] 8th September.

it was adjudged that he should be drawn and hanged, beheaded, disembowelled, and dismembered, and that his entrails should be burnt; which was done. And his head was exposed
A.D. 1305. upon London Bridge, his right arm on the bridge of Newcastle-upon-Tyne, his left arm at Berwick, his right foot at Perth, and his left foot at Aberdeen.

The vilest doom is fittest for thy crimes,
Justice demands that thou shouldst die three times.
Thou pillager of many a sacred shrine,
Butcher of thousands, threefold death be thine!
So shall the English from thee gain relief,
Scotland! be wise, and choose a nobler chief.[1]

In the same year, on the fourth of the Ides of February, to wit, on the festival of S. Scholastica virgin,[2] Sir Robert Bruce, Earl of Carrick, sent seditiously and treacherously for Sir John Comyn, requiring him to come and confer with him at the house of the Minorite Friars in Dumfries; and, when he came, did slay him and his uncle Sir Robert Comyn in the church of the Friars, and afterwards took [some] castles of Scotland and their wardens, and on the Annunciation of the Blessed Virgin next following[3] was made King of Scotland at Scone, and many of the nobles and commonalty of that land adhered to him.

MS. fo. 211[b] When the King of England heard of this, he sent horse and foot to Carlisle and Berwick to protect the Border. But

[1] *Sunt tua demerita misero dignissima fine,*
Esque pati dignus necis infortunia trinæ;
Qui vastare soles sacras hostiliter ædes,
Et nimis atroces hominum committere cædes,
Turpiter occisus, Anglos non amodo lædes;
Si sapis ergo duci tali te, Scotia, ne des.

[2] 10th February, 1305-6.

[3] 25th March, 1305-6. The real date of the coronation was the 27th.

CARLISLE CATHEDRAL

FROM DRAWING BY T. HEARNE, F.S.A. 1802

because the men of Galloway refused to join the aforesaid Robert in his rebellion, their lands were burnt by him, and, pursuing one of the chiefs of Galloway, he besieged him in a certain lake, but some of the Carlisle garrison caused him to raise the siege, and he retreated, after burning the engines and ships that he had made for the siege.[1] A.D. 1306.

But those who were in garrison at Berwick, to wit, Sir Robert Fitzroger, an Englishman who was warden of the town, and Sir John Mowbray, Sir Ingelram de Umfraville, and Sir Alexander de Abernethy, Scotsmen, with their following, over all of whom Sir Aymer de Valence was in command—all these, I say, entered Scotland and received to the King of England's peace some of those who at first had been intimidated into rebellion with Sir Robert. Him they pursued beyond the Scottish sea,[2] and there engaged him in battle near the town of St. John (which is called by another name Pert), killed many of his people, and in the end put him to flight.[3]

Meanwhile the King of England, having assembled an army, sent my lord Edward, his son aforesaid (whom he had knighted in London together with three hundred others), and the Earl of Lincoln, by whose advice the said lord Edward was to act, in pursuit of the said Robert de Brus, who had caused himself to be called King. When they entered Scotland they received many people to peace on condition that they should in all circumstances observe the law; then marching forward to the furthest bounds of Scotland, where the said Robert might be found, they found him not, but

[1] This does not coincide with anything that is known of Bruce's movements after his coronation.

[2] *I.e.* the firths of Forth and Clyde.

[3] 26th June, 1306.

they took all the castles with a strong hand. But they hanged those who had part in the aforesaid conspiracy, design and assistance in making him king, most of whom they caused first to be drawn at the heels of horses and afterwards hanged them ; among whom were the Englishman Christopher de Seton, who had married the sister of the oft-mentioned Robert, and John and Humphrey, brothers of the said Christopher, and several others with them. Among those who were hanged were not only simple country folk and laymen, but also knights and clerics and prebendaries, albeit these protested that, as members of the Church, justice should be done to them accordingly.[1] Then Sir Simon Fraser, a Scot, having been taken to London, was first drawn, then hanged, thirdly beheaded, and his head set up on London Bridge beside that of William Wallace. They also took to England and imprisoned the Bishop of S. Andrews, whom the King of England had appointed Guardian of Scotland, and who had entered into a bond of friendship with the said Robert, as was proved by letters of his which were found ; also the Bishop of Glasgow, who had been principal adviser in that affair, and the Abbot of Scone, who assisted the aforesaid Robert when he was received into royal honour. Howbeit in the meantime Robert called de Brus was lurking in the remote isles of Scotland.[2]

Throughout all these doings the King of England was not in

[1] Benefit of clergy, *i.e.* to be dealt with by ecclesiastical authority.

[2] Fabyan and some other English writers state that Bruce spent this winter in Norway. It is usually believed that he spent it in the island of Rachrin, off the coast of Antrim. This belonged to Bysset of the Glens, to whom orders were sent from King Edward in January, 1306-7, to join Sir John de Menteith and Sir Simon de Montacute with his ships 'to put down Robert de Brus and destroy his retreat in the Isles between Scotland and Ireland.' Bain's *Calendar*, iii. 502

Scotland, but his son, with the aforesaid army. But the King was slowly approaching the Scottish border with the Queen, by many easy stages and borne in a litter on the backs of horses on account of his age and infirmity; and on the feast of S. Michael[1] he arrived at the Priory of Lanercost, which is eight miles from Carlisle, and there he remained until near Easter.[2] Meantime his kinsman, the Earl of Athol, who had encouraged the party of the said Robert to make him king, had been captured, and by command of the King was taken to London, where he was drawn, hanged, MS. fo. 212
and beheaded, and his head was set upon London Bridge above the heads of William Wallace and Simon Fraser, because he was akin to the King.

After this, on the vigil of S. Scholastica virgin,[3] two brothers of Robert de Brus, Thomas and Alexander, Dean of Glasgow, and Sir Reginald de Crawford, desiring to avenge themselves upon the people of Galloway, invaded their country with eighteen ships and galleys, having with them a certain kinglet of Ireland, and the Lord of Cantyre and other large following. Against them came Dougal Macdoual (that is the son of Doual), a chief among the Gallovidians, with his countrymen, defeated them and captured all but a few who escaped in two galleys. He ordered the Irish kinglet and the Lord of Cantyre to be beheaded and their heads to be carried to the King of England at Lanercost.[4]

Thomas de Brus and his brother Alexander and Sir Reginald de Crawford, who had been severely wounded in their capture by lances and arrows, he likewise took alive to the King, who

[1] 29th September.

[2] 26th March, 1307. His writs are dated from Lanercost till 4th March, 1306-7.

[3] 10th February, 1306-7.

[4] Bain's *Cal. Doc. Scot.* ii. 1905.

pronounced sentence upon them, and caused Thomas to be drawn at the tails of horses in Carlisle on the Friday after the first Sunday in Lent,[1] and then to be hanged and afterwards beheaded. Also he commanded the other two to be hanged on the same day and afterwards beheaded; whose heads, with the heads of the four others aforesaid, were set upon the three gates of Carlisle, and the head of Thomas de Brus upon the keep of Carlisle. Nigel, the third brother of Robert, had been hanged already at Newcastle.

About the same time a certain cardinal named Peter came to England, sent *a latere* from my lord the Pope to establish peace between the King of France and the King of England; and it so happened that both my lord the King and my lord the said cardinal entered Carlisle on Passion Sunday.[2] Then in the cathedral church on the Wednesday following my lord cardinal explained the object of his legation before a very great number of people and clergy, and showed them the excellent manner in which my lord the Pope and my lord the King of France had agreed, subject to the consent of the King of England—to wit, that my lord Edward, son and heir of the King of England, should marry Isabella, daughter of the King of France. When this had been said, uprose William of Gainsborough, Bishop of Worcester, and on the part of the King briefly informed my lord cardinal and all who had come thither of the manner of Sir John Comyn's assassination, praying that he would deign to grant some indulgence for his soul, and that he would pronounce sentence of excommunication upon the murderers; whereupon the legate liberally granted one year [of indulgence] for those who should pray for the said soul so long as he [the cardinal] should remain in

[1] 17th February, 1306-7. [2] 19th March, 1306-7.

England, and for one hundred days afterwards. Then straightway, having doffed his ordinary raiment and donned his pontificals, he denounced the murderers of the said Sir John as excommunicate, anathematised, and sacrilegious, together with all their abettors, and any who offered them counsel or favour; and expelled them from Holy Mother Church until they should make full atonement; and thus those who were denounced were excommunicate for a long time throughout all England, especially in the northern parts and in the neighbourhood where the murder was committed.

On the following Friday, in the same place, peace was proclaimed between the said kings by the Archbishop of York, and [it was announced] that the King of England's son was to marry the King of France's daughter, accordingly as had been previously decreed by my lord Pope Boniface.

In the same year, about the feast of S. Matthew the Apostle,[1] the most noble King Edward being laid up at Newbrough near Hexham, his consort the illustrious Margaret Queen of England, came to the house of Lanercost with her honourable household. And my lord the King came thither on the vigil of S. Michael[2] next following, and remained there nearly half a year. And on the first day of March[3] they left the said monastery for Carlisle, and there he held a parliament with all the great men of the realm.

In the same year Friar N. de M^or^ was sent by the Queen to Oseney.

On Easter Day[4] the aforesaid Dungal[5] was knighted by the

[1] 21st September. [2] 28th September. [3] 1306-7. [4] 26th March.

[5] Dungal or Doual, one of the Pictish chiefs of Galloway, head of a powerful clan of the same blood as the M'Doualls of Lorn. The lands of Logan in Wigtownshire are still held by his descendants.

King's hand ; and in the same week Sir John Wallace was captured and taken to the King at Carlisle, who sent him to London, that he should there undergo the same doom as his brother

A.D. 1307.

William had suffered. Howbeit, notwithstanding the terrible vengeance inflicted upon the Scots who adhered to the party of the aforesaid Robert de Brus, the number of those willing to establish him in the realm increased from day to day.[1] Wherefore the King of England caused all the chief men of England who owed him service to attend at Carlisle with the Welsh infantry within fifteen days after the nativity of S. John the Baptist.[2] But alas ! on the feast of the translation of S. Thomas, Archbishop of Canterbury and Martyr,[3] in the year of our Lord aforesaid, this illustrious and excellent King, my lord Edward, son of King Henry, died at Burgh-upon-Sands, which is distant about three miles to the north from Carlisle, in the thirty-sixth[4] year of his reign and the sixty-seventh of his age. Throughout his time he had been fearless and warlike, in all things strenuous and illustrious ; he left not his like among Christian princes for sagacity and courage. He is reported to have said to the Lord before his death :—Have mercy upon me, Almighty God ! *Ita veraciter sicut nunquam aliquem* [ ][5] *nisi tantum te, Dominum Deum meum.*

Messengers were sent in haste to my lord Edward Prince of Wales, his son and heir, who arrived at Carlisle on the eleventh day, to wit, on the festival of S. Symphorosa,[6] and on the next day

[1] In this sentence is well expressed the national character of the Scots—they are willing to be led but will not be driven.

[2] 8th July. [3] 7th July. [4] Really the thirty-fifth.

[5] The verb here is wanting in the original, which leaves the sense doubtful.

[6] 18th July.

he went to Burgh to mourn for his father, with the nobles of the land and prelates of the Church, who were assembled there in great number.

On the following day, to wit, on the festival of S. Margaret, Virgin and Martyr,[1] he received at Carlisle Castle fealty and homage from nearly all the chief men of England, who were assembled there for the expedition to be made into Scotland, and was proclaimed king. Thus Edward A.D. 1307. the younger succeeded the elder, but in the same manner as Rehoboam succeeded Solomon, which his career and fate were to prove. Meanwhile, the obsequies and funeral rites of his father were being arranged, and when these were ready, the corpse was taken to Carlisle, and so on to the south, liberal offerings in money and in wax being made for it in those churches by MS. fo. 212b which it passed, most of all in those where it rested for the night. The new king, and Antony Bek, Bishop of Durham (who had previously been ordained by the Pope Patriarch of Jerusalem), accompanied the corpse through several days' journey, together with the nobles of England and a great multitude of Secular and Regular clergy; and afterwards the king returned to Carlisle to arrange for the expedition into Scotland; and thither came to him first Patrick, Earl of Dunbar, and made homage and fealty to him.

On the vigil of S. Peter ad Vincula[2] he moved his army into Scotland in order to receive homage and fealty from the Scots, as he had forewarned them, having summoned by his letters all the chief men of the country to appear before him at Dumfries, there to render him the service due. Afterwards he divided

[1] 20th July. [2] 31st July.

his army into three columns to search for the oft-mentioned Robert; but, this time, as formerly, he was not to be found, so they returned empty-handed to England after certain guardians had been appointed in Scotland.[1]

Meanwhile there came in great pomp to the king a certain knight of Gascony, Piers de Gaveston by name, whom my lord, the elder Edward, had exiled from the realm of England, and in accordance with the unanimous advice of parliament had caused solemnly to swear that he would never re-enter England; this because of the improper familiarity which my lord Edward the younger entertained with him, speaking of him openly as his brother. To this fellow, coming by the new king's command to join him while he was still in Scotland, the king gave the noble earldom of Cornwall and the Isle of Man, and preferred him in affection to all the other nobles of the country, whether of his own kin or otherwise. When this was done, the whole of England murmured against the king, and was indignant against the aforesaid Piers. Moreover, the new king apprehended Walter de Langton, my lord Bishop of Chester, a man as worthy as any in the realm, who had been treasurer to his [Edward's] father until his death, and imprisoned him in Wallingford Castle.[2] He did this, as was alleged, because the said bishop had been prime mover in advising that the aforesaid Piers should be exiled from the realm in the time of his [Edward's]

[1] Aymer de Valence was appointed guardian of Scotland on 28th August, but he was superseded on 8th September by John de Bretagne, Earl of Richmond. In this may be traced the influence of Piers de Gaveston, no friend to de Valence, whom, because of his swarthy complexion, he nicknamed 'Joseph the Jew,' a term of special opprobrium in the fourteenth century.

[2] In Berkshire.

father. He also caused many other leading men, who had been with his father, to be dismissed from their offices, and viler and worse men to be appointed. Howbeit, he had some cause for punishing the bishop, because, as was said, he found in his possession more of the treasure which he had collected under his [Edward's] father than was in his father's treasury after his death.

Later, after the feast of S. Michael,[1] the king held his parliament at Northampton, and there confirmed the gift of the said earldom [of Cornwall], and allowed the bishop to remain in the aforesaid castle [of Wallingford], which was at that time the castle of Piers himself; and after the parliament he went to London with the clergy and people, and caused his father to be interred at Westminster among the kings; for since the day of his death his body had been kept above ground in the abbey of Walsingham.

While all these affairs were being transacted, Robert Bruce, with his brother Edward and many of his adherents, was moving through Scotland wherever he liked, in despite of the English guardians, and chiefly in Galloway, from which district he took tribute under agreement that it should be left in peace; for they were unable to resist him because of the large number of the people who then adhered to him.

About the same time died Friar William of Gainsborough, Bishop of Worcester, beyond the sea, when returning from the court of France, whither he had been sent to arrange the king's nuptials. He lies at Beauvais among the Minorite Friars. Almost all his household died there with him, whence it was believed that they had perished by poison.

[1] 29th September. *Mortem* in Stevenson's text ought manifestly to be *festum*, for, as the Rev. Dr. James Wilson has reminded me, archangels are immortal!

Later, about the feast of the chair of S. Peter,[1] the King of England sailed across to France, and with solemnity and great state married his wife Isabella, daughter of the King of France, at Boulogne, as had been arranged in the presence of her father and the leading men of that country, and of many from England. He brought her back to England, and was crowned in London. The people of the country and the leading men complained loudly at his coronation against the aforesaid Piers, and unanimously wished that he should be deprived of his earldom; but this the king obstinately refused. The murmurs increased from day to day, and engrossed the lips and ears of all men, nor was there one who had a good word either for the king or for Piers. The chief men agreed unanimously in strongly demanding that Piers should be sent back into exile, foremost among them being the noble Earl of Lincoln and the young Earl of Gloucester, whose sister, however, Piers had received in marriage by the king's gift.[2]

About Easter[3] the king held a parliament, in which it was unanimously declared that the said Piers should be banished within fifteen days from all the lands which are under

A.D. 1308.

the King of England's dominion. Howbeit the king, though he gave verbal assent to this, did not in fact keep faith, any more than in some other things which he promised, and Piers remained in England. Wherefore about Pentecost the

[1] 22nd February, 1307-8.

[2] Margaret de Clare, the king's niece, being daughter of his elder sister, Joan of Acre. The marriage took place on 1st November, 1307, although Walsingham says it was after Gaveston had been appointed Lord Lieutenant of Ireland, 16th June, 1308.

[3] 14th April.

earls and barons, with horses and arms and a strong force, came to Northampton, where the king was staying at that time with the said Piers, and there at length it was arranged by force and fear that he should immediately be sent back into exile, in the manner aforesaid, and the Pope's excommunication was procured upon him in the event of his ever after re-entering England. But while it was decreed that he should embark at Dover and have an annuity for life of £200 sterling for himself and £100 for his wife, if she were willing to leave the country with him, the king secretly caused him to sail to Ireland with his wife, furnishing him with letters to the effect that, wheresoever he should go within the lands of the King of England, he should be received with the glory and honour due to the person of the king himself. Also he gave him, as was said, such precious and valuable articles as he could find in his treasury, and also he gave him many charters sealed with his great seal, but in blank, whereon Piers might write whatever he chose; and accordingly he was received in Ireland with great glory.

In all these proceedings no one in the kingdom supported the king, except four persons, to wit, my lord Hugh le Despenser, MS. fo. 213 baron, Sir Nicholas de Segrave, Sir William de Burford, and Sir William de Enge, against whom the earls and barons rose, demanding that they should be banished as deceivers of the king and traitors to the realm, or else that they should be removed immediately and utterly from the king's presence and council.

About the same time, grievous to relate, the Master of the Order of Templars, with many brethren of his order, publicly confessed, as was said, before my lord the King of France and the clergy and people, that for sixty years and more he and his brethren had performed mock-worship before a statue of a certain brother of the Order, and had trodden the image of the Crucified One under foot, spitting in its face, and that they had habitually committed sodomy among themselves, and had perpetrated many other iniquities against the faith. On account of which all the Templars in France were apprehended and imprisoned, not undeservedly, and their goods were confiscated, and the same was done in England, pending what the Pope and the clergy should decide what should be done with them.

Meanwhile, taking advantage of the dispute between the King of England and the barons, Edward de Brus, brother of the oft-mentioned Robert, and Alexander de Lindsey and Robert Boyd and James de Douglas,[1] knights, with their following which they had from the outer isles of Scotland, invaded the people of Galloway, disregarding the tribute which they took from them, and in one day slew many of the gentry of Galloway, and made nearly all that district subject to them. Those Gallovidians, however, who could escape came to England to find refuge. But it was said that the King of England desired, if he could, to ally himself with Robert de Brus, and to grant him peace upon such terms as would help him to contend with his own earls and barons. Howbeit, after the feast of S. Michael[2] some kind of peace and agreement was patched up between the King of England and his people, on condition that the king should do nothing important without the advice and consent of the Earl of Lincoln; but from day to day the king, by gifts and promises, drew to his side some of the earls and barons.

[1] First mention of 'the good Sir James,' son of Sir William 'le Hardi.'

[2] 29th September.

About the beginning of the following Lent[1] an embassy was sent to the King of England by order of the Pope and at the instance of the King of France, desiring him to desist from attacking the Scots, and that he should hold meanwhile only what he possessed at the preceding feast of S. James the Apostle;[2] and likewise an embassy was sent to Robert de Brus desiring him to keep the peace, and that meanwhile he should enjoy all that he had acquired at the preceding feast of the same S. James, and no more; and that the truce should endure until the festival of All Saints next to come.[3] But Robert and his people restored nothing to the King of England of that which he had wrongously usurped between the said feast of S. James and the beginning of Lent aforesaid; rather were they continually striving to get more.

In the summer the king held his parliament at Northampton; whereat, contrary to the hope of all England, the said Piers de Gaveston, through privy procurement of the king beforehand, was confirmed as formerly in the earldom of Cornwall, with the assent of the earls and barons, on condition that he should have nothing in the kingdom except the earldom. For already, before the aforesaid parliament, the sentence of excommunication pronounced by my lord the Pope against the said Piers in England had been suspended for ten months, and all Englishmen were absolved from whatever oath they had taken in any manner affecting the said Piers; and meanwhile he received license to return from Ireland to England, and obtained in parliament the earldom of Cornwall as before.

A.D. 1309.

[1] 12th February, 1308-9. [2] 25th July, 1308.

[3] 1st November.

But in the aforesaid parliament there was read a fresh sentence of excommunication pronounced against Robert de Brus and against all who should give him aid, counsel, or favour.

Now about the feast of All Saints,[1] when the said truce was due to expire, the King of England sent Sir John de Segrave and many others with him to keep the march at Berwick; and to defend the march at Carlisle [he sent] the Earl of Hereford and Baron Sir Robert de Clifford, Sir John de Cromwell, knight, and others with them. But a little before the feast of S. Andrew[2] they made a truce with the oft-mentioned Robert de Brus, and he with them, subject to the King of England's consent, until the twentieth day after Christmas,[3] and accordingly Robert de Clifford went to the king to ascertain his pleasure. On his return, he agreed to a further truce with the Scots until the first Sunday in Lent,[4] and afterwards the truce was prolonged until summer; for the English do not willingly enter Scotland to wage war before summer, chiefly because earlier in the year they find no food for their horses.

About the feast of the Assumption[5] the king came to Berwick with Piers, Earl of Cornwall, and the Earl of Gloucester and the Earl of Warenne, which town the King of England
A.D. 1310. had caused to be enclosed with a strong and high wall and ditch; but the other earls refused to march with the king by reason of fresh dispute that had arisen. But he [the king] advanced with his suite further into Scotland in search for the oft-mentioned Robert, who fled in his usual manner, not daring to

[1] 1st November.
[2] 30th November.
[3] 14th January, 1309-10.
[4] 8th March, 1309-10.
[5] 15th August.

meet them, wherefore they returned to Berwick.[1] So soon as they had retired, Robert and his people invaded Lothian and inflicted much damage upon those who were in the king of England's peace. The king, therefore, pursued them with a small force, but the Earl of Cornwall remained at Roxburgh with his people to guard that district, and the Earl of Gloucester [remained at] Norham.

After the feast of the Purification[2] the king sent the aforesaid Earl of Cornwall with two hundred men-at-arms to the town of S. John beyond the Scottish Sea,[3] in case Robert de Brus, who was then marching towards Galloway, should go beyond the said sea to collect troops. But the king remained on at Berwick. The said earl received to peace all beyond the Scottish Sea, as far as the Mounth. After the beginning of Lent[4] the Earls of Gloucester and Warenne rode through the great Forest of Selkirk, receiving the foresters and others of the Forest to peace.

About the same time died the noble Henry, Earl of Lincoln, who was Guardian of England in the king's absence, in place of whom the Earl of Gloucester was elected with the king's consent, and therefore returned from Scotland to England.

In the same year died Antony Bek, Patriarch of Jerusalem and MS. fo. 213b
Bishop of Durham (Patriarch, however, only in name), and was buried with great solemnity in the cathedral church of Durham,

[1] This Fabian strategy was very exasperating to the chronicler, but it was the means whereby Bruce won and kept his kingdom.

[2] 2nd February, 1310-11.

[3] *I.e.* Perth, beyond the Firth of Forth.

[4] 24th February, 1310-11.

at the northern corner of the east end; in which church none had hitherto been buried save S. Cuthbert.[1]

To him succeeded Richard of Kelso, a monk of that monastery

A.D. 1311. [Durham], soon after Easter,[2] and was consecrated at York by the archbishop on the feast of Pentecost.[3]

In the same year my lord Thomas, Earl of Lancaster, came to the king in Scotland, to do homage for the earldom of Lincoln which had come to him through his wife after the death of the aforesaid earl. But, forasmuch as the king was in Berwick, the earl was advised not to go before him outside the realm to render homage, neither would the king come across the river to him; wherefore there was much apprehension of civil war in England, because the earl, having four other earldoms besides that of Lincoln, threatened to return immediately with one hundred knights whom he had brought with him (without taking account of foot-soldiers besides), and to enter upon the lands of the said earldom whereof he had offered homage to the king, who had declined to receive it. But by God's influence the king followed wiser counsel, crossed the water of Tweed, and came to the earl at Haggerston, about four miles from Berwick, where they saluted each other amicably and exchanged frequent kisses. Although hitherto they had been much at discord because of Piers de Gaveston, yet [that person] came thither with the king; but the earl would neither kiss him, nor even salute him, whereat Piers was offended beyond measure.

[1] Considering the effusive eulogy or scathing criticism passed by the chronicler upon other deceased dignitaries of the Church, it is strange that he should have nothing to say about the character of this most redoubtable prelate.

[2] 11th April.

[3] 30th May.

In the same year the Templars of England were tried upon the aforesaid crimes with which they were charged by inquisitors sent by my lord the Pope, all of which they denied at York, but three of them pled guilty to them all in London.

Forasmuch as the king, two years before, had granted in a certain parliament, and confirmed by establishing it under his great seal, that he would submit to the authority of certain persons, earls and bishops,[1] partly for councillors (for he was not very wise in his acts, though he may have spoken rationally enough), and likewise partly for the better governance of his house and household, and that the term of two years should be given them for dealing with these matters and deliberating, which time had now elapsed, therefore the Guardian of England and the nobles of the land sent forward envoys to the king in Scotland about the feast of S. Laurence,[2] humbly beseeching that it would please him to come to London and hear in parliament what they had ordained for his honour and the welfare of his realm. Wherefore the king, unwillingly enough, went to London, where all the great men of the realm were assembled, and in that parliament the said ordainers announced publicly what they had ordained, and these were approved by the judgment of all as being very expedient for the king and realm, and specially so for the community and the people. Among these [ordinances] it was decreed now, as it had been frequently before, that Piers de Gaveston

[1] These Lord Ordainers were the Archbishop of Canterbury, the Bishops of London, Salisbury, Chichester, Norwich, S. David's and Llandaff; the Earls of Gloucester, Lancaster, Lincoln, Hereford, Pembroke, Richmond, Warwick and Arundel; the Barons Hugh de Vere, William le Mareschal, Robert Fitz Roger, Hugh Courtenay, William Martin, and John de Grey.

[2] 10th August.

should depart from the soil of England within fifteen days after the feast of S. Michael the Archangel,[1] never to return, nor should he thereafter be styled nor be an earl, nor be admitted to any country which might be under the king's dominion; and sentence of excommunication was solemnly pronounced by the Archbishop of Canterbury upon all who should receive, defend, or entertain him in England after the aforesaid fixed limit of time. He himself, confident that he had been confirmed for life in his earldom, albeit he was an alien and had been preferred to so great dignity solely by the king's favour, had now grown so insolent as to despise all the nobles of the land; among whom he called the Earl of Warwick (a man of equal wisdom and integrity) 'the Black Dog of Arden.' When this was reported to the earl, he is said to have replied with calmness: 'If he call me a dog, be sure that I will bite him so soon as I shall perceive my opportunity.'

But let us have done with him [Piers] till another time and return to Robert de Brus to see what he has been about meanwhile. The said Robert, then, taking note that the king and all the nobles of the realm were in such distant parts, and in such discord about the said accursed individual [Piers], having collected a large army invaded England by the Solway on Thursday before the feast of the Assumption of the Glorious Virgin,[2] and burnt all the land of the Lord of Gillesland and the town of Haltwhistle and a great part of Tynedale, and after eight days returned into Scotland, taking with him a very large booty in cattle. But he had killed few men besides those who offered resistance.

About the feast of the Nativity of the Blessed Virgin,[3] Robert

[1] 13th October. [2] 12th August. [3] 8th September.

returned with an army into England, directing his march towards Northumberland, and, passing by Harbottle and Holystone and Redesdale, he burnt the district about Corbridge, destroying everything; also he caused more men to be killed than on the former occasion. And so he turned into the valleys of North and South Tyne, laying waste those parts which he had previously spared, and returned into Scotland after fifteen days; nor could the wardens whom the King of England had stationed on the marches oppose so great a force of Scots as he brought with him. Howbeit, like the Scots, they destroyed all the goods in the land, with this exception, that they neither burnt houses nor killed men.

Meanwhile the Northumbrians, still dreading lest Robert should return, sent envoys to him to negotiate a temporary truce, and they agreed with him that they would pay two thousand pounds for an exceedingly short truce—to wit, until the Purification of the Glorious Virgin.[1] Also those of the county of Dunbar, next to Berwick, in Scotland, who were still in the King of England's peace, were very heavily taxed for a truce until the said date.

In all these aforesaid campaigns the Scots were so divided among themselves that sometimes the father was on the Scottish side and the son on the English, and *vice versa*; also one brother might be with the Scots and another with the English; yea, even the same individual be first with one party and then with the MS. fo. 214
other. But all those who were with the English were merely feigning, either because it was the stronger party, or in order to save the lands they possessed in England; for their hearts were always with their own people, although their persons might not be so.

[1] 2nd Feb., 1311-12.

From the feast of S. Michael[1] until the feast of S. John Lateran,[2] Pope Clement held a council at Vienne[3] with the cardinals and three patriarchs and one hundred and thirty archbishops and bishops, and abolished the Order of Templars so that it should no longer be considered an Order. Also he caused many new constitutions to be enacted there, which were compiled in seven books in the time of his successor, John XXII.

Now let us return to Piers. That oft-mentioned Piers de Gaveston left England and went to Flanders within the time appointed him, to wit, within fifteen days after the feast of S. Michael.[4] But whereas in Flanders he met with a reception far from favourable (through the agency of the King of France, who cordially detested him because, as was said, the King of England, having married his daughter, loved her indifferently because of the aforesaid Piers), to his own undoing he returned to England, but clandestinely, through fear of the earls and barons; and the king received him and took him with him to York, where they plundered the town and country, because they had not wherewithal to pay their expenses. For the earls and barons had ordained, and enforced execution thereof after the return of the said Piers, that the king, who would not agree with his lieges in anything, should not receive from his exchequer so much as a half-penny or a farthing.[5] The king, then, fearing lest the earls and barons should come upon him there, took Piers to Scarborough with him; but he who was then warden of the castle[6] refused to allow, on any account, the king to enter accompanied

[1] 29th September, 1311. [2] 6th May, 1312. [3] In Dauphiny.

[4] 12th October. [5] *Obolum nec quadrantem.*

[6] Henry de Percy, First Lord Percy of Alnwick, 1272-1315.

by Piers, wherefore the king turned aside with him to Newcastle, and there, as at York, they plundered the town and country. When Thomas, Earl of Lancaster, heard this, being most hostile to the said Piers, he marched secretly and suddenly through the wooded parts of England, avoiding the high roads, about the feast of the Invention of the Holy Cross.[1]

In the same year the said Robert de Brus, King of Scotland,[2] came with a great army in the month of August to the monastery of Lanercost, and remained there three days, making many of the canons prisoners and doing an infinity of injury; but at last the canons were set at liberty by himself.

The said Earl [of Lancaster] entered Newcastle with a large body of men-at-arms in order to seize the said Piers, according to what had been ordained by the earls and barons; A.D. 1312. but it so happened that the king and he had gone to Tynemouth, which is about six miles from Newcastle, and, hearing that the earl was after them, they embarked in an open boat and made for Scarborough, and were then received there. But the king, having dismissed Piers there and Henry de Beaumond (likewise an alien) with some others for the defence of the castle, left them and went to Knaresborough Castle, and thence forward to York, thinking thereby to cause the siege of Scarborough to be raised if the castle should be besieged; but he failed to effect what he wished. For the Earl of Lancaster, hearing that the king and Piers had separated, and that Piers was in the castle,

[1] 3rd May.

[2] This is the first time the chronicler admits King Robert's regal rank. But neither he nor any of his successors ever called themselves King of Scotland; they were Kings of Scots.

attacked it most vigorously, so that very shortly Piers was forced to surrender himself. This, however, he did upon terms which, as I have not heard them, I have not written. Having surrendered, he was committed to the custody of Sir Aymer de Valence, Earl of Pembroke, who had ever before been his chief enemy, and about the feast of the nativity of John the Baptist,[1] in the absence of Aymer de Valence, he was beheaded on the high road near the town of Warwick by command of the Earl of Lancaster and the Earl of Warwick.

On the third of the nones of July,[2] on the vigil of the octave of the Apostles Peter and Paul was a new moon,[3] and an eclipse of the sun about the first hour of the day,[4] and the sun appeared like a horned moon, which was small at first and then larger, until about the third hour it recovered its proper and usual size; though sometimes it seemed green, but sometimes of the colour which it usually has.

Now, while the aforesaid things were getting done with Piers, the march of England had no defender against the Scots, and therefore they rendered tribute to Robert in order to have peace for a while. Meanwhile, however, the Scots burnt the town of Norham, because the castle did them great injury, and they took away men as prisoners and also cattle.

When the king heard of the slaughter of the oft-mentioned Piers, he flared up in anger, and gave all his thoughts to the means whereby he might avenge himself on the slayers.

My lord Aymer de Valence, Earl of Pembroke, then attached himself to the king, chiefly because the said Piers had been

[1] 24th June. The actual date of decollation was 19th June. [2] 5th July.

[3] *Luna tricesima, i.e.* the thirtieth lunation. [4] 6 a.m.

committed to his custody and had been killed without his knowledge. It was said also that the Earl of Warenne and some others joined the king's party against the Earl of Lancaster. Therefore the king caused his parliament to be summoned in London, in case he could there seize the earl, notwithstanding that they were the sons of two brothers, to wit, Edward and Edmund.[1] But this was not unknown to the earl, wherefore he gathered to himself out of his five earldoms a mounted force so strong and numerous that he had no fear of the king's party, and he came to London for the parliament. When the king heard this he dissimulated, nor would he attempt anything against him, but prolonged the parliament from day to day in order to vex him [Lancaster] and the others, both earls and barons who had come to his aid and for the confirmation of the aforesaid ordinances. But the Earl of Gloucester and the Earl of Richmond were mediators of peace between the opposing parties, albeit they were not able to pacify them.

When Robert de Brus heard of this discord in the south, having assembled a great army, he invaded England about the feast of the Assumption of the Blessed Virgin,[2] and burnt the towns of Hexham and Corbridge and the western parts, and took booty and much spoil and prisoners, nor was there anyone MS. fo. 214b
who dared resist. While he halted in peace and safety near Corbridge he sent part of his army as far as Durham, which, arriving there suddenly on market day, carried off all that was found in the town, and gave a great part of it to the flames,

[1] Lancaster was Edward II.'s first cousin, being the son of Edmund 'Crouch-back.'

[2] 15th August.

cruelly killing all who opposed them, but scarcely attacking the castle and abbey. The people of Durham, fearing more mischief from them, and despairing of help from the king, compounded with them, giving two thousand pounds to obtain truce for that bishopric until the nativity of John the Baptist;[1] which, however, the Scots refused to accept unless on condition that they might have free access and retreat through the land of the bishopric whensoever they wished to make a raid into England. The Northumbrians also, fearing that they would visit them, gave them other two thousand pounds to secure peace until the aforesaid date; and the people of Westmorland, Copland, and Cumberland redeemed themselves in a similar way; and, as they had not so much money in hand as would pay them, they paid a part, and gave as hostages for the rest the sons of the chief lords of the country. Having achieved this, Robert returned to Scotland with his army.

Meanwhile a cardinal legate came to England with my lord Louis, brother of my lord the King of France, to effect concord between the king and the earls and barons; but they did not succeed, although they spent many days in attempting to bring about agreement.

In winter, about the feast of S. Martin, to wit, on the feast day of S. Bricius,[2] a first-born son was born and was named Edward, like his father and grandfather.

Now the oft-mentioned Robert, seeing that thus he had the whole March of England under tribute, applied all his thoughts to getting possession of the town of Berwick, which was in the King of England's hands. Coming unexpectedly to the castle

[1] 24th June, 1313. [2] 13th November.

on the night of S. Nicholas,[1] he laid ladders against the walls and began to scale them; and had not a dog betrayed the approach of the Scots by loud barking, it is believed that he would quickly have taken the castle and, in consequence, the town.

Now these ladders which they placed against the walls were of wonderful construction, as I myself, who write these lines, beheld with my own eyes.[2] For the Scots had made two strong ropes as long as the height of the wall, making a knot at one end of each cord. They had made a wooden board also, about two feet and a half long and half a foot broad, strong enough to carry a man, and in the two extremities of the board they had made two holes, through which the two ropes could be passed; then the cords, having been passed through as far as the knots, they had made two other knots in the ropes one foot and a half higher, and above these knots they placed another log or board, and so on to the end of the ropes. They had also made an iron hook, measuring at least one foot along one limb, and this was to lie over the wall; but the other limb, being of the same length, hung downwards towards the ground, having at its end a round hole wherein the point of a lance could be inserted, and two rings on the two sides wherein the said ropes could be knotted.

Having fitted them together in this manner, they took a strong spear as long as the height of the wall, placing the point thereof in the iron hole, and two men lifted the ropes and boards with that spear and placed the iron hook (which was not a round one) over the wall. Then they were able to climb up by those wooden steps just as one usually climbs ordinary ladders, and the greater the weight of the climber the more firmly the iron hook clung

[1] 6th December. [2] *Fide occulata conspexi.*

over the wall. But lest the ropes should lie too close to the wall and hinder the ascent, they had made fenders round every third step which thrust the ropes off the wall. When, therefore, they had placed two ladders upon the wall, the dog betrayed them as I have said, and they left the ladders there, which our people next day hung upon a pillory to put them to shame. And thus a dog saved the town on that occasion, just as of old geese saved Rome by their gaggle, as saith S. Augustine in *de Civitate Dei*, book iii. chapter 4, *de magnis*, and Ambrose in *Exameron in Opere Quintæ Diei.*

Robert, having failed in his attempt on Berwick, marched with his army to the town of S. John,[1] which was then still in the King of England's hands; and he laid siege thereto, and on Monday of the octave of Epiphany[2] it was taken by the Scots, who scaled the walls by night on ladders, and entered the town through the negligence of sentries and guards. Next day Robert caused those citizens of the better class who were of the Scottish nation to be killed,[3] but the English were allowed to go away free. But the Scottish Sir William Oliphant, who had long time held that town for the King of England against the Scots, was bound and sent far away to the Isles. The town itself the Scots utterly destroyed.

About the day of S. Peter in cathedra [ ][4] Master Robert of Winchelsea, Archbishop of Canterbury, died; in whose room Master Thomas of Cobham, Doctor of Theology, was elected; but at the king's request the archbishopric was conferred by the Pope upon my lord Walter Reynald, Bishop of Wor-

[1] Perth.

[2] 10th January, 1312-13.

[3] And English too, according to Fordun, ch. cxxix.

[4] Blank in original.

cester, a man almost illiterate, and, in public opinion, unworthy of any degree of dignity both on the score of his mode of life and his [want of] learning. Behold! what evils the king wrought among the clergy (besides the confusion he brought upon his people) when he procured the appointment of such a man to be Primate of all England! However, as he had hindered the election made of Master Thomas, he obtained his appointment as Bishop of Worcester.

After the feast of the Nativity of S. John the Baptist,[1] when the English truce on the March had lapsed, Robert de Brus threatened to invade England in his usual manner. The people of Northumberland, Westmorland and Cumberland, and other Borderers, apprehending this, and neither having nor hoping for any defence or help from their king (seeing that he was engaged in distant parts of England, seeming not to give them a thought), offered to the said Robert no small sum of money, indeed a very large one, for a truce to last till the feast of S. Michael in the following year.[2]

A.D. 1313.

MS. fo. 215

All this time the body of Piers de Gaveston remained above ground unburied with the Friars Preachers of Oxford, who daily said for his soul a placebo, a dirige, and a mass with nones, receiving from the king half a mark for their trouble.

In the same year about the feast of the Assumption of the Blessed Virgin[3] the Emperor[4] was poisoned, as was said, by a certain monk.

After the feast of S. Michael[5] the king caused the earls and barons to be summoned to parliament in London, and there an

[1] 24th June. [2] 29th Sept., 1314. [3] 15th August.

[4] Henry VII., Count of Luxembourg. [5] 29th September.

agreement, such as it was, was made between them on Sunday next before the feast of S. Luke,[1] and they made to him such an humbling and obeisance as befitted a king, which afterwards they did not observe.

Now at the beginning of Lent[2] the Scots cunningly entered the castle of Roxburgh at night by ladders, and captured all the castle except one tower, wherein the warden of the castle, Sir Gillemin de Fiennes, a knight of Gascony, had taken refuge with difficulty, and his people with him; but the Scots got possession of that tower soon afterwards. And they razed to the ground the whole of that beautiful castle, just as they did other castles which they succeeded in taking, lest the English should ever hereafter be able to lord it over the land through holding the castles.

In the same season of Lent they captured Edinburgh Castle in the following manner. In the evening one day the besiegers of that castle delivered an assault in force upon the south gate,[3] because, owing to the position of the castle there was no other quarter where an assault could be made. Those within gathered together at the gate and offered a stout resistance; but meanwhile the other Scots climbed the rocks on the north side, which was very high and fell away steeply from the foot of the wall. There they laid ladders to the wall and climbed up in such numbers that those within could not withstand them; and thus they threw open the gates, admitted their comrades, got possession of the whole castle and killed the English. They razed the said castle to the ground, just as they had done to Roxburgh Castle.

[1] Sunday, 14th October.

[2] 28th February, 1313-14.

[3] It was really the east gate.

Having accomplished this success, they marched to Stirling and besieged that castle with their army.

In the same year died Sir Thomas de Multan, Lord of Gillesland, on the sixth of the kalends of December,[1] leaving an only daughter as his heir, named Margaret, whom Robert de Clifford, son of Robert of the same name, married at Hoffe[2] in the seventh year of her age, he himself lying on his bed. And in the life of the said Robert, Ralph de Dacre, son of Sir William de Dacre, married the same Margaret, having a right to her through a contract concluded between Thomas de Multan, father of the said Margaret, and William de Dacre, before her former marriage.

On Tuesday after the octave of Easter,[3] Edward de Brus, Robert's brother, invaded England by way of Carlisle with an army, contrary to agreement, and remained there three days at the bishop's manor house, to wit, at Rose, A.D. 1314. and sent a strong detachment of his army to burn the southern and western districts during those three days. They burnt many towns and two churches, taking men and women prisoners, and collected a great number of cattle in Inglewood Forest and elsewhere, driving them off with them on the Friday;[4] they killed few men except those who made determined resistance; but they made attack upon the city of Carlisle because of the knights and country people who were assembled there. Now the Scots did all these wrongs at that time because the men of that March had not paid them the tribute which they had pledged themselves to pay on certain days. Although the Scots had hostages from the sons and heirs of the knights of that

[1] 26th November.
[2] Near Appleby.
[3] 16th April.
[4] 19th April.

country in full security for covenanted sums, yet they did not on that account refrain from committing the aforesaid wrongs.

Now about the feast of Pentecost[1] the King of England approached the March of Scotland; also the Earl of Gloucester, the Earl of Hereford, the Earl of Pembroke, and the Earl of Angus, Sir Robert de Clifford, Sir John Comyn (son of the murdered John), Sir Henry de Beaumont, Sir John de Segrave, Sir Pagan de Typtoft, Sir Edmund de Mauley, Sir Ingelram de Umfraville, with other barons, knights, and a splendid and numerous army, if only they had had the Lord as ally. But the Earl of Lancaster and the other English earls who were of his party remained at home with their men (except those with whom they were bound in strict obligation to furnish the king in war), because the king as yet had refused to agree with them or to perform what he had promised before. And whereas when his noble father Edward went on a campaign in Scotland, he used to visit on his march [the shrines of] the English saints, Thomas of Canterbury, Edmund, Hugh, William, and Cuthbert, offering fair oblations, commending himself to their prayers, and also bestowing liberal gifts to monasteries and the poor, this [king] did none of these things; but marching with great pomp and elaborate state, he took goods from the monasteries on his journey, and, as was reported, did and said things to the prejudice and injury of the saints. In consequence of this and other things it is not surprising that confusion and everlasting shame overtook him and his army, which was foretold at the time by certain religious men of England.

[1] 26th May.

Thus before the feast of the Nativity of S. John the Baptist,[1] the king, having massed his army, advanced with the aforesaid pomp towards Stirling Castle, to relieve it from siege and to engage the Scots, who were assembled there in all their strength. On the vigil of the aforesaid Nativity[2] the king's army arrived after dinner near Torwood; and, upon information that there were Scots in the wood, the king's advanced guard, commanded by Lord de Clifford, began to make a circuit of the wood to prevent the Scots escaping by flight. The Scots did not interfere until they [the English] were far ahead of the main body, when they showed themselves, and, cutting off the king's advanced MS.
guard from the middle and rear columns, they charged and killed fo. 215b
some of them and put the rest to flight.[3] From that moment began a panic among the English and the Scots grew bolder.

On the morrow—an evil, miserable and calamitous day for the English—when both sides had made themselves ready for battle, the English archers were thrown forward before the line, and the Scottish archers engaged them, a few being killed and wounded on either side; but the King of England's archers quickly put the others to flight. Now when the two armies had approached very near each other, all the Scots fell on their knees to repeat *Pater noster*, commending themselves to God and seeking help from heaven; after which they advanced boldly against the English. They had so arranged their army that two columns went abreast in advance of the third, so that neither should be in advance of the other;

[1] 24th June. [2] 23rd June.

[3] This is a very inaccurate account, obviously from confused hearsay, of de Clifford's repulse by young Randolph. The true narrative is given best in Gray's *Scalacronica*.

and the third followed, in which was Robert.[1] Of a truth, when both armies engaged each other, and the great horses of the English charged the pikes of the Scots, as it were into a dense forest, there arose a great and terrible crash of spears broken and of destriers wounded to the death ; and so they remained without movement for a while. Now the English in the rear could not reach the Scots because the leading division was in the way, nor could they do anything to help themselves, wherefore there was nothing for it but to take to flight. This account I heard from a trustworthy person who was present as eye-witness.

In the leading division were killed the Earl of Gloucester, Sir John Comyn, Sir Pagan de Typtoft, Sir Edmund de Mauley and many other nobles, besides foot soldiers who fell in great numbers. Another calamity which befel the English was that, whereas they had shortly before crossed a great ditch called Bannockburn, into which the tide flows, and now wanted to recross it in confusion, many nobles and others fell into it with their horses in the crush, while others escaped with much difficulty, and many were never able to extricate themselves from the ditch ; thus Bannockburn was spoken about for many years in English throats.

[Here follows a long dirge in Latin hexameters, which will not repay translation.]

The king and Sir Hugh le Despenser (who, after Piers de Gaveston, was as his right eye) and Sir Henry de Beaumont (whom he had promoted to an earldom in Scotland), with many others mounted and on foot, to their perpetual shame fled like

[1] This again is not correct. The Scots order of battle was three columns or 'schiltromes' in the first line, supported by the fourth commanded by King Robert.

miserable wretches to Dunbar Castle, guided by a certain knight of Scotland who knew through what districts they could escape. Some who were not so speedy in flight were killed by the Scots, who pursued them hotly; but these, holding bravely together, came safe and sound through the ambushes into England. At Dunbar the king embarked with some of his chosen followers in an open boat for Berwick, leaving all the others to their fate.

In like manner as the king and his following fled in one direction to Berwick, so the Earl of Hereford, the Earl of Angus, Sir John de Segrave, Sir Antony de Lucy and Sir Ingelram de Umfraville, with a great crowd of knights, six hundred other mounted MS.
men and one thousand foot, fled in another direction towards fo. 216
Carlisle. The Earl of Pembroke left the army on foot and saved himself with the fugitive Welsh; but the aforesaid earls and others, who had fled towards Carlisle were captured on the way at Bothwell Castle, for the sheriff, the warden of the castle,[1] who had held the castle down to that time for the King of England, perceiving that his countrymen had won the battle, allowed the chief men who came thither to enter the castle in the belief that they would find a safe refuge, and when they had entered he took them prisoners, thereby treacherously deceiving them. Many,

[1] Sir Walter Gilbertson. A full list of the officers and garrison is given in King Edward's *Wardrobe Accounts*. In this, as in many other details, Barbour is singularly accurate.

> The Erle of Hertfurd fra the mellé
> Departyt with a gret menye,
> And straucht to Bothwell tok the vai,
> That then in the Ingliss mennys fay
> Was, and haldyn as place of wer.
> Schyr Waltre Gilbertson was ther
> Capitane, and it had in ward.—*The Brus*, ix. 582.

also, were taken wandering round the castle and hither and thither in the country, and many were killed; it was said, also, that certain knights were captured by women, nor did any of them get back to England save in abject confusion. The Earl of Hereford, the Earl of Angus, Sir [John] de Segrave, Sir Antony de Lucy, Sir Ingelram de Umfraville and the other nobles who were in the castle were brought before Robert de Brus and sent into captivity, and after a lengthy imprisonment were ransomed for much money. After the aforesaid victory Robert de Brus was commonly called King of Scotland by all men, because he had acquired Scotland by force of arms.

About the same time died King Philip of France.[1]

Shortly afterwards, to wit, about the feast of S. Peter ad Vincula,[2] Sir Edward de Brus, Sir James of Douglas, John de Soulis and other nobles of Scotland invaded England by way of Berwick with cavalry and a large army, and, during the time of truce, devastated almost all Northumberland with fire, except the castles; and so they passed forward into the bishopric of Durham; but there they did not burn much, for the people of the bishopric ransomed themselves from burning by a large sum of money. Nevertheless, the Scots carried off a booty of cattle and what men they could capture, and so invaded the county of Richmond beyond, acting in the same manner there without resistance, for nearly all men fled to the south or hid themselves in the woods, except those who took refuge in the castles.

The Scots even went as far as the Water of Tees on that occasion, and some of them beyond the town of Richmond, but they did not enter that town. Afterwards, reuniting their forces,

[1] 29th Nov., 1314. [2] 1st August.

they all returned by Swaledale and other valleys and by Stanemoor, whence they carried off an immense booty of cattle. Also they burnt the towns of Brough and Appleby and Kirkoswald, and other towns here and there on their route, trampling down the crops by themselves and their beasts as much as they could; and so, passing near the priory of Lanercost, they entered Scotland, having many men prisoners from whom they might extort money ransom at will. But the people of Coupland,[1] fearing their return and invasion, sent envoys and appeased them with much money.

On the day[2] after the feast of the Nativity of the Blessed Mary the King of England's parliament opened at York, whereat the king and the Earl [of Lancaster] with his adherents came to an agreement, and all of them approved of the ordinances above mentioned, which were confirmed by the seals of the king and the earl.

Now about the feast of S. Michael[3] the Earl of Hereford, who had married the King of England's sister, returned from Scotland, and in exchange for him were released the Bishop of Glasgow, the Earl of Mar (who had been reared in England), and the wife, sister, and daughter of my lord Robert de Brus.[4] Howbeit, the Earl of Mar, having arrived at Newcastle, refused to go with them into Scotland, preferring to remain in England. From day to day sundry prisoners were released from the hands of the Scots, but only through very heavy pecuniary ransoms. About

[1] A ward of southern Cumberland.

[2] 9th September.

[3] 29th September.

[4] Queen Elizabeth was maintained at the king's charges during her captivity. In the year 1312-13 her expenses amounted to £125 5s. 2d. (*Wardrobe Accounts*, 5 Edward II.).

the feast of our Lord's birth[1] the Earl of Angus was released, also Sir John de Segrave, and a little later Sir Antony de Lucy.

About the feast of the Epiphany the illustrious King of France died, not having reigned a full year.[2]

Meanwhile the Scots occupied both north and south Tynedale —to wit Haltwhistle, Hexham, Corbridge, and so on towards Newcastle, and Tynedale did homage to the King of Scots and forcibly attacked Gillesland and the other adjacent districts of England.

At this time also the Scots again wasted Northumberland; but from the aforesaid Nativity of Our Lord until the Nativity of S. John[3] the Baptist the county of Cumberland alone paid 600 marks in tribute to the King of Scots.

The Scots, therefore, unduly elated, as much by their victory in the field as by the devastation of the March of England and the receipt of very large sums of money, were not satisfied with their own frontiers, but fitted out ships and sailed to Ireland in the month of May, to reduce that country to subjection if they could. Their commanders were my lord Edward Bruce, the king's brother, and his kinsman my lord Thomas Randolf, Earl of Moray, both enterprising and valiant knights, having a very strong force with them. Landing in Ireland, and receiving some slight aid from the Irish, they captured from the King of England's dominion much land and many towns, and so prevailed as to have my lord Edward made king

A.D. 1315.

[1] 25th December.

[2] The date is wrong, Philip IV. died 29th November, 1314, Louis X. died 5th June, 1316—June instead of January.

[3] 25th December, 1314–24th June, 1315.

by the Irish. Let us leave him reigning there for the present, just as many kinglets reign there, till we shall describe elsewhere how he came to be beheaded, and let us return to Scotland.

The Scots, then, seeing that affairs were going everywhere in their favour, invaded the bishopric of Durham about the feast of the Apostles Peter and Paul,[1] and plundered the town of Hartlepool, whence the people took to the sea in ships; but they did not burn it. On their return they carried away very much booty from the bishopric.

Also, a little later in the same year, on the feast of S. Mary Magdalene,[2] the King of Scotland, having mustered all his forces, came to Carlisle, invested the city and besieged it for ten days, trampling down all the crops, wasting the suburbs and all within the bounds, burning the whole of that district, and driving in a very great store of cattle for his army from Allerdale, Copland, and Westmorland. On every day of the siege they assaulted one MS. fo. 216b
of the three gates of the city, sometimes all three at once; but never without loss, because there were discharged upon them from the walls such dense volleys of darts and arrows, likewise stones, that they asked one another whether stones bred and multiplied within the walls. Now on the fifth day of the siege they set up a machine for casting stones next the church of Holy Trinity, where their king stationed himself, and they cast great stones continually against the Caldew gate[3] and against the wall, but they did little or no injury to those within, except that they killed one man. But there were seven or eight similar machines within the city, besides other engines of war, which are called springalds, for discharging long darts, and staves with sockets for

[1] 29th June. [2] 22nd July. [3] On the west of the town.

casting stones, which caused great fear and damage to those outside. Meanwhile, however, the Scots set up a certain great berefrai like a kind of tower, which was considerably higher than the city walls. On perceiving this, the carpenters of the city erected upon a tower of the wall against which that engine must come if it had ever reached the wall, a wooden tower loftier than the other ; but neither that engine nor any other ever did reach the wall, because, when it was being drawn on wheels over the wet and swampy ground, having stuck there through its own weight, it could neither be taken any further nor do any harm.

Moreover the Scots had made many long ladders, which they brought with them for scaling the wall in different places simultaneously ; also a sow [1] for mining the town wall, had they been able ; but neither sow nor ladders availed them aught. Also they made great numbers of fascines of corn and herbage to fill the moat outside the wall on the east side, so as they might pass over dry-shod. Also they made long bridges of logs running upon wheels, such as being strongly and swiftly drawn with ropes might reach across the width of the moat. But during all the time the Scots were on the ground neither fascines sufficed to fill the moat, nor those wooden bridges to cross the ditch, but sank to the depths by their own weight.

Howbeit on the ninth day of the siege, when all the engines were ready, they delivered a general assault upon all the city gates and upon the whole circuit of the wall, attacking manfully, while the citizens defended themselves just as manfully, and they did the same next day. The Scots also resorted to the same kind of

[1] A siege engine which was constructed to contain men, who, when the sow was wheeled up to the wall, should proceed to sap the foundation under shelter.

stratagem whereby they had taken Edinburgh Castle; for they employed the greater part of their army in delivering an assault upon the eastern side of the city, against the place of the Minorite Friars, in order to draw thither the people who were inside. But Sir James of Douglas, a bold and cautious knight, stationed himself, with some others of the army who were most daring and nimble, on the west side opposite the place of the Canons and Preaching Friars, where no attack was expected because of the height [of the wall] and the difficulty of access. There they set up long ladders which they climbed, and the bowmen, whereof they had a great number, shot their arrows thickly to prevent anyone showing his head above the wall. But, blessed be God! they met with such resistance there as threw them to the ground with their ladders, so that there and elsewhere round the wall some were killed, others taken prisoners and others wounded; yet throughout the whole siege no Englishman was killed, save one man only who was struck by an arrow (and except the man above mentioned), and few were wounded.

Wherefore on the eleventh day, to wit, the feast of S. Peter ad Vincula,[1] whether because they had heard that the English were approaching to relieve the besieged or whether they despaired of success, the Scots marched off in confusion to their own country, leaving behind them all their engines of war aforesaid. Some Englishmen pursuing them captured John de Moray, who in the aforesaid battle near Stirling[2] had for his share twenty-three English knights, besides esquires and others of meaner rank, and had taken very heavy ransom for them. Also they captured with the aforesaid John, Sir Robert Bardolf, a man specially

[1] 1st August. [2] Bannockburn.

ill-disposed to the English, and brought them both to Carlisle Castle; but they were ransomed later for no small sum of money.

In the octave of the Epiphany[1] the King of Scotland came stealthily to Berwick one bright moonlit night with a strong force, and delivered an assault by land and by sea in boats, intending to enter the town by stealth on the waterside between Brighouse and the castle, where the wall was not yet built, but they were manfully repulsed by the guards and by those who answered to the alarm, and a certain Scottish knight, Sir J. de Landels, was killed, and Sir James of Douglas escaped with difficulty in a small boat. And thus the whole army was put to confusion.

About the same time, on the morrow of the Conception of the Blessed Mary,[2] my lord Henry de Burgh, Prior of Lanercost, died, and was succeeded by Sir Robert de Meburne.

About the feast of the Nativity of S. John the Baptist[3] the Scots invaded England, burning as before and laying waste all things to the best of their power; and so they went as far as Richmond. But the nobles of that district, who

A.D. 1316.

took refuge in Richmond Castle and defended the same, compounded with them for a large sum of money so that they might not burn that town, nor yet the district, more than they had already done. Having received this money, the Scots marched away some sixty miles to the west, laying waste everything as far as Furness, and burnt that district whither they had not come before, taking away with them nearly all the goods of that district, with men and women as prisoners. Especially were

[1] 14th January, 1315-16. It was full moon. [2] 9th December.
[3] 24th June.

they delighted with the abundance of iron which they found there, because Scotland is not rich in iron.

Now in that year there was such a mortality of men in England and Scotland through famine and pestilence as had not been heard of in our time. In some of the northern parts of England the quarter of wheat sold for forty shillings. MS. fo. 217

After the Scots had returned to their own country, their King Robert provided himself with a great force and sailed to Ireland, in order to conquer that country, or a large part thereof, for his brother Edward. He freely traversed nearly all that part of it which was within the King of England's dominion, but he did not take walled towns or castles.

About the same time died Master William de Grenefeld, Archbishop of York, to whom succeeded my lord William de Meltoun; who, albeit he was one of the king's courtiers, yet led a religious and honourable life. Also in the same year there died my lord Richard de Kellow, Bishop of Durham, to whom succeeded my lord Louis de Belmont, a Frenchman of noble birth, but lame on both feet, nevertheless liberal and agreeable. He was appointed by the Pope, as was reported, because of a deceitful suggestion, whereby the Pope was led to believe that he [Louis] himself would hold the March of England against the Scots.

After the feast of S. Michael,[1] the Earl of Lancaster with his adherents marched toward Scotland as far as Newcastle in compliance with the king's behest; but the king declined to follow him as they had agreed upon together, wherefore the earl marched back again at once; for neither of them put any trust in the other.

[1] 29th September.

In the month of October in that year, in the night after the day of S. Remigius,[1] and rather more than an hour after midnight, there was a total eclipse of the moon, and the whole moon was hidden for the space of one hour.

About the same time a certain knight of Northumberland, to wit, Sir Gilbert de Middleton, seized and robbed two cardinals who had landed in England not long before, because they came in the company of the aforesaid Louis de Belmont in order to consecrate him Bishop of Durham, as had been commanded by the Pope.

Also at the same time a certain knight of Richmond county, to wit, Sir John de Cleasby, having gathered together a number of malefactors and rogues, rose and devastated the district, plundering, robbing, and wasting, at his own and his people's pleasure, just as Sir Gilbert was doing in Northumberland with his accomplices and rogues. But, by God's ordinance, both of them were soon taken. Sir John was put to his penance,[2] because he refused to speak when brought before the justiciaries, and he soon afterwards died in prison. Sir Gilbert, after [suffering] other punishments, was cut into four quarters, which were sent to different places in England.

About Pentecost[3] the King of Scotland returned to his own land from Ireland. In the same year before noon on the sixth day of September there was an eclipse of the sun.

A.D. 1317. After the feast of S. Michael[4] the Pope sent a bull to England wherein he advised a truce between England and

[1] 1st October. [2] *Positus est ad pœnitentiam suam.* [3] 22nd May.

[4] 29th September. This is the famous bull which King Robert refused to read, as described by the Cardinals in their letter to the Pope (printed in *Fœdera*

Scotland to last for two years after the receipt of the said bull. Now the English received the said bull with satisfaction, both on account of the dissension between the king and the Earl of Lancaster and because of excessive molestation by the Scots arising out of the said dissension, and they hung the bull according to the Pope's command in the cathedral churches and other important places. But the Scots refused to accept it, and paid it no manner of respect, and therefore came deplorably under the sentence of excommunication delivered by the Pope and contained in the said bull.[1]

In the middle of the said truce Pope Clement the Fifth died, and Pope John the Twenty-second was elected.

On the second day of the month of April, in mid-Lent, about midnight on Saturday, the Scots treacherously took the town of Berwick through means of a certain Englishman, Peter of Spalding, living in the town, who, being bribed by a great sum of money received from them and by the promise of land, allowed them to scale the wall and to enter by that part of the

and given in abstract by Lord Hailes, ii. 74). The Pope's letter contained the following apology for not addressing Robert as king. 'Forasmuch as the matter of dispute regarding the kingdom of Scotland is still pending between thee and the aforesaid king [of England], we cannot with propriety address to thee the name of the royal title, and thy wisdom will not take it amiss that we have omitted to name thee as King of Scots in the same letters; especially as the council of our brethren would by no means sanction a denomination of that kind: nor would thy mother the Roman Church, who weigheth all her course and actions in the balance of equity, be doing according to her practice if she interfered between disputants to the detriment of either.'

[1] The sentence of excommunication is printed in *Fœdera*. King Edward obtained it from the Pope by representing to him that King Robert and Edward Bruce were the only obstacles to his undertaking a crusade as recommended by the Council of Vienna.

wall where he himself was stationed as guard and sentry. After they had entered and obtained full possession of the town, they expelled all the English, almost naked and despoiled of all their property; howbeit, in their entrance they killed few or none, except those who resisted them.

A.D. 1318.

Also the castles of Wark and Harbottle, to which they had already laid siege, were surrendered to them in that season of Lent,[1] because relief did not reach them on the appointed day. Also they took the castle of Mitford by guile, and subdued nearly the whole of Northumberland as far as the town of Newcastle, except those castles which have not been mentioned above. Howbeit the castle of the town of Berwick defended itself manfully against the town, but at length capitulated through want of victual.

About the same time there arrived in England for the first time the seventh book of Decretals, and the statute of Pope Boniface VIII. was renewed—*Super cathedram et cætera*—dealing with the relations between prelates of the churches and the Orders of Preachers and Minorites, and the statute of Pope Benedict XI. was revoked, because it seemed to be too much in favour of the Friars. Also there came the decree of Pope John XXII., under a bull and with the addition of severe penalty, that no cleric should have more than one church; whereas before that time a single rector or parson of a church could accept and hold as many churches as different patrons might be willing to confer upon him, notwithstanding that each such church depended upon his ministrations alone. During the whole of that time these two cardinals remained in England.

[1] *In illo tempore inedio.*

LANERCOST

In the month of May the Scottish army invaded England further than usual, burning the town of Northallerton and Boroughbridge and sundry other towns on their march, pressing forward as far as the town of Ripon, which town they despoiled of all the goods they could find; and from those who entered the mother church and defended it against the Scottish army they exacted one thousand marks instead of burning the town itself.

After they had lain there three days, they went off to Knaresborough, destroying that town with fire, and, searching the woods in that district whither the people had fled for refuge with their cattle, they took away the cattle. And so forth to the town of Skipton in Craven, which they plundered first and then burnt, returning through the middle of that district to Scotland, burning MS.
in all directions and driving off a countless quantity of cattle. fo. 217b
They made men and women captives, making the poor folks drive the cattle, carrying them off to Scotland without any opposition.

In the same year, about the Nativity of the blessed John the Baptist,[1] there arrived in Oxford a certain unknown and ignoble individual, who, establishing himself in the king's manor (where the Carmelite Friars now dwell), made claim to the kingdom of England, alleging that he was the true heir of the realm as the son of the illustrious King Edward who had long been dead. He declared that my lord Edward, who at that time possessed the kingdom, was not of the blood royal, nor had any right to the realm, which he offered to prove by combat with him or with any one else in his place. When this was reported the whole community became excited and greatly wondered, certain

[1] 24th June.

foolish persons yielding adherence to this fellow, all the more readily because the said lord Edward resembled the elder lord Edward in none of his virtues. For it was commonly reported that he [Edward II.] had devoted himself privately from his youth to the arts of rowing and driving chariots, digging pits and roofing houses; also that he wrought as a craftsman with his boon companions by night, and at other mechanical arts, besides other vanities and frivolities wherein it doth not become a king's son to busy himself.[1] So when the said report reached the king, who was then at Northampton, he commanded that this man should be brought before him. When he came, the king addressed him derisively—'Welcome, my brother!' but he answered—'Thou art no brother of mine, but falsely thou claimest the kingdom for thyself. Thou hast not a drop of blood from the illustrious Edward, and that I am prepared to prove against thee, or against any one else in thy room.'

When he heard these rough words, the king commanded that he should be imprisoned as guilty of lese-majesty, and took counsel with his advisers what should be done with him. After a few days, when the council had been held and a very large number of the people had been assembled, he was brought before the king's steward sitting in judgment, who asked the said man before the people what was his name. He answered that he was called John of Powderham. Whereupon the steward straightway pronounced sentence upon him, saying—'John of Powderham, whereas, either by the most wicked counsel of some other, or

[1] When John XXII. became Pope he addressed a long letter to Edward II. rebuking him for his fondness for light and boyish pursuits, and reminding him that, now he was king, he should put away childish things.

out of the iniquity and device of thine own heart, thou hast dared falsely and presumptuously to usurp and claim for thyself the right of inheritance of the realm of England, and whereas thou hast no right in that realm, but art an ignoble and unknown man, I pronounce upon thee as doom that thou be first drawn at the heels of horses, and secondly be hanged on the gallows, and thirdly be burnt.'

When this sentence had been pronounced and horses had been brought up to draw him, he, seeing none of the succour at hand which had been promised to him, and perceiving that he had been deceived, he besought a hearing for the love of God the Lord of Heaven. Having obtained a hearing he began to relate how a certain evil spirit[1] had appeared to him in dreams on various occasions before that time, and had promised him carnal pleasures and many other things that he desired; and always those things which that spirit promised him came to pass shortly afterwards. On one occasion as he was going to walk abroad alone in the fields, a certain man met him, who, after some little familiar conversation, asked him—'Wouldst thou become rich?' When he replied in the affirmative, the other enquired further whether he would like to be King of England. And when he, greatly wondering, replied that he would like to reign if that were by any means possible, the other said to him—'I, who now appear to thee in the likeness of a man, am that spirit which hath often before this appeared to thee in dreams'; and then he added—'Hast thou ever found me untruthful? Have I not fulfilled in act all that I promised thee in words?' He

[1] *Spiritus Domini*, in Stevenson's edition, probably a misreading for *spiritus demonis*.

answering said—'I have found no falsehood in thee, but all that thou hast promised thou hast faithfully fulfilled.' Then said the other—'Nor shalt thou find me faithless now. Do homage unto me and I will cause thee to reign. And if the king, or any one else in his name, will offer to fight thee for the realm, I will assist thee and cause thee to conquer.'

Whereupon he made homage to him, who said—'Go to Oxford, taking with thee a dog, a cock and a tom-cat; enter the king's manor, and there publicly claim thy right to the realm of England, and I will cause the hearts of the people to turn to thee, forasmuch as King Edward is by no means deeply beloved by the people.'

And when he [John] had related these things—'Thus did that evil spirit beguile me, and behold! I die a shameful death.' After this confession had been listened to, he was immediately drawn to the gallows, hanged there and afterwards burnt. Wherefore let everybody beware of the devil's falsehood and his cunning, nor pay any heed to the dreams which he may dream, according to the precept of Jeremy the prophet, as is said in the Book of Wisdom—'Dreams excite the unwary, and as one who catcheth at a shadow and pursueth the wind, so is he who taketh heed to the deceptive visions of a dream.'

In the same year, about the feast of the Nativity of the Blessed Virgin,[1] the Cardinals, who then were still in England, wrote to all the prelates of England that in every solemn mass on ordinary days as well as festivals, they should thrice denounce Robert de Brus, with all his counsellors and adherents, as excommunicate; and, by the Pope's authority, they proclaimed him infamous and

[1] 8th September.

bereft of all honour, and placed all his lands and the lands of all his adherents under ecclesiastical interdict, and disqualified the offspring of all his adherents to the second generation from holding any ecclesiastical office or benefice. Also against all prelates of Scotland and all religious men, whether exempt or not exempt from episcopal jurisdiction, who should adhere to the said Robert or show him favour they promulgated sentence of excommunication and interdict, with other most grievous penalties. Howbeit the Scots, stubbornly pertinacious, cared nothing for any excommunication, nor would they pay the slightest attention to the interdict. It is not to be wondered at, therefore, that afterwards MS. fo. 218 the weighty vengeance of God, in the appearance of a true heir of the realm, visited so rebellious a people, whose head (I will not call him king, but usurper) showed such contempt for the keys of Holy Mother Church.

Let us now hear what happened to his brother Edward in Ireland. Within fifteen days after the feast of St. Michael,[1] he came to the town of Dundalk with his Irish adherents and a great army of Scots which had newly arrived in Ireland to enable him to invade and lay waste that land and [to harass] the King of England's people to the best of their power. But by God's help, nearly all these were killed by a few of the commonalty, excepting only those who saved themselves by flight; for they were in three columns at such a distance from each other that the first was done with before the second came up, and then the second before the third, with which Edward was marching, could render any aid. Thus the third column was routed, just as the two preceding ones had been. Edward fell at the same time and was

[1] That is, 14th October, the actual date of the battle of Dundalk.

beheaded after death ; his body being divided into four quarters, which quarters were sent to the four chief towns of Ireland.

About the feast of the Nativity of S. John the Baptist the Christians were defeated by the Saracens in Spain.[1]

A.D. 1319.

Also in the same year a permanent agreement, as was thought, having been come to between the king and the Earl of Lancaster, they entered Scotland together, with a large army, about the feast of the Assumption of the Glorious Virgin, and set themselves to attack the town of Berwick, and almost scaled the wall in the first assault delivered with great fury, which when those within the wall perceived, many of them fled to the castle; but later, when the English slackened their attack, the inhabitants regained courage and defended themselves with spirit, manning the walls better than before and burning the sow[2] which had been brought up to the wall to mine it.

Meanwhile my lord Thomas Randolf, Earl of Moray and Sir James of Douglas, not daring to encounter the King of England and the earl [of Lancaster], invaded England with an army, burning the country and taking captives and booty of cattle, and so pressed as far as Boroughbridge. When the citizens of York heard of this, without knowledge of the country people and led by my lord Archbishop William de Meltoun and my lord the Bishop of Ely, with a great number of priests and clerics, among whom were sundry religious men, both beneficed and mendicant, they attacked the Scots one day after dinner near the town of Mytton, about twelve miles north of York; but, as men unskilled in war, they marched all scattered through the fields and in no kind of array. When the Scots beheld men rushing to

[1] At Granada, on 24th June.

[2] See note to p. 214, *supra*.

fight against them, they formed up according to their custom in a single schiltrom, and then uttered together a tremendous shout to terrify the English, who straightway began to take to their heels at the sound. Then the Scots, breaking up their schiltrom wherein they were massed, mounted their horses and pursued the English, killing both clergy and laymen, so that about four thousand were slain, among whom fell the mayor of the town, and about one thousand, it was said, were drowned in the water of Swale. Had not night come on, hardly a single Englishman would have escaped. Also many were taken alive, carried off to Scotland and ransomed at a heavy price.[1]

When the King of England, occupied in the siege of Berwick, heard of such transactions in his own country, he wished to send part of his forces to attack the Scots still remaining in England, and to maintain the siege with the rest of his people; but by advice of his nobles, who objected either to divide their forces or to fight the Scots, he raised the siege and marched his army into England, expecting to encounter the Scots. But they got wind of this and entered Scotland with their captives and booty of cattle by way of Stanemoor, Gilsland and those western parts. Then the king disbanded his army, allowing every one to return home, without any good business done.

But the excommunicate Scots, not satisfied with the aforesaid misdeeds, invaded England with an army commanded by the aforesaid two leaders, to wit, Thomas Randolf and James of Douglas, about the feast of All Saints,[2] when the crop had been

[1] This affair was called 'the Chapter of Mytton' because of the number of clergy engaged.

[2] 1st November.

stored in barns, and burnt the whole of Gilsland, both the corn upon which the people depended for sustenance during that year and the houses wherein they had been able to take refuge; also, they carried off with them both men and cattle. And so, marching as far as Borough under Stanemoor, they laid all waste, and then returned through Westmorland, doing there as they had done in Gilsland, or worse. Then, after ten or twelve days, they fared through part of Cumberland, which they burnt on their march, and returned to Scotland with a very large spoil of men and cattle.[1]

Howbeit, before the Nativity of our Lord, the wise men of both nations met, and by common consent arranged a truce between the kingdoms, to last for two years, and that truce was proclaimed on the march on the octave of the Nativity of our Lord.[2]

At the same time the plague and the murrain of cattle which had lasted through the two preceding years in the southern districts, broke out in the northern districts among oxen and cows, which, after a short sickness, generally died; and few animals of that kind were left, so that men had to plough that year with horses. Howbeit, men used to eat cattle dying in the aforesaid manner, and, by God's ordinance, suffered no ill consequences. At the same time sea fishes were found dead on the shores in great multitude, whereof neither man nor other animal nor bird did eat. Also in the southern parts of England the birds fought

[1] These incessant raids provide very monotonous reading; but nothing short of constant repetition could give any adequate notion of the horror and cruelty of this kind of warfare, or of the utterly defenceless condition into which the lamentable rule of Edward II. allowed the northern counties to fall.

[2] 1st January, 1320.

most fiercely among themselves, and were found dead in great numbers; and all these three [phenomena] seem to have happened either in vengeance upon sinners or as omens of future events.

About the feast of S. Michael[1] a mandate came from the Pope for the denunciation of Robert de Brus as excommunicate with all who held intercourse with him. This, however, was no addition to the sentence pronounced before; and he [Robert] paying no attention thereto, remained as obstinate as ever. MS. fo. 218b A.D. 1320.

All lepers who could be found in nearly all parts across the sea as far as Rome, were burnt; for they had been secretly hired at a great price by the Pagans to poison the waters of the Christians and thereby to cause their death. A.D. 1321.

In summer of the same year Humfrey de Bohun, Earl of Hereford, Sir John de Mowbray, Sir Roger de Clifford, with many other barons, knights, esquires and a great force of other horse and foot, entered the March of Wales, and speedily took and occupied without opposition the various castles of Sir Hugh Despenser the younger, who was, as it were, the King of England's right eye and, after the death of Piers de Gavestoun, his chief counsellor against the earls and barons. These castles they despoiled of treasure and all other goods, and put keepers therein of their own followers; also they seized the king's castles in those parts, and although they removed the king's arms and standard from the same, they declared that they were doing all these things, not against the crown, but for the crown and law of the realm of England. But all these things were done by advice and command

[1] 29th September.

of the Earl of Lancaster. These earls and barons were specially animated against the said Sir Hugh because he had married one of the three sisters among whom the noble earldom of Gloucester had been divided, and because, being a most avaricious man, he had contrived by different means and tricks that he alone should possess the lands and revenues, and for that reason had devised grave charges against those who had married the other two sisters, so that he might obtain the whole earldom for himself.

The aforesaid [knights], then, holding the castles in this manner and prevailing more and more against the king from day to day, in the following autumn they, as it were, compelled the king to hold a parliament in London and to yield to their will in all things. In this parliament Sir Hugh Despenser the younger was banished for ever, with his father and son, and all their property was confiscated.

Now after the Epiphany,[1] when the truce between the kingdoms lapsed, the Scottish army invaded England and marched into the bishopric of Durham, and the Earl of Moray remained at Darlington. But James of Douglas and the Steward of Scotland went forward plundering the country in all directions, one of them raiding towards Hartlepool and the district of Cleveland, the other towards Richmond. The people of Richmond county, neither having nor hoping to have any defender now as formerly, bought off the invaders with a great sum of money. This time the Scots remained in England a fortnight and more; and when the northern knights came to the Earl of Lancaster at Pontefract, where he usually dwelt, ready to fight against the Scots if he would assist them, he feigned excuse; and no wonder! seeing that he

[1] 6th January, 1322.

cared not to take up arms in the cause of a king who was ready to attack him.

Howbeit, as time went on, the king, through the efforts of some of his adherents, drew to his party by large gifts and promises the citizens of London and other southerners, earls as well as barons and knights. And he granted leave for the said two exiles to return,[1] received them to his peace, and caused this to be publicly proclaimed in London.

When this report was received, the party of the Earl of Lancaster besieged the king's castle of Tykhill with a large army; and thus war was declared and begun in England, and the enmity between the king and the earl was made manifest.

When, therefore, the whole strength of the king's party south of Trent was assembled at Burton-upon-Trent, some 60,000 fighting men, in the second week of Lent, about the feast of the Forty Martyr Saints,[2] the Earl of Lancaster and the Earl of Hereford (who had married the king's sister) attacked them with barons, knights and other cavalry, and with foot archers; but the earl's forces were soon thrown into confusion and retired before the king's army, taking their way towards Pontefract, where the earl usually dwelt. The king followed him with his army at a leisurely pace, but there was no slaughter to speak of on either side; and although the earl would have awaited the king there and given him battle, yet on the advice of his people he retired with his army into the northern district.

Now when that valiant and famous knight, Sir Andrew de Harcla, Sheriff of Carlisle, heard of their approach, believing that they intended to go to Scotland to ally themselves with the Scots

[1] The Despensers. [2] 10th March, 1322.

against the King of England, acting under the king's commission and authority, he summoned, under very heavy penalties, the knights, esquires and other able men of the two counties, to wit, Cumberland and Westmorland, all who were able to bear arms, to assemble for the king's aid against the oft-mentioned earl. But when the said Sir Andrew, on his march towards the king with that somewhat scanty following, had spent the night at Ripon, he learnt from a certain spy that the earl and his army were going to arrive on the morrow at the town of Boroughbridge, which is only some four miles distant from the town of Ripon. Pressing forward, therefore, at night, he got a start of the earl, occupying the bridge of Boroughbridge before him, and, sending his horses and those of his men to the rear, he posted all his knights and some pikemen on foot at the northern end of the bridge, and other pikemen he stationed in schiltrom, after the Scottish fashion, opposite the ford or passage of the water, to oppose the cavalry wherein the enemy put his trust. Also he directed his archers to keep up a hot and constant discharge upon the enemy as he approached. On Tuesday, then, after the third Sunday in Lent, being the seventeenth of the kalends of April,[1] the aforesaid earls arrived in force, and perceiving that Sir Andrew had anticipated them by occupying the north end of the bridge, they arranged that the Earl of Hereford and Sir Roger de Clifford (a man of great strength who had married his daughter) should advance with their company and seize the bridge from the pikemen
MS. fo. 219 stationed there, while the Earl of Lancaster with the rest of the cavalry should attack the ford and seize the water and the ford from the pikemen, putting them to flight and killing all who

[1] 16th March, 1322.

resisted; but matters took a different turn. For when the Earl of Hereford (with his standard-bearer leading the advance, to wit, Sir Ralf de Applinsdene) and Sir Roger de Clifford and some other knights, had entered upon the bridge before the others as bold as lions, charging fiercely upon the enemy, pikes were thrust at the earl from all sides; he fell immediately and was killed with his standard-bearer and the knights aforesaid, to wit, Sir W. de Sule and Sir Roger de Berefield; but Sir Roger de Clifford, though grievously wounded with pikes and arrows, and driven back, escaped with difficulty along with the others.

The Earl [of Lancaster's] cavalry, when they endeavoured to cross the water, could not enter it by reason of the number and density of arrows which the archers discharged upon them and their horses. This affair being thus quickly settled, the Earl of Lancaster and his people retired from the water, nor did they dare to approach it again, and so their whole array was thrown into disorder. Wherefore the earl sent messengers to Sir Andrew, requesting an armistice until the morning, when he would either give him battle or surrender to him. Andrew agreed to the earl's proposal; nevertheless he kept his people at the bridge and the river all that day and throughout the night, so as to be ready for battle at any moment.

But during that night the Earl of Hereford's men deserted and fled, because their lord had been killed, also many of the Earl of Lancaster's men and those of my Lord de Clifford and others deserted from them. When morning came, therefore, the Earl of Lancaster, my Lord de Clifford, my Lord de Mowbray and all who had remained with them, surrendered to Sir Andrew, who himself took them to York as captives, where they were confined in the castle to await there the pleasure of my lord the king.

The king, then, greatly delighted by the capture of these persons, sent for the earl to come to Pontefract, where he remained still in the castle of the same earl; and there, in revenge for the death of Piers de Gaveston (whom the earl had caused to be beheaded), and at the instance of the earl's rivals (especially of Sir Hugh Despenser the younger), without holding a parliament or taking the advice of the majority, caused sentence to be pronounced that he should be drawn, hanged and beheaded. But, forasmuch as he was the queen's uncle and son of the king's uncle, the first two penalties were commuted, so that he was neither drawn nor hanged, only beheaded in like manner as this same Earl Thomas had caused Piers de Gaveston to be beheaded. Howbeit, other adequate cause was brought forward and alleged, to wit, that he had borne arms against the King of England in his own realm; but those who best knew the king's mind declared that the earl never would have been summarily beheaded without the advice of parliament, nor so badly treated, had not that other cause prevailed, but that he would have been imprisoned for life or sent into exile.

This man, then, said to be of most eminent birth and noblest of Christians, as well as the wealthiest earl in the world, inasmuch as he owned five earldoms, to wit, Lancaster, Lincoln, Salisbury, Leycester and Ferrers, was taken on the morrow of S. Benedict Abbot[1] in Lent and beheaded like any thief or vilest rascal upon a certain hillock outside the town, where now, because of the miracles which it is said God works in his honour, there is a great

[1] 22nd March, 1321-22.

concourse of pilgrims, and a chapel has been built. In the aforesaid town Sir Garin de l'Isle, a king's baron, also was drawn and hanged, and three knights with him. But the aforesaid Sir Andrew [de Harcla] was made Earl of Carlisle for his good service and courage.

Besides the decollation of the most noble Earl of Lancaster at Pontefract, and the slaying of the Earl of Hereford and two knights at Boroughbridge, eight English barons, belonging to the party and policy of the earl and his friends, were afterwards drawn and hanged, as I have been informed, and one other died in his bed, it is believed through grief. Four others were taken and immediately released; ten others were imprisoned and released later. Also fifteen knights were drawn and hanged; one died in his bed, and five escaped and fled to France; five were taken and released at once, and sixty-two were taken and imprisoned, but were released later. O the excessive cruelty of the king and his friends!

In addition to all these aforesaid, the following barons were taken with the earl at Boroughbridge and in the neighbourhood: Sir Hugh de Audley,[1] who owned a third part of the earldom of Gloucester, Sir John Giffard,[2] Sir Bartholomew de

[1] Sir Hugh de Audley of Stratton Audley, youngest son of James Audley or de Aldithley of Heleigh, co. Stafford: created baron by writ in 1321. After being taken at Boroughbridge he was confined in Wallingford Castle, whence he is said to have escaped and afterwards to have been pardoned. His second son, Hugh, was created baron by writ during his father's life, 1317. He also was taken at Boroughbridge, but was pardoned and summoned again to parliament in 1326. He was created Earl of Gloucester in 1336-37. He married Margaret de Clare, Countess of Cornwall, widow of Piers Gavestoun.

[2] Sir John Giffard, called *le Rych*, of Brimsfield, Gloucestershire, was son of that John Giffard who took prisoner Llewelyn, Prince of Wales, and beheaded him in 1282. He was Constable of Glamorgan and Morgannoe Castles, and was hanged at Gloucester.

Badlesmere,[1] Sir Henry de Tyes,[2] Sir John de Euer,[3] Sir William Touchet,[4] Sir Robert de Holand,[5] Sir Thomas Maudent.[6] Now Sir John de Mowbray[7] and Sir Roger de Clifford,[8] were drawn and

[1] Sir Bartholomew de Badlesmere in Kent, summoned as baron by writ 1309-21; hanged at Canterbury, 22nd April, 1322. His wife Margaret, aunt and co-heir of Thomas de Clare, refused to admit Queen Isabella to the royal castle of Leeds (Kent) in 1321, was besieged there, and, having been taken on 11th November, 1321, was imprisoned in the Tower, but was afterwards released.

[2] Sir Henry de Tyes of Shirburn, Oxon., baron by writ, 1313-21, was beheaded. He was brother-in-law of Sir Warine de Lisle.

[3] Sir John de Euer. I find no baron summoned under this name till 1544, when Sir William Eure or Evers of Wilton, co. Durham, appears as Lord Eure, Baron of Wilton. His father and he were successive Wardens of the East Marches, and his son and grandson Wardens of the Middle Marches.

[4] Sir William Touchet was probably the same who was summoned as baron by writ, 1299-1306. He belonged to Northamptonshire, and subscribed the famous letter to the Pope in 1301 as *Willielmus Touchet dominus de Levenhales.*

[5] Sir Robert de Holand, co. Lancaster, baron by writ, 1314-21. He married Maud, 2nd daughter of Alan, Lord Touche of Ashley, and acted as secretary to Thomas, Earl of Lancaster; but, having failed to support him in his rebellion, he was taken by some of the earl's adherents near Windsor as late as 1328, and beheaded on 7th October.

[6] Sir Thomas Maudent. There is no trace of a baron of this name in Edward II.'s parliaments; though Sir John Mauduit of Somerford Mauduit, Wilts., was summoned in 1342 to Edward III.'s parliament.

[7] Sir John de Mowbray of the Isle of Axholme, co. Lincoln, had done excellent service in the Scottish war. That he was concerned in Lancaster's rebellion is one of the many proofs of the despair which the best men in the realm entertained of any good coming from Edward II. He was Warden of the Marches and Sheriff of Yorkshire in 1312-13, and was hanged at York in 1322. But there was no attainder, and the present Lord Mowbray claims, as 24th baron, to be the senior of his degree.

[8] Sir Roger de Clifford of the county of Hereford, son of Sir Robert killed at Bannockburn. According to some accounts, he was alive in the reign of Edward III. He was the second baron: the present Lord de Clifford is the 26th baron.

hanged at York with Sir Jocelyn de Dayvile, a knight notorious for his misdeeds; but Sir Bartholomew de Badlesmere was taken near Canterbury, and was there drawn, hanged and beheaded. Sir Henry Tyes was drawn and hanged in London, each of them in his own district for their greater disgrace, except the aforesaid Sir Hugh de Audley and others. Also there were imprisoned at York about sixty-seven knights, but most of these afterwards obtained the king's pardon.

After this the king held his parliament at York, and there Hugh Despenser the elder, sometime exiled from England, was made Earl of Winchester.

About this time the question was raised and discussed in various consistories and before the Pope, whether it was heresy to say that Christ owned no private property nor even anything in common; the Preaching Friars held that it was [heresy] and the Minorite Friars that it was not, chiefly on the strength of that decretal in Sextus—*Exiit qui seminat.* Of the cardinals and other seculars, some held one opinion, others another.

The king mustered an army in order to approach Scotland about the feast of S. Peter ad Vincula;[1] hearing of which Robert de Brus invaded England with an army by way of Carlisle MS. fo. 219b
in the octave before the Nativity of S. John the A.D. 1322.
Baptist,[2] and burnt the bishop's manor at Rose,[3] and Allerdale, and plundered the monastery of Holm Cultran, notwithstanding that his father's body was buried there; and thence proceeded to waste and plunder Copeland, and so on beyond the sands of Duddon to Furness. But the Abbot of Furness went to meet him, and paid ransom for the district of Furness that it should

[1] 1st August. [2] 17th June. [3] About seven miles from Carlisle.

not be again burnt or plundered, and took him to Furness Abbey. This notwithstanding, the Scots set fire to various places and lifted spoil. Also they went further beyond the sands of Leven to Cartmel, and burnt the lands round the priory of the Black Canons,[1] taking away cattle and spoil: and so they crossed the sands of Kent[2] as far as the town of Lancaster, which they burnt, except the priory of the Black Monks and the house of the Preaching Friars. The Earl of Moray and Sir James of Douglas joined them there with another strong force, and so they marched forward together some twenty miles to the south, burning everything and taking away prisoners and cattle as far as the town of Preston in Amoundness, which also they burnt, except the house of the Minorite Friars. Some of the Scots even went beyond that town fifteen miles to the south, being then some eighty miles within England; and then all returned with many prisoners and cattle and much booty; so that on the vigil of S. Margaret Virgin[3] they came to Carlisle, and lay there in their tents around the town for five days, trampling and destroying as much of the crops as they could by themselves and their beasts. They re-entered Scotland on the vigil of S. James the Apostle,[4] so that they spent three weeks and three days in England on that occasion.

The King of England came to Newcastle about the feast of S. Peter ad Vincula,[5] and shortly afterwards invaded Scotland with his earls, barons, knights and a very great army; but the

[1] Austin Canons.

[2] The river Kent, between Westmorland and Lancashire whence Kendal takes its name, *i.e.* Kent dale.

[3] 12th July. [4] 24th July. [5] 1st August.

Scots retired before him in their usual way, nor dared to give him battle. Thus the English were compelled to evacuate Scottish ground before the Nativity of the Glorious Virgin,[1] owing as much to want of provender as to pestilence in the army; for famine killed as many soldiers as did dysentery.

After the retreat of the King of England the King of Scotland collected all his forces, both on this side of the Scottish sea[2] and beyond it, and from the Isles and from Bute and Arran,[3] and on the day after the feast of S. Michael[4] he invaded England by the Solway and lay for five days at Beaumond, about three miles from Carlisle, and during that time sent the greater part of his force to lay waste the country all around; after which he marched into England to Blackmoor[5] (whither he had never gone before nor laid waste those parts, because of their difficulty of access), having learned for a certainty from his scouts that the King of England was there. The king, however, hearing of his approach, wrote to the new Earl of Carlisle,[6] commanding him to muster all the northern forces, horse and foot, of his county and Lancaster, that were fit for war, and to come to his aid against the Scots. This he [Carlisle] did, having taken command of the county of Lancaster, so that he had 30,000 men ready for battle; and whereas the Scots were in the eastern district, he brought his forces by the western district so as to reach the king. But the Scots burnt

[1] 8th September. [2] The Firths of Forth and Clyde.

[3] *De Brandanis:* the Atlantic was known as *Brendanicum mare.*

[4] 30th September.

[5] *Blakehoumor*, Blackmoor in the North Riding, the old name of the moorland south of Cleveland.

[6] Sir Andrew de Harcla.

the villages and manors in Blackmoor, and laid waste all that they could, taking men away as prisoners, together with much booty and cattle.

Now my lord John of Brittany, Earl of Richmond, having been detached with his division by the king to reconnoitre the army of the Scots from a certain height between Biland Abbey and Rievaulx Abbey, and being suddenly attacked and surprised by them, attempted by making his people hurl stones to repel their assault by a certain narrow and steep pass in the hill; but the Scots forced their way fiercely and courageously against them; many English escaped by flight and many were made prisoners, including the aforesaid earl. Justly, indeed, did he incur that punishment, seeing that it was he himself who had prevented peace being made between the realms.

When this became known to the King of England, who was then in Rievaulx Abbey, he, being ever chicken-hearted and luckless in war and having [already] fled in fear from them in Scotland, now took to flight in England, leaving behind him in the monastery in his haste his silver plate and much treasure. Then the Scots, arriving immediately after, seized it all and plundered the monastery, and then marched on to the Wolds, taking the Earl [of Richmond] with them, laying waste that country nearly as far as the town of Beverley, which was held to ransom to escape being burnt by them in like manner as they had destroyed other towns.

Now when the aforesaid Earl of Carlisle heard that the king was at York, he directed his march thither in order to attack the Scots with him and drive them out of the kingdom; but when he found the king all in confusion and no army mustered, he disbanded his own forces, allowing every man to return home. The Scots on that occasion did not go beyond Beverley, but returned laden with spoil and with many prisoners and much booty; and on the day of the Commemoration of All Souls[1] they entered Scotland, after remaining in England one month and three days. Wherefore, when the said Earl of Carlisle perceived that the King of England neither knew how to rule his realm nor was able to defend it against the Scots, who year by year laid it more and more waste, he feared lest at last he [the king] should lose the entire kingdom; so he chose the less of two evils, and considered how much better it would be for the community of each realm if each king should possess his own kingdom freely and peacefully without any homage, instead of so many homicides MS. fo. 220 and arsons, captivities, plunderings and raidings taking place every year. Therefore on the 3rd January [1323] the said Earl of Carlisle went secretly to Robert the Bruce at Lochmaben and, after holding long conference and protracted discussion with him, at length, to his own perdition, came to agreement with him in the following bond. The earl firmly pledged himself, his heirs and their adherents to advise and assist with all their might in maintaining the said Robert as King of Scotland, his heirs and successors, in the aforesaid independence, and to oppose with all their force all those who would not join in nor even consent to the said treaty, as hinderers of the public and common welfare. And the said Robert, King of Scotland, pledged himself upon honour to assist and protect with all his might the said earl and all his heirs and their adherents according to the aforesaid compact, which he was willing should be confirmed by six persons each [kingdom] to be

[1] 1st November.

nominated by the aforesaid king and earl. And if the King of England should give his assent to the said treaty within a year, then the King of Scots should cause a monastery to be built in Scotland, the rental whereof should be five hundred merks, for the perpetual commemoration of and prayer for the souls of those slain in the war between England and Scotland, and should pay to the King of England within ten years 80,000 merks of silver, and that the King of England should have the heir male of the King of Scotland in order to marry to him any lady of his blood.

On behalf of the King of Scotland my Lord Thomas Randolf, Earl of Moray, swore to the faithful fulfilment of all these conditions without fraud, and the said Earl of Carlisle in his own person, touching the sacred gospels; and written indentures having been made out, their seals were set thereto mutually.

Now the Earl of Carlisle made the aforesaid convention and treaty with the Scots without the knowledge and consent of the King of England and of the kingdom in parliament; nor was he more than a single individual, none of whose business it was to transact such affairs. But the said earl, returning soon after from Scotland, caused all the chief men in his earldom to be summoned to Carlisle, both regulars and laymen, and there, more from fear than from any liking, they made him their oath that they would help him faithfully to fulfil all the things aforesaid. But after all these things had been made known for certain to the King and kingdom of England, the poor folk, middle class and farmers in the northern parts were not a little delighted that the King of Scotland should freely possess his own kingdom on such terms that they themselves might live in peace. But the king and his council were exceedingly put out (and no wonder!) because he whom the king had made an earl so lately had allied himself to the Scots, an excommunicated enemy, to the prejudice of the realm and crown, and would compel the lieges of the King of England to rebel with him against the king; wherefore they [the king and council] publicly proclaimed him as a traitor. So the king sent word to Sir Antony de Lucy that he should endeavour to take him [Harcla] by craft; and if he should succeed in doing so by any means, the king would reward him and all who helped and assisted him. Therefore Sir Antony, taking advantage of a time when the esquires[1] of the aforesaid earl and his other people had been scattered hither and thither on various affairs, entered Carlisle Castle on the morrow after S. Matthew the Apostle's day,[2] as if to consult with him as usual upon some household matters. With him went three powerful and bold knights, to wit, Sir Hugh de Lowther, Sir Richard de Denton, and Sir Hugh de Moriceby, with four men-at-arms of good mettle, and some others with arms concealed under their clothing. When they had entered the castle, they were careful to leave armed men behind them in all the outer and inner parts thereof to guard the same; but Sir Antony, with the aforesaid three knights, entered the great hall where the earl sat dictating letters to be sent to different places, and spoke as follows to the earl: 'My lord earl, thou must either surrender immediately or defend thyself.' He, perceiving so many armed knights coming in upon him on a sudden, and being himself unarmed, surrendered to Sir Antony.

Meanwhile the sound arose of the earl's household crying—'Treason! treason!' and when the porter at the inner gate tried

[1] *Armigeri.* [2] 25th February, 1322-23.

to shut it against the knights who had entered, Sir Richard de Denton killed him with his own hand. Nobody else was killed when the earl was arrested, for all the earl's men who were in the castle surrendered and the castle was given up to the aforesaid Sir Antony. But one of the earl's household ran off to the pele of Highhead and informed Master Michael, the earl's cousin (an ecclesiastic) of all that had been done at Carlisle. Michael went off in haste to Scotland, and with him Sir William Blount, a knight of Scotland, and sundry others who had been particular friends of the earl. Then a messenger was sent to the king at York, to announce to him the earl's arrest and all that had taken place, that he might send word to Sir Antony how he wished the oft-mentioned earl to be dealt with.

Meanwhile, to wit, on the morning after his arrest, the earl made confession to the parish priest about his whole life, and afterwards, before dinner on the same day, to a Preaching Friar, and later to a Minorite Friar, and on the following day to the Warden of the Minorite Friars—each and all of these about the whole of his life, and afterwards repeatedly to the aforesaid Minorite; all of whom justified him and acquitted him of intention and taint of treason. Whence it may be that, albeit he merited death according to the laws of kingdoms, his aforesaid good intention may yet have saved him in the sight of God.

On the feast of S. Cedda Bishop[1] (that is, on the sixth day after the earl's arrest), there arrived in Carlisle from the king a number of men-at-arms, with whom was the justiciary Sir Galfrid
MS. fo. 220b de Scrope, who on the next day, to wit, the 3rd of March, sat in judgment in the castle, and pronounced sentence upon the earl as

[1] 2nd March, 1322-23.

if from the mouth and in the words of the king, condemning him first to be degraded and stripped of the dignity of earldom by being deprived of the sword given him by the king, and in like manner of knightly rank by striking off from his heels the gilded spurs, and thereafter to be drawn by horses from the castle through the town to the gallows of Harraby and there to be hanged and afterwards beheaded; to be disembowelled and his entrails burnt; his head to be taken and suspended on the Tower of London; his body to be divided into four parts, one part to be suspended on the tower of Carlisle, another at Newcastle-on-Tyne, a third at Bristol and the fourth at Dover.[1]

When this sentence was pronounced the earl made answer: 'Ye have divided my carcase according to your pleasure, and I commend my soul to God.' And so, with most steadfast countenance and bold spirit, as it seemed to the bystanders, he went to suffer all these pains, and, while being drawn through the town, he gazed upon the heavens, with hands clasped and held aloft and likewise his eyes directed on high. Then under the gallows, whole in body, strong and fiery in spirit and powerful in speech, he explained to all men the purpose he had in making the aforesaid convention with the Scots, and so yielded himself to undergo the aforesaid punishment.[2]

[1] It appears from the Parliamentary Writs (ii. 3,971) that the destination of the earl's quarters was to Carlisle, Newcastle, York and Shrewsbury.

[2] It is not difficult to discern in this most tragic fate of a gallant knight the influence upon the king of men who were jealous of Harcla's rapid rise. Harcla had been appointed by the king to treat with King Robert: he agreed to little more than what the king two months later was obliged to concede at Newcastle in fixing a truce for thirteen years. The terms of Harcla's indenture with King Robert are given in Bain's *Cal. Doc. Scot.* iii. 148.

The king made ample recognition to Sir Antony and the others who arrested the earl, to wit—Sir Antony de Lucy [received] the manor of Cockermouth, Sir Richard de Denton the village of Thursby close to Carlisle, Sir Hugh de Moriceby of part of the village of Culgaythe, being the part belonging to the aforesaid Earl Andrew, Sir Hugh de Lowther [. . .],[1] Richard de Salkeld the village of Great Corby.

Before Christmas came the bull of my lord Pope John XXII.—*Cum inter nonnullos*, wherein he pronounced it to be erroneous and heretical to affirm obstinately that our

A.D. 1323.

Lord Jesus Christ and his apostles possessed no private property even in common, since this is expressly contrary to Scripture; and likewise that consequently it is heretical to affirm obstinately that the Lord Jesus Christ and his apostles had no legal right to those things which Holy Scripture testifies that they possessed, but only actual use of them, and that they had not the right to sell or give away those things, or of themselves acquiring other things, which aforesaid things Holy Scripture testifies to their having done, because such use of them would have been illegal. Friar Michael, Minister General, appealed against this finding of the Pope, wherefore the Pope had him arrested, as is explained below, in the year 1328.

In the same year, about the feast of the Ascension of the Lord[2] Sir Aymer de Valence, Earl of Pembroke, and Sir Hugh Despenser the younger, with four other official personages, came to Newcastle-on-Tyne on the part of the King of England; and on the part of the King of Scotland came my lord Bishop of S. Andrews and Sir Thomas Randolph, Earl of Moray, and four

[1] Blank in original. [2] 5th May.

other duly authorised persons, to treat for peace between the kingdoms, or, at least, for a prolonged truce, and, by God's will, they speedily agreed upon a truce for thirteen years fully reckoned. When this was made public about the feast of S. Barnabas the Apostle,[1] that truce was ratified and proclaimed in both kingdoms, on condition, however, that, because of the excommunication of the Scots, neither people should buy of or sell to the other, nor hold any intercourse with each other, nor even go from one kingdom to the other without special letters of conduct. For the granting of such letters and licenses three notable persons for England and three persons for Scotland were appointed on the marches of the aforesaid kingdoms, and patrols were set on the marches to watch lest anyone should cross the march in any other manner.

With the bull of Pope John, whereof mention was made in the preceding year, came four other bulls from the same; one revoking the decision conveyed in that Decretal—*Exiit quod seminat*, lest anyone should twist it into different and injurious meanings, and that none might disparage the rule or state of the Minorite Friars. Another, beginning *Cum ad conditorem canonum*, lays down that none can have simple usufruct without legal right of user, because use cannot be separated from possession in things consumed in the using. The third is lengthy, beginning *Quia quarumdam*, wherein it is laid down that the Pope can decree and do all the aforesaid things, and the arguments of those who declare he cannot are dealt with. There is a fourth, wherein it is ordered that the four preceding bulls be read in the schools in like manner as the other letters decretal. A.D. 1324.

[1] 11th June.

The new King of France[1] invaded Gascony and other lands of the King of England beyond the sea, because the King of England would not go and pay him the due and accustomed homage for the lands which he held in that kingdom. So the King of England sent his brother-german, my lord Edmund, Earl of Kent, to Gascony with an army for the defence of his lands.

On the feast of All Saints in the same year died my lord Bishop Prebendary of Carlisle at the manor of Rose; in place of whom my lord William de Ermyn was elected by the canons on the morrow of Epiphany following;[2] but the election did not take effect, because Master John de Rose, a south-countryman, was consecrated Bishop of Carlisle by the Pope in the Curia on the first Sunday in Lent.

The Pope excommunicated my lord Louis, the Duke of Bavaria's son, who had been elected Emperor; but Louis formally summoned [the Pope] to a council, undertaking to prove that

MS. fo. 221

he was a heretic—aye, an arch-heretic, that is a prince and doctor of heretics; and through the clergy whom he had with

A.D. 1325.

him he answered all the arguments which the Pope put forward on his part. Now the clergy and people of all Germany and Italy drew more each day to the Emperor's side, and unanimously approved of his election, and crowned him, first with the iron crown at Milan,[3] secondly with the silver crown at Aachen, and thirdly he was crowned afterwards with the golden crown in the city of Rome, having been very honourably received

[1] Charles IV.

[2] 7th January, 1324-5.

[3] In 1327. From this it appears that this part of the chronicle was not written quite contemporaneously; but, as was the usual custom, compiled from information recorded in various monasteries.

by the Romans. Many battles were fought between the Pope's army and the Emperor's, but the Pope's side was generally beaten.[1]

In the same year the King of England sent his consort the queen to her brother, the King of France, hoping that, by God's help, peace might be established between himself and the King of France through her, according to her promise. But the queen had a secret motive for desiring to cross over to France; for Hugh Despenser the younger, the King's agent in all matters of business, was exerting himself at the Pope's court to procure divorce between the King of England and the queen, and in furtherance of this business there went to the court a certain man of religion, acting irreligiously, by name Thomas de Dunheved, with an appointed colleague, and a certain secular priest named Master Robert de Baldock. These men had even instigated the king to resume possession of the lands and rents which he had formerly bestowed upon the queen, and they allowed her only twenty shillings a day for herself and her whole court, and they took away from her her officers and body servants, so that the wife of the said Sir Hugh was appointed, as it were, guardian to the queen, and carried her seal; nor could the queen write to anybody without her knowledge; whereat my lady the queen was equally indignant and distressed, and therefore wished to visit her brother in France to seek for a remedy.

When, therefore, she had arrived there she astutely contrived that Edward, her elder son and heir of England, should cross over to his uncle, the King of France, on the plea that if he came and did homage to his uncle for Gascony and the other lands of the king beyond the sea, the King [of France] would transfer to him

[1] The Papal Court during these years was at Avignon.

all these lands from the King [of England]; and he [Prince Edward] was made Duke of Aquitaine. But when he wished to appoint his men and bailiffs in those lands to take seisin thereof, the King of England's men, who had been in possession hitherto of those lands and certain cities, would not allow it. Hence arose disagreement between the King of England's men and those of his son, the duke.

Meanwhile it was publicly rumoured in England that the Queen of England was coming to England with her son, the duke, and the army of France in ships, to avenge herself upon Sir Hugh Despenser, and upon his father, the Earl of Winchester, by whose advice the King of England had caused the Earl of Lancaster, the Queen's uncle, to be executed, and upon the said Master Robert de Baldock and upon sundry others, by whose most pernicious counsel the King of England, with his whole realm, was controlled in everything. For this reason the king ordered that all the harbours of England should be most carefully guarded.

But there were contradictory rumours in England about the queen, some declaring that she was the betrayer of the king and kingdom, others that she was acting for peace and the common welfare of the kingdom, and for the removal of evil counsellors from the king; but it is horrible to tell what was done by the aforesaid evil counsellors of the king.

Public proclamation was made in London that if [the queen] herself or her son (albeit he was heir of the realm) should enter England, they were to be arrested as enemies of the
A.D. 1326. king and kingdom. Meanwhile it was said that a very large sum of money was sent to sundry nobles and leading men in France, to induce them to cause the Queen of England and her

son to be arrested by craft and sent over to England. Some of them, bribed with the money, endeavoured to do this, but she was forewarned by the Count of Hainault or Hanonia and saved. Then there was a treaty made, under which her son, Duke of Aquitaine and heir of the realm of England, should marry the daughter of the aforesaid count, provided that with his army he assisted the queen and her son, the duke, to cross over to England in safety: which was duly accomplished.

In the same year, on Wednesday next before the feast of the Dedication of the Church of S. Michael the Archangel,[1] she landed at the port of Harwich, in the east of England, with her son, the duke, and Messire Jehan, brother of the Count of Hainault or Hanonia, and my lord Edmund, Earl of Kent, the King of England's brother, and Sir Roger de Mortimer, a baron of the King of England, who had fled from him previously to France to save his life, and sundry others who had been exiled from England on account of the Earl of Lancaster. They had with them a small enough force (for there were not more at the outside than fifteen hundred men all told), but the Earl Marshal, the King of England's brother, joined them immediately, and my lord Henry, Earl of Leicester, brother of the executed Earl of Lancaster; and soon after the other earls and barons and the commonalty of the southern parts adhered to them. They proceeded against the king because he would not dismiss from his side Sir Hugh Despenser and Master Robert de Baldock.

Meanwhile, however, the people of London, holding in detestation the king and his party, seized my lord the Bishop of Exeter, the king's treasurer, whose exactions upon their community

[1] 24th September.

in the past had been excessively harsh, and who was then in London, and, dreadful to say, they beheaded him with great MS. fo. 221b ferocity. Thereafter, having assembled the commonalty of the city, they violently assaulted the Tower of London, wherein were at that time the wife of the aforesaid Sir Hugh, and many State prisoners, adherents of the aforesaid Earl of Lancaster. Some townsmen within, to whom custody of the Tower had been entrusted, hearing and understanding all the aforesaid events, and seeing their fellow citizens fiercely attacking the Tower, surrendered it to them, with everything therein, both persons and property. But they appointed as warden thereof the king's younger son, my lord John of Eltham, who was in the Tower, a boy about twelve years old, for the use of his mother and brother, handing it over to him with a strong armed garrison.

Shortly afterwards Sir Hugh Despenser the elder, Earl of Winchester, was captured, and drawn at Bristol in his coat of arms (so that those arms should never again be borne in England),[1] and afterwards hanged and then beheaded. After a short interval the Earl of Arundel[2] was captured likewise. He had married the daughter of Sir Hugh the younger, and had been, with Hugh, one of the king's counsellors. He was condemned to death in secret, as it were, and afterwards beheaded. Meanwhile all who were captives and prisoners in England on account of their adherence to the oft-mentioned Earl of Lancaster were released, and the exiles were recalled, and their lands and heritages, whereof they had been disinherited, were restored to them in full; where-

[1] Having been thereby irremediably dishonoured. Nevertheless, they are borne at this day by Earl Spencer. Winchester was about 90 years old when executed.

[2] Edmund Fitzalan, Earl of Arundel (1285-1326).

fore they joined the party of the queen and her son eagerly and gladly.

During all these proceedings my lord the Earl of Leicester, Sir Roger de Mortimer, and Messire Jehan of Hainault, were pursuing with their forces the king, Sir Hugh Despenser, and Master Robert de Baldock to the west, lest they should embark there and sail across to Ireland, there to collect an army and oppress England as they had done before. Also, the aforesaid lords feared that if the king could reach Ireland he might collect an army there and cross over into Scotland, and by the help of the Scots and Irish together he might attack England. For already, alarmed at the coming to England of the French and some English with the queen, the king had been so ill-advised as to write to the Scots, freely giving up to them the land and realm of Scotland, to be held independently of any King of England, and (which was still worse) bestowed upon them with Scotland great part of the northern lands of England lying next to them, on condition that they should assist him against the queen, her son, and their confederates. But, by God's ordaining, the project of Achitophel was confounded, the king's will and purpose were hindered, nor were he and his people able to cross to Ireland, although they tried with all their might to do so.

The baffled king's following being dispersed, he wandered houseless about Wales with Hugh Despenser and Robert de Baldock, and there they were captured before the feast of S. Andrew.[1] The king was sent to Kenilworth Castle, and was there kept in close captivity. Hugh was drawn, hanged, and beheaded at Hereford; his body was divided into four parts and sent to

[1] 30th November.

four cities of England, and his head was suspended in London. But Baldock, being a cleric, was put to his penance in Newgate in London, and died soon after in prison.

After Christmas, by common advice of all the nobles of England, a parliament was held in London, at the beginning whereof two bishops—Winchester and Hereford—were sent to the king at Kenilworth, begging him humbly and urgently on the part of my lady the queen, of her son, the Duke of Aquitaine, and of all the earls, barons, and commonalty of the whole country assembled in London, that he would be pleased to come to the parliament to perform and enact with his lieges for the crown of England what ought to be done and what justice demanded. When he received this request he utterly refused to comply therewith; nay, he cursed them contemptuously, declaring that he would not come among his enemies—or rather, his traitors. The aforesaid envoys returned, therefore, and on the vigil of the octave of Epiphany[1] they entered the great hall of Westminster, where the aforesaid parliament was being held, and publicly recited the reply of the two envoys before all the clergy and people.

On the morrow, to wit, the feast of S. Hilary, the Bishop of Hereford preached, and, taking for his text that passage in Ecclesiasticus—'A foolish king shall ruin his people'—dwelt weightily upon the folly and unwisdom of the king, and upon his childish doings (if indeed they deserved to be spoken of as childish), and upon the multiple and manifold disasters that had befallen in England in his time. And all the people answered with one voice—'We will no longer have this man to reign over us.'

Then on the next day following the Bishop of Winchester

[1] 12th January, 1326-7.

preached, and, taking for his text that passage in the fourth of Kings—'My head pains me'—he explained with sorrow what a feeble head England had had for many years. The Archbishop of Canterbury preached on the third day, taking for his text—'The voice of the people is the voice of God,' and he ended by announcing to all his hearers that, by the unanimous consent of all the earls and barons, and of the archbishops and bishops, and of the whole clergy and people, King Edward was deposed from his pristine dignity, never more to reign nor to govern the people of England; and he added that all the above-mentioned, both laity and clergy, unanimously agreed that my lord Edward, his MS. fo. 222
first-born son, should succeed his father in the kingdom.

When this had been done, all the chief men, with the assent of the whole community, sent formal envoys to his father at Kenilworth to renounce their homage, and to inform him that he was deposed from the royal dignity and that he should govern the people of England no more. The aforesaid envoys were two bishops, Winchester and Hereford; two earls, Lancaster and Warren; two barons, de Ros and de Courtney;[1] two abbots, two priors, two justiciaries, two Preaching Friars, two Carmelite Friars. But at the instance of my lady the queen, Minorite Friars were not sent, so that they should not be bearers of such a dismal message, for he greatly loved the Minorites.[2] Then there were two knights from beyond Trent, and two from this

[1] William 3rd Baron de Ros, d. 1343, and Hugh de Courtenay afterwards 1st Earl of Devon, d. 1340. The present Baroness de Ros is 25th in descent from William, and the present Earl of Devon is directly descended from Sir Philip de Courtenay, grandson of Hugh, 1st Earl.

[2] *Quia Minores multum amabat*; it is not clear whether it was the hapless king or the queen who loved the Minorites.

side of Trent ; two citizens of London and two from the Cinque Ports ; so that altogether there were four-and-twenty persons appointed to bear that message.

Meanwhile public proclamation was made in the city of London that my lord Edward, son of the late king, was to be crowned at Westminster upon Sunday, being the vigil of the Purification of the Glorious Virgin,[1] and that he would there assume the diadem of the realm. Which took place with great pomp, such as befitted so great a king.

On the night of the king's coronation in London, the Scots, having already heard thereof, came in great force with ladders to Norham Castle, which is upon the March and had been very offensive to them. About sixteen of them boldly mounted the castle walls ; but Robert de Maners, warden of the castle, had been warned of their coming by a certain Scot within the castle, and, rushing suddenly upon them, killed nine or ten and took five of them alive, but severely wounded. This mishap ought to have been a sign and portent of the ills that were to befal them in the time of the new king.

Howbeit, this did not cause them [the Scots] to desist in the least from their long-standing iniquity and evil habits ; for, hearing that the King of England's son had been crowned and confirmed in the kingdom, and that his father, who had yielded to them their country free, together with a large part of the English march, had been deposed and was detained in custody, they invaded England, before the feast of S. Margaret Virgin and Martyr,[2] in three columns, whereof one was commanded by the oft-mentioned Earl of Moray, another

A.D. 1327.

[1] 1st February, 1326-7.

[2] 20th July.

by Sir James of Douglas, and the third by the Earl of Mar,[1] who for many years previously had been educated at the King of England's court, but had returned to Scotland after the capture of the king, hoping to rescue him from captivity and restore him to his kingdom, as formerly, by the help of the Scots and of certain adherents whom the deposed king still had in England. My lord Robert de Brus, who had become leprous, did not invade England on this occasion.

On hearing reports of these events, the new King of England assembled an army and advanced swiftly against the Scots in the northern parts about Castle Barnard and Stanhope Park; and as they kept to the woods and would not accept battle in the open, the young king, with extraordinary exertion, made a flank march with part of his forces in a single day to Haydon Bridge, in order to cut off their retreat to Scotland. But, as the Scots continued to hold their ground in Stanhope Park, the king marched back to their neighbourhood, and, had he attacked them at once with his army, he must have beaten them, as was commonly said by all men afterwards. Daily they lost both men and horses through lack of provender, although they had gathered some booty in the country round about; but the affair was put off for eight days in accord with the bad advice of certain chief officers of the army, the king lying all that time between the Scots and Scotland;[2] until one night the Scots, warned, it is said, by an Englishman in the king's army that the king had decided to attack them next morning, silently decamped from the park, and, marching round the king's army, held their way

[1] Donald, 8th Earl of Mar in the ancient line (1300?—1332).

[2] *Inter eos et Scottos*, an obvious error for *Scotiam*.

to Scotland; and thus it was made clear how action is endangered by delay.

One night, when they were still in the park, Sir James of Douglas, like a brave and enterprising knight, stealthily penetrated far into the king's camp with a small party, and nearly reached the king's tent; but, in returning he made known who he was, killed many who were taken by surprise, and escaped without a scratch.[1]

When the king heard that the Scots had decamped he shed tears of vexation, disbanded his army, and returned to the south; and Messire Jehan, the Count of Hainault's brother, went back with his following to his own country. But after the king's departure, the Scots assembled an army and harried almost the whole of Northumberland, except the castles, remaining there a long time. When the people of the other English marches saw this, they sent envoys to the Scots, and for a large sum of money obtained from them a truce to last till the following feast of Pentecost.[2]

About the same time a certain friar of the Order of Preachers, by name Thomas of Dunheved, who had gone more than two years before with the envoys of the king, now deposed, to the MS. fo. 222b court of my lord the Pope to obtain a divorce between the king and the queen, albeit he had not obtained his object, now travelled through England, not only secretly but even openly, stirring up the people of the south and north to rise for the

[1] The above was known hereafter as the campaign of Weardale, remarkable, says Barbour, for two notable things never before seen, viz. (1) 'Crakis of weir,' *i.e.* artillery; (2) crests worn on the helmets of knights (*The Brus*, xiv., 168-175).

[2] 22nd May, 1328.

deposed and imprisoned king and restore the kingdom to him, promising them speedy aid. But he was unable to fulfil what he promised; wherefore that foolish friar was arrested at last, thrown into prison, and died there.

The deposed king died soon after, either by a natural death or by the violence of others, and was buried at Gloucester, among the monks, on the feast of S. Thomas the Apostle,[1] and not in London among the other kings, because he was deposed from reigning.

Meanwhile ambassadors were appointed between the kingdoms of England and Scotland to arrange a temporary truce or confirm the former truce for thirteen years, or to come to any treaty for a perpetual peace if that could be done.

About Christmastide the aforesaid Messire Jehan, brother of the Count of Hainault, returned to England, bringing with him Philippa, daughter of the said count, whom the King of England married with great pomp at York shortly after, to wit, on Sunday in the vigil of the Conversion of Paul the Apostle.[2]

In the same year died the King of France without heir born of his body, just as his brother had died before him. When the King of England heard of his uncle's death without an heir, and holding himself to be the nearest rightful heir to the throne of France, fearing also, nevertheless, that the French would not admit this, but would elect somebody else of the blood (which they did immediately, to wit, the son of Charles, uncle of their deceased king), acting on the pestilent advice of his mother and Sir Roger de Mortimer (they being the chief controllers of the king, who was barely fifteen years of age), he was forced

[1] 21st December. Edward II. died on 21st September.

[2] 4th January, 1327-8.

to release the Scots by his public deed from all exaction, right, claim or demand of the overlordship of the kingdom of Scotland on his part, or that of his heirs and successors in perpetuity, and from any homage to be done to the Kings of England. He restored to them also that piece of the Cross of Christ which the Scots call the Black Rood, and likewise a certain instrument or deed of subjection and homage to be done to the Kings of England, to which were appended the seals of all the chief men of Scotland, which they delivered, as related above, to the king's grandsire, and which, owing to the multitude of seals hanging to it, is called 'Ragman' by the Scots. But the people of London would no wise allow to be taken away from them the Stone of Scone, whereon the Kings of Scotland used to be set at their coronation at Scone. All these objects the illustrious King Edward, son of Henry, had caused to be brought away from Scotland when he reduced the Scots to his rule.

Also, the aforesaid young king gave his younger sister, my lady Joan of the Tower, in marriage to David, son of Robert de Brus, King of Scotland, he being then a boy five years old. All this was arranged by the king's mother the Queen [dowager] of England, who at that time governed the whole realm. The nuptials were solemnly celebrated at Berwick on Sunday next before the feast of S. Mary Magdalene.[1]

The King of England was not present at these nuptials, but the queen mother was there, with the king's brother and his elder sister and my lords the Bishops of Lincoln, Ely

A.D. 1328.

and Norwich, and the Earl of Warenne, Sir Roger de Mortimer and other English barons, and much people, besides

[1] 17th July.

those of Scotland, who assembled in great numbers at those nuptials. The reason, or rather the excuse, for making that remission or gratuitous concession to the Scots (to wit, that they should freely possess their kingdom and not hold it from any King of England as over-lord) was that unless the king had first made peace with the Scots, he could not have attacked the French who had disinherited him lest the Scots should invade England.

'To all Christ's faithful people who shall see these letters, Edward, by the grace of God, King of England, Lord of Ireland, Duke of Aquitaine, greeting and peace everlasting in the Lord. Whereas, we and some of our predecessors, Kings of England, have endeavoured to establish rights of rule or dominion or superiority over the realm of Scotland, whence dire conflicts of wars waged have afflicted for a long time the kingdoms of England and Scotland: we, having regard to the slaughter, disasters, crimes, destruction of churches and evils innumerable which, in the course of such wars, have repeatedly befallen the subjects of both realms, and to the wealth with which each realm, if united by the assurance of perpetual peace, might abound to their mutual advantage, thereby rendering them more secure against the hurtful efforts of those conspiring to rebel or to attack, whether from within or from without: We will and grant by these presents, for us, our heirs and successors whatsoever, with the common advice, assent and consent of the prelates, princes, earls and barons, and the commons of our realm in our parliament, that the kingdom of Scotland, within its own proper marches as they were held and maintained in the time of King Alexander of Scotland, last deceased, of good memory, shall belong[1] to our dearest ally and friend, the magnificent prince, Lord Robert, by God's grace illustrious King of Scotland, and to his heirs and successors, separate in all things from the kingdom of England, whole, free and undisturbed in perpetuity, without any kind of subjection, service, claim or demand. And by these presents we renounce and demit to the King of Scotland, his heirs and successors, whatsoever right we or our predecessors have put forward in any way in bygone times to the aforesaid kingdom of Scotland. And, for ourselves and our heirs and successors, we cancel wholly and MS.
utterly all obligations, conventions and compacts undertaken in whatsoever manner fo. 223
with our predecessors, at whatsoever times, by whatsoever kings or inhabitants, clergy or laity, of the same kingdom of Scotland concerning the subjection of the realm of Scotland and its inhabitants. And wheresoever any letters, charters, deeds

[1] *Remaneat.*

or instruments may be discovered bearing upon obligations, conventions, and compacts of this nature, we will that they be deemed cancelled, invalid, of no effect and void, and of no value or moment. And for the full, peaceful and faithful observance of the foregoing, all and singular, for all time, we have given full power and special command by our other letters patent to our well-beloved and faithful Henry de Percy, our kinsman, and William de la Zouche of Ashby,[1] and to either of them to make oath upon our soul. In testimony whereof we have caused these letters patent to be executed.

'Given at York, on the first day of March, in the second year of our reign.'

The same King Edward of England granted other letters, wherein he declared that he expressly and wholly withdrew from every suit, action or prosecution arising out of processes or sentences laid by the Supreme Lord Pontiff and the Cardinal-legates, Sir Joceline the priest, and Luke the deacon, against the said Lord Robert, King of Scotland, and the inhabitants of his kingdom, and would henceforth be opposed to any renewal of the Pope's processes. In testimony whereof, *et coetera.* But it is to be observed that these notable acts were done in the sixteenth year of the king's age.

In the same year, the clergy and people of Rome, chiefly at the instigation of Louis of Bavaria (who had been elected Emperor), deposed Pope John XXII. (whose seat was then in Avignon in the kingdom of France) after the ancient manner, because they held all the cardinals who were with the Pope to be supporters of heretical wickedness, and because of divers manifest heresies which they publicly laid to his charge, and obliged themselves to prove solemnly, in writing, by time and place, whatever was charged against him. Then they elected a Pope (if that ought to be called an election where no cardinal was present), a certain friar of the Order of Minorites by name Peter of Corvara, who, after his election (such

[1] William, 1st Baron Zouche (1276-1352) ancestor of the 15th and present baron.

as it was) was called Nicholas the Fifth. And the said Lord Louis, with the whole clergy and people of Rome, decreed that thenceforward neither the said John, who was called Pope, nor his predecessor Clement, should come near the city of Rome, where was the seat of Peter, the chief of the Apostles; and further, that if any future Lord Pope should leave the city of Rome beyond two days' journey according to common computation, and not return within one month to the city or its neighbourhood, the clergy and people of Rome should be thereby entitled to elect another as Pope, and when this had been done he who should so absent himself should be straightway deposed.

In the same year Friar Michael, Minister-General of the Minorite Order, was arrested by Pope John at Avignon, and received his injunction that, upon his obedience and under pain of excommunication he should not depart from his [the Pope's] court unless by license received and not assumed. This notwithstanding, he did depart in the company of Friar Bona Gratia and Friar William of Ockham,[1] an Englishman, being supported by the aid and armed force of the Emperor and the Genoese who took him with his companions away by sea, wherefore the Pope directed letters of excommunication against them because of their flight; but [this was] after he had made proclamation under the hand of a notary public before he [Michael] should depart from the court, which proclamation, beginning *Innotescat universis Christi fidelibus*, he afterwards published throughout Italy and Germany, and it was set upon the door of S. Paul's church in London about the Feast of All Saints.

[1] *Doctor singularis et invincibilis*, born at Ockham in Surrey, c. 1275, d. 1349.

Note—that the deliverance of the Chapter General of the Minorite Friars assembled at Paris in the year of Our Lord MCCCXXVIIJ was as follows—'We declare that it is not heretical, but reasonable, catholic and faithful, to say and affirm that Christ and his apostles, following the way of perfection, had no property or private rights in special or in common.' But Pope John XXII. pronounced this deliverance to be heretical, and as the Minister-General defended it, he caused him to be arrested by the Court.

My lord Robert de Brus, King of Scotland, died a leper; he had made for himself, however, a costly sepulchre. His son, David, a boy of six or seven years, succeeded him. He had married the sister of the King of England, as has been explained above; but he was not crowned immediately, nor anointed, although his father had obtained [authority] from the [Papal] Court for such anointing of the Kings of Scotland in future.[1]

A.D. 1329.

In the same year, on the 16th day of March, my lord Edmund of Woodstock, Earl of Kent, the king's uncle and son of the late illustrious King Edward the son of Henry, was taken at Winchester as a traitor to the king, and there before many nobles of the realm acknowledged that (both by command of my lord the Pope and at the instigation of certain bishops of England, whom he named expressly, and by advice of many great men of the land, whom he also named and proved by sure tokens, and especially at the instigation of a certain preaching friar of the

[1] The bull conveying this right is dated at Avignon on the Ides of June, 1329. The Bishops of Glasgow and S. Andrews were directed to exact from King Robert and his successors an oath that they would preserve the immunity of the ecclesiastical order and extirpate heretics.

convent of London, to wit, Friar Thomas of Dunheved, who had told the said earl that he had raised up the devil, who asserted that my lord King Edward, lately deposed, was still alive, and at the instigation of three other friars of the aforesaid Order (to wit, Edmund, John and Richard) he intended to act, and did act with all his power, so that the said Lord Edward, the deposed king, should be released from prison and restored to the kingdom, and that for such purpose my lord the Pope and the said lord bishops and nobles aforesaid had promised him plenty of money, besides advice and aid in carrying it out.

In consequence of this confession, the said Edmund, Earl of Kent, was condemned to death and was cruelly beheaded. Moreover, it was said that his death was procured chiefly through the agency of Sir Roger de Mortimer, Earl of March, who at that time was more than king in the kingdom, forasmuch as the queen-mother and he ruled the whole realm. The bishops, also, and the other nobles who were the Earl of Kent's advisers and promoters of the aforesaid business were severely punished. MS.
And the aforesaid Preaching Friar was delivered to perpetual fo. 223b
imprisonment, wherein he died, as has been described above. But the marvel is that the said friar, or any other very learned person, should trust the devil, seeing that it is said by God in the holy gospel according to John that he is a liar and the father, that is the inventor, of lies. My lord Thomas de Wake, a baron and faithful subject of England and loyal to the realm,[1] and sundry other Englishmen, fearing the cruelty and tyranny of

[1] Ancestor of Sir Herewald Wake of Courteenhall, Northampton. The Wakes claim to be of Saxon descent, and this Thomas or his father was first summoned as a baron of Parliament in 1295.

the said Earl of March, crossed over to France until such time as they should see better conditions and more peace in the realm.

In the same year the Scottish friars obtained a certain Vicar of the Minister-General and were totally separated from the friars of England.

About the feast of S. Luke the Evangelist,[1] the king held a parliament at Nottingham, whereat the said Earl of March was privily arrested by order of the king and taken

A.D. 1330. thence to London, and there on the vigil of S. Andrew the Apostle next following[2] in parliament was condemned to death, and on the evening of the same day was drawn and hanged on the gallows, where he hung for three days, being afterwards taken down and buried at the Minorite Friars.[3] The charge upon which he was condemned is said to have been manifold—that he seemed to aspire to the throne—that it was said that he himself had caused the king's father to be killed, or at least had been consenting to his death—that he had procured the death of the aforesaid Earl of Kent—that it was through him and the Queen-mother that the Scots, so far as in them lay, had gained the kingdom of Scotland, free and independent of the lordship of England for ever, without having to do homage to the Kings of England, thereby causing serious detriment to the heritage of the King and Crown of England—that there was a liaison suspected between him and the lady Queen-mother, as according to public

[1] 18th October. [2] 29th November.

[3] But the king's letter is extant, directing that the body should be delivered to the widowed Countess and her son Edmund for interment with his ancestors at Wigmore.

report. There was hanged also on account of the aforesaid earl one Symon of Hereford, formerly the king's justiciary.

Now the lady Queen-mother, seeing the earl's death and hearing the charge upon which he was condemned, took alarm on her own account, as was said, assumed the habit of the Sisters of the Order of S. Clare and was deprived of the towns and castles and wide lands which she possessed in England. Howbeit she enjoyed a competent and honourable sufficiency, as was becoming for the king's mother.

Meanwhile the son and heir of the Earl of Arundel, my lord Thomas le Wake, Sir Henry de Beaumont,[1] Sir Thomas de Rosslyn, Sir Fulk Fitzwarren, Sir Griffin de la Pole, and many others, who had been exiles in France, returned to England, and their lands were restored to them, with all that the king had received from these lands during the time of their exile.[2]

In the same year the new Pope came to the old one and was received to favour, on condition that he should not leave the curia, and there he remained till the day of his death, when the Pope caused him to be buried with ceremony.

In the same year a son named Edward was born to my lord King Edward the Third.

[1] Ancestor of Sir George H. W. Beaumont of Coleorton Hall, Ashby-de-la-Zouch. This Henry was styled *consanguineus regis*, and was summoned as a baron of Parliament, 4th March, 1309.

[2] Some of these lands were in Scotland, over which Edward III. had resigned all claim by the Treaty of Northampton. But it was stipulated in that treaty that these lords should receive back their Scottish possessions, a condition that the Scottish Government was not in a position to fulfil. Hence all the subsequent trouble about the Disinherited Lords.

About the feast of S. Andrew[1] David, son of the late Robert de Brus, was anointed and crowned King of Scotland at Scone, and it was publicly proclaimed at his coronation that he claimed right to the kingdom of Scotland by no hereditary succession, but in like manner as his father, by conquest alone.

A.D. 1331.

In the same year died my lord Thomas Randolph, Earl of Moray, who had been appointed Guardian of Scotland until David should come of age; wherefore Donald, Earl of Mar, was elected to the guardianship of Scotland, notwithstanding that he had always hitherto encouraged my lord Edward de Balliol to come to Scotland in order to gain the kingdom by his aid; but when he found himself elected to the guardianship of the realm, he deserted Edward and adhered to the party of David.

On the feast of the Holy Martyrs Sixtus, Felicissimus and Agapetus, to wit, the sixth day of the month of August, the aforesaid Sir Edward de Balliol, son of the late Sir John of that ilk, King of Scotland (having first taken counsel privately with the King of England, and bringing with him the English who had been disinherited of their lands in Scotland, and the Frenchman, Sir Henry de Beaumont, who had married the heiress of the earldom of Buchan, and who was in England; bringing also with him my lord the Earl of Athol,[2] who had been expelled from Scotland,[3] and the Earl of Angus[4] and the

A.D. 1332.

[1] 30th November.

[2] David of Strathbogie, 11th earl in the Celtic line.

[3] He is noted in Fordun (cxlvii.) as one of the disinherited lords.

[4] Gilbert de Umfraville, 4th earl in the English line.

Baron of Stafford,[1] and a small force of English mercenaries) took ship and invaded Scotland in the Earl of Fife's land near the town of Kinghorn, effecting a landing where no ship had ever yet been known to land. The whole force did not exceed fifteen hundred, all told; or, according to others, two thousand and eighty. Oh what a small number of soldiers was that for the invasion of a realm then most confident in its strength! No sooner had they disembarked than the Earl of Fife[2] attacked them with 4000 men; but he was quickly repulsed, many of his men being killed and the rest put to flight. So my lord Edward and his men remained there in peace without molestation that night and the following day, but on the third day they marched as far as the monastery of Dunfermline.

On the day following the feast of S. Lawrence the Martyr[3] they marched to the Water of Earn, where the Scots from the other side of the river came against them with 30,000 fighting men. But on that day they would not cross the water to the English, nor would the English cross over to them; but the English, having held council, crossed the water in the night and fell upon the Scottish infantry, of whom they killed 10,000, put to flight the others unarmed, and pursued them. And when they returned in the morning light, believing that the armed men had run away in the same manner, behold! they were confronted by the Earl of Mar, Guardian of Scotland, having in his following MS. fo. 224

[1] Ralph, Lord de Stafford, created Earl of Stafford in 1351. He was one of Edward III.'s ablest officers.

[2] Duncan, 10th Earl of Fife (1285-1353), who, although he often changed sides, is distinguished as having been the first to sign the famous letter to the Pope in 1320, declaring the independence of Scotland.

[3] 11th August.

the Earls of Fife, of Moray,[1] of Menteith,[2] of Atholl (whom the Scots had created),[3] and Sir Robert de Brus, Earl of Carrick, son of the late Sir Robert de Brus their king, but not born in wedlock.[4] They were formed in two great divisions, with twelve banners displayed on the hard ground at Gledenmore,[5] about two miles from S. John's town.[6] They began to fight at sunrise and the action lasted till high noon; but my lord Edward was strengthened by God's protection and the justice of his cause, so that the Scots were defeated chiefly by the English archers, who so blinded and wounded the faces of the first division of the Scots by an incessant discharge of arrows, that they could not support each other; so that, according to report, of that whole army, scarcely a dozen men-at-arms escaped, but that all were killed or captured, and that the number of killed and prisoners was 16,000 men. Howbeit in the first onset, when English and Scots were fighting with their spears firmly fixed against each other, the Scots drove back the English some twenty or thirty feet, when the Baron of Stafford cried out:

[1] Thomas, 2nd Earl of Moray, succeeded his father on 20th July and was killed on 12th August.

[2] Murdach, 8th Earl of Menteith in the Celtic line.

[3] David of Strathbogie having been forfeited in 1314, King Robert bestowed the earldom on his brother-in-law, Sir Neil Campbell (d. c. 1316). The earl named in the text was Sir Neil's son John, who was killed next year at Halidon Hill.

[4] There is confusion here. David (afterwards King of Scots), was created Earl of Carrick previous to his marriage in 1328 to Princess Joan of England. Afterwards, in 1332 or 1333, Alexander, natural son of Edward Bruce, Earl of Carrick (brother of King Robert I.), was created Earl of Carrick and was killed soon after at Halidon Hill.

[5] Dupplin Moor.

[6] Perth.

'Ye English! turn your shoulders instead of your breasts to the pikes.' And when they did this they repulsed the Scots immediately.

There was also much advantage in what a certain English knight said that day, who, perceiving that the fighting was very severe on both sides, cunningly cried out: 'Cheer up, Englishmen! and fight like men, for the Scots in rear have now begun to fly.' Hearing these words the English were encouraged and the Scots greatly dismayed. One most marvellous thing happened that day, such as was never seen or heard of in any previous battle, to wit, that the pile of dead was greater in height from the earth toward the sky than one whole spear length.

Thus, therefore, in this battle and in others that followed there fell vengeance upon the heads of the Scots through the Pope's excommunication for breach of the aforesaid truce, and through the excommunication by the cardinal and the Anglican Church because of the support and favour shown to Robert the Bruce after the murder of John Comyn.

My lord Edward caused all the slain aforesaid to be buried at his expense. Having, therefore obtained this truly marvellous victory aforesaid, they entered S. John's town and abode there to rest themselves.

Now on the feast of S. Francis the Confessor, to wit, the fourth day of the month of October, my lord Edward was created King of Scotland at the Abbey of Scone according to the custom of that kingdom, with much rejoicing and honour. In which solemn ceremony it is said that this miracle took place, namely, whereas there were in that place an immense multitude of men and but slight means of feeding them, God nevertheless looked down and multiplied the victuals there as he did of old in the desert, so that there was ample provision for all men.

Meanwhile the Bishop of Dunkeld came to the king's place, and undertook to bring over to the king all the bishops of Scotland, except the Bishop of S. Andrews. The Abbots of Dunfermline, of Cupar-in-Angus, of Inchaffray, of Arbroath and of Scone came to peace also; and likewise the Earl of Fife with thirteen knights, to wit, David de Graham,[1] Michael de Wemyss, David de Wemyss, Michael Scott,[2] John de Inchmartin, Alexander de Lamberton, John de Dunmore, John de Bonvile, William de Fraser, W. de Cambo, Roger de Morton, John de Laundel and Walter de Lundy. But the other chief men of Scotland who had been deserted, seeing the king in the unwalled town of S. John,[3] as it were in the heart of the kingdom with such a small force, assembled in great numbers and besieged him. When the people of Galloway, whose special chieftain was the king,[4] heard this they invaded the lands of these Scots in their rear under their leader Sir Eustace de Maxwell, and thus very soon caused the siege to be raised. Upon this Earl Patrick, and the new Earl of Moray by the Scottish creation,[5] with Sir Andrew de Moray,[6] and Sir Archi-

[1] Sir David Graham of Kincardine and Old Montrose, afterwards one of the plenipotentiaries for the release and ransom of David II. in 1357; lineal ancestor of the Duke of Montrose.

[2] Of Balwearie, ancestor of the Scotts of Ancrum, etc.

[3] Perth.

[4] Edward Baliol inherited the lordship of Galloway through his father John and his grandmother Devorguila, daughter and co-heiress of Alan, last of the Celtic Lords of Galloway.

[5] John, 3rd and last Earl of Moray in this line, 2nd son of Thomas Randolph, 1st Earl, killed at Neville's Cross, 1346.

[6] Son of the younger Andrew de Moray (killed at Stirling in 1297) and afterwards Regent of Scotland. See Bain's *Calendar*, ii. pp. xxx.-xxxi.

bald Douglas,[1] having collected an army, invaded and burnt Galloway, taking away spoil and cattle, but killing few people, because they found but few. And for this reason the Scots and the men of Galloway were long at war with each other.

Meanwhile the king strengthened and fortified S. John's town, appointing the Earl of Fife with his men as garrison there, while he with his army rode about and perambulated the country beyond the Firth of Forth, and then returned. But before he got back, the Scots, by stratagem and wiles, had captured the Earl of Fife and burnt S. John's town.

Now after the king's return and when he had arrived at Roxburgh on the feast of S. Calixtus, to wit, the fourteenth day of the month of October, he dismissed his army in the town and went himself, for the sake of greater quiet, with a small retinue, to be entertained in the Abbey of Kelso, which is on the other side of the town bridge. But when the said Sir Andrew de Moray heard this, with other knights and troops, he continually dogged the king and his people in order to harass them. They broke down the bridge between the king and his army by night, so that they might capture him with his small following in the abbey, or kill him if he would not surrender to them. But the king's army hearing of this repaired the bridge with utmost speed; and some of them, not waiting till this was done, plunged into the great river armed and mounted, swam across and MS.
pursued the flying Scots for eight miles, in which pursuit many fo. 224b
were killed and others captured, among whom was the aforesaid Sir Andrew de Moray, Guardian of Scotland since the death of

[1] Regent of Scotland, youngest brother of the 'Good Sir James.' Killed at Halidon Hill, 1333.

the Earl of Mar, and a certain cruel and determined pirate called Crab, who for many years preceding had harassed the English by land and sea. Both of them were sent to the King of England that he might dispose of them according to his will.[1] Howbeit this Crab, having been granted his life by the King of England, became afterwards a most bitter persecutor of his people, because of the ingratitude of the Scots of Berwick, who, at the time of the siege of that town refused afterwards to ransom him and even killed his son. But Sir Andrew de Moray was ransomed afterwards for a large sum of money.

About the feast of S. Nicholas the Bishop,[2] the King of England held a parliament at York, to which the King of Scotland sent my lord Henry de Beaumont, Earl of Buchan, and the Earl of Atholl, and many others with them, to negociate and establish good peace and firm concord between my lord the King of England and himself; and this business, by God's ordinance, was carried to a prosperous conclusion, as will be shown anon.

But meanwhile the new young Earl of Mar (by the Scottish creation),[3] and the steward of Scotland, and Sir Archibald Douglas, having assembled a strong troop of men-at-arms on the 17th of the kalends of January, to wit, the ninth day before Christmas, came secretly early in the morning to the town of Annan, which is on the march between the two kingdoms, where the King of

[1] John Crab, a Flemish engineer, served Walter the Steward well in the defence of Berwick in 1319 (see Bain's *Catalogue*, iii. 126, Maxwell's *Robert the Bruce*, pp. 266-268, Barbour's *Brus*, c. xxx.).

[2] 6th December.

[3] Thomas, 9th Earl of Mar, can have been but an infant at the time. The reference is to the Earl of Moray.

Scotland aforesaid was staying with the small force he kept together, intending to remain there over Christmas. They found the king and his people in bed, like those who were too confident in the safety secured through many different victories already won, and they rushed in upon them, naked and unarmed as they were and utterly unprepared for their coming, killing about one hundred of them, among whom were two noble and valiant Scots, to wit, Sir J. Moubray and Sir Walter Comyn, whose deaths were deeply lamented,[1] but the king afterwards caused them all to be buried. Meanwhile the king and most of the others made their escape, scarcely saving their persons and a few possessions which they carried with them across the water into England. Of the Scots, as was reported, about thirty were killed in the brave defence offered by the naked men aforesaid.[2]

The king therefore came to Carlisle, and there kept his Christmas in the house of the Minorite Friars, receiving money and gifts and presents which were sent to him both from the country and the town; for the community greatly loved him and his people because of the mighty confusion he caused among the Scots when he entered their land, although that confusion had now befallen himself.

At the feast of S. Stephen Protomartyr,[3] the king departed from Carlisle into Westmorland, where he was honourably received, and he stayed with my Lord de Clifford at his

[1] Sir Henry Balliol, Edward's brother, was also among the slain.

[2] The chronicler does not here allude to an allegation made by both Hemingburgh and Walsingham, viz. that Douglas in this exploit broke a truce which he and March had made with Edward Balliol for the safety of their own lands.

[3] 26th December.

expense, to whom he granted Douglasdale in Scotland (which formerly had been granted to his grandfather in the time of the illustrious King Edward the son of Henry), provided that God should vouchsafe him prosperity and restoration to his kingdom. After that he stayed with his near relative the Lady de Gynes at Moorholm,[1] from whom he received gifts of money and jewels and promised that, if he should prosper, he would give her wide lands and rents in Scotland to which he was hereditarily entitled of old.

After the aforesaid overthrow of the king and his expulsion from the realm, forasmuch as Sir Archibald Douglas had been the prime mover in planning and prosecuting the said overthrow of the king (albeit that expulsion may be attributed to the Earl of Moray as being of nobler rank and more powerful) they treacherously captured my lord the Earl of Fife when he was travelling beyond the Scottish sea, because he was true to the King of Scotland and put him in prison, making Archibald guardian of the realm of Scotland.[2] In course of time, however, Archibald afterwards released the earl from prison and granted him lands beyond the Scottish sea, so that he should have the earldom.

Now it is held by many people that the said overthrow and expulsion, inflicted upon the king at that time, were really to his advantage, enabling him to know what men of the realm would be faithful to him; but many of his former adherents

[1] This lady died in 1334, leaving extensive estates to her son William.

[2] This Archibald Douglas (there were many of that name) was the youngest brother of the good Sir James. He was known as 'The Tineman,' because he lost so many battles.

utterly deserted him after his expulsion; whence he also learnt to be more careful in dealing with the Scots, and look better after his own safety.

On the tenth day of March following,[1] to wit, on the morrow of the Forty Holy Martyrs, being the season when, as Scripture testifieth, kings were wont to go forth to war, the King of Scotland,[2] supported by a strong armed force of English and some Scots, entered Scotland directing his march towards Berwick, and there applied himself and his army to the siege of that city, which was well fortified. My lord the Earl of Atholl, being young and warlike, raided the neighbouring country with his following and supplied the army with cattle; also the ships of England in great number brought plenty of victual, and closely maintained the blockade by sea. The Scots, seeing the king re-enter his realm with so great an army, dared not risk an engagement with him, but invaded Northumberland, slaying and burning, carrying off prey and booty, and then returned to Scotland.

Also on the twenty-second day of the aforesaid month of March, to wit, on the morrow of S. Benedict, they invaded Gillesland by way of Carlisle, slaying and burning in the same manner, carrying off cattle and booty, and on the following day they returned.

On the next day, to wit, on the vigil of the Annunciation of MS. fo. 225
the Glorious Virgin, Sir Antony de Lucy, having collected a strong body of English Marchmen, entered Scotland and marched as far as twelve miles therein, burning many villages. But as he was returning on the following day with the booty he had taken, the

[1] 1332-3. [2] Edward Balliol.

Scottish garrison of Lochmaben attacked him near the village of Dornock at the Sand Wath, to wit, Sir Humphrey de Boys and Sir Humphrey de Jardine, knights, William Baird and William of Douglas, notorious malefactors, and about fifty others well armed, together with their followers from the whole neighbouring country. They charged with one intent and voice upon the person of Sir Antony, but, by God's help and the gallant aid of his young men, these two knights aforesaid were slain, together with four-and-twenty men-at-arms. William Baird and William of Douglas were captured, and all the rest fled disgracefully. No Englishmen were killed, except two gallant esquires, to wit, Thomas of Plumland and John of Ormsby, who had ever before been a thorn in the eyes of the Scots. Their bodies were straightway taken to Carlisle on horses and honourably interred. Sir Antony, however, was wounded in the foot, the eye and the hand, but he afterwards recovered well from all these wounds.[1]

On the same day of the Annunciation,[2] which was the first day of the year of our Lord MCCCXXXIIJ, the Scots were defeated in Northumberland, and likewise others near the town of Berwick. Now when the King of England heard that the Scots had thus invaded his land and done all the evils aforesaid, notwithstanding that he had not yet broken the peace and concord arranged between himself and David, son of Robert the Bruce, who had married his sister who was with him [David] in Scotland, he approached Berwick about the feast of the apostles

A.D. 1333.

[1] See a paper, by Mr. George Neilson, on *The Battle of Dornock*, in the *Transactions* of the Dumfries and Galloway Antiquarian Society, 1895-6, pp. 154-158.

[2] 25th March, which was New Year's Day according to the Calendar then in vogue.

Philip and James,[1] to make war upon the Scots in aid of his kinsman, the King of Scotland.[2] With him were his brother-german, my lord John of Eltham,[3] and many other noble earls, barons, knights, esquires, and 30,000 picked men. The King of Scotland was still maintaining the siege of the said town; and on the octave of the Ascension of our Lord,[4] both kings delivered a violent assault with their army upon the said city; but those within resisted so strongly, and defended themselves so manfully, by means of the strength and height of the wall (which the father of the King of England had caused to be built while the town was in his possession), that the English could not obtain entrance against them; nevertheless, they maintained the siege without interruption. After dinner, on the fourteenth of the Kalends of August, to wit, on the vigil of S. Margaret, virgin and martyr,[5] the Scots came up in great strength (to their own destruction) in three columns towards the town of Berwick, against the two kings and their armies occupied in the siege, who, however, were forewarned and prepared against their coming. Now the Scots marching in the first division were so grievously wounded in the face and blinded by the host of English archery, just as they had been formerly at Gledenmore,[6] that they were helpless, and quickly began to turn away their faces from the arrow flights and to fall. And whereas the English, like the Scots, were arrayed in three divisions, and the King of Scotland[7] was in the rear division,

[1] 1st May.

[2] The chronicler continues thus to designate Edward Balliol, although King David had never been deposed. Moreover, the kinship between the two Edwards was exceedingly remote.

[3] Second son of Edward II. and Earl of Cornwall.

[4] 20th May. [5] 19th July. [6] Dupplin. [7] Edward Balliol.

so the Scots diverted their course in order that they might first meet and attack the division of him who, not without right, laid claim to the kingdom. But, as has been explained, their first division was soon thrown into confusion and routed by his [Balliol's] division before the others came into action at all. And like as the first division was routed by him [Edward Balliol], so the other two were shortly defeated in the encounter by the other English divisions. The Scots in the rear then took to flight, making use of their heels; but the English pursued them on horseback, felling the wretches as they fled in all directions with iron-shod maces. On that day it is said that among the Scots killed were seven earls, to wit, Ross,[1] Lennox,[2] Carrick,[3] Sutherland,[4] and three others:[5] twenty-seven knights banneret and 36,320 foot soldiers—fewer, however, according to some, and according to others, many more. Among them also fell Sir Archibald de Douglas, who was chiefly responsible for leading them to such a fate; and, had not night come on many more would have been killed. But of the English there fell, it is said [. . . . .][6]

Before the Scottish army arrived at Berwick a certain monk who was in their company and had listened to their deliberations exclaimed in a loud voice—'Go ye no further but let us all turn

[1] Hugh, 4th Celtic Earl of Ross.

[2] Malcolm, 5th Earl of Lennox in the Celtic line. He was one of the earliest to espouse the cause of Bruce in 1306.

[3] Alexander de Brus, natural son of Edward, Earl of Carrick.

[4] Kenneth, 3rd Earl of Sutherland.

[5] The Earls of Menteith and Athol made up six: there is no record of a seventh.

[6] Blank in original.

back, for I behold in the air the crucified Christ coming against you from Berwick brandishing a spear!' But they, like proud and stubborn men, trusting in their numbers, which were double as many as the English, hardened their hearts and would not turn back. This story was told by one of the Scots who had been knighted before that battle, and who was taken prisoner in the same and ransomed. He added that whereas before the battle there were two hundred and three newly-made knights, none escaped death but himself and four others.

Now on the day after the battle the town of Berwick was surrendered to my lord the King of England on this condition—that all its inhabitants should be safe in life and limb with all their goods, movable and immovable, subject, however, to the rights of any petitioner. Also Earl Patrick surrendered the castle of the town to my lord the King of England, on condition that he should retain his earldom as formerly, and he made oath that for ever after he would remain faithful to the king's cause. Therefore the King of England entered the town and castle and took possession of them for himself and the crown of England for all future time, together with the county of Berwick and the other four counties of Scotland next the March (to be named presently), according to the convention formerly made between him and the King of Scotland,[1] when the King of Scotland had been expelled from his kingdom, and the King of England
pledged himself and his people to restore the kingdom to him; MS. fo. 225b
and he[1] promised and confirmed it by a charter that he would hold the kingdom of Scotland from him, as from a Lord Para-

[1] Edward Balliol. See Bain's *Calendar*, iii. pp. 200, 201.

mount, in like manner as his father had held it from his [Edward III.'s] grandfather.

The king appointed my lord Henry de Percy warden of the castle and town, and Sir Thomas Gray, knight,[1] under him. He made William de Burnton Mayor of the town, who had previously been Mayor of Newcastle. The king also commanded that three justiciaries should come there, to wit, Sir William de Denholm, knight, Richard de Embleton, Mayor of Newcastle, and Adam de Bowes, to make inquest as to what Englishmen had been disinherited in the town of Berwick, and at what time, and to restore their houses and lands to them.[2]

When these matters had been settled satisfactorily, the king returned to England about the feast of S. Lawrence,[3] and the aforesaid justiciaries coming to Berwick, performed the duties assigned to them; but, whereas the clergy of the town had given great offence to the king during the siege, all the clergy of Scottish birth were expelled according to his instructions, and English clergy brought in to replace them.[4]

Note, that when the Scottish friars had to leave the convent of Berwick and two English friars were introduced, the Scots provided them with good cheer; and while some of them entertained them at dinner with talk, others broke open the wardrobe, collected all the books, chalices and vestments, packed them in

[1] Father of the author of *Scalacronica*.

[2] All these appointments, except that of William de Burnton, may be seen in *Rotuli Scotiæ*, i. 256-7.

[3] 10th August.

[4] The writs expelling the Scottish friars are printed in *Rotuli Scotiæ*, i. 258.

silken and other wrappings, and carried them off, declaring that all these had been gifts from my lord Earl Patrick.[1]

Now it must not pass without mention how, before warlike operations were undertaken against Berwick, an offer was made to David, son of my lord Robert de Brus, whom the Scots had anointed as their king, that he might come in safety to the King of Scotland[2] to renounce the kingdom in his favour, whereupon he [Edward] would straightway grant him all the lands in Scotland which his father or grandfather had at any time possessed in Scotland. But he [David], being a boy of about nine years, acting on the advice of his council, utterly refused that offer, and, after the aforesaid battle, hearing sinister rumours about disaster to the Scots, betook himself with his people to Dunbarton castle as a secret place of safety.

Meanwhile, on the morrow of the octave of the Nativity of the Glorious Virgin,[3] the King of Scotland[4] held a parliament at S. John's town[5] in Scotland, wherein he utterly revoked and quashed all the deeds and grants of my lord Robert de Brus, who had forced himself treacherously and violently upon the throne, ordaining and commanding that all that he [Robert] had granted away should be restored to such of the original and true heirs who had not borne arms against him in the aforesaid wars. [To the widows of those who][6] had fought and been killed

[1] Ninth Earl of Dunbar, and second or fourth Earl of March (1282-1360). During his sixty years' tenure of the earldom he changed sides very often, giving shelter to Edward II. in his flight from Bannockburn; but the invasion of Scotland in 1334, when the English did not spare his own lands, finally sent him over to the cause of Scotland.

[2] Edward Balliol. [3] 17th September. [4] Edward Balliol. [5] Perth.

[6] Hiatus in original.

he did not give their terce, but charitably and graciously granted them a fifth part only, on condition that they should not marry again except by his special license or command.

In the same year died Master John de Ross, Bishop of Carlisle, who was taken away for burial in the south of England, whereof he was a native. Sir John of Kirkby, canon regular of Carlisle, succeeded him in the bishopric.

Also in winter of the same year died my lord Louis de Beaumont, Bishop of Durham, and was buried there in the monk's choir under a great, remarkable and beautiful stone. In his place the monks of Durham elected one of their confraternity, Sir Robert of Greystanes, a man in every respect worthy of such a dignity and a doctor of sacred theology. When he came before the king and besought his grace for the baronies and lands belonging to the bishopric, the king received him graciously enough; but in the end replied that he had sent his own clerk, Master Richard de Bury,[1] Doctor in Theology, to the court of my lord the Pope upon certain important affairs of the realm, and that among other things he had requested him that Richard might be made Bishop of Durham; but, in the event of his not obtaining what he asked from the Pope then he would willingly grant him [Robert] all the grace he craved.

This reply notwithstanding, that monk went before his Archbishop of York, was consecrated by him, was afterwards installed, received the submission of the clergy of the diocese, and performed other acts pertaining to the office of bishop.

[1] Richard Aungerville (1281-1345), better known as Richard de Bury, a great scholar and patron of learning, author of *Philobiblon*. At the dissolution of the monasteries, some of his books went to the Bodleian and others to Balliol College.

After this, the aforesaid Master Richard returned from the Pope's court bringing with him to England a bull wherein it was set forth that the Pope had granted him the bishopric of Durham, and that he might be consecrated by any bishop whom he should choose. And consecrated he was in England, but not by the Archbishop of York. Thus were there two bishops consecrated for one bishopric; but one of them, to wit the monk, shortly after went the way of all flesh; whereby Master Richard remained as Bishop of Durham, and held a most solemn festival on the day of his installation, to wit, the fifth day of June in the year 1334. My lord the King of England was present, also the Queen, my lord King Edward of Scotland, two English earls, to wit, the king's brother the Earl of Cornwall and the Earl of Warenne, four Scottish earls, the Archbishop of York, the Bishop of Carlisle and a great multitude of clergy and people. A.D. 1334.

On the nineteenth day of the said month, to wit, on the feast of the Holy Martyrs Gervase and Prothasius, the King of Scotland came to Newcastle-on-Tyne, accompanied by the Earls of Atholl,[1] Dunbar, Mar[2] and Buchan, and there in presence of the two English earls aforesaid, four Scottish earls, the archbishop, the aforesaid bishops and an almost innumerable multitude of clergy and people, the same Edward de Balliol, King of Scotland, MS. fo. 226 performed his homage to my lord Edward the Third, King of England, in token of holding the kingdom of Scotland from him as Lord Paramount, and so from his heirs and successors for all

[1] David of Strathbogie, 11th Celtic Earl of Atholl (1309-1335).

[2] Thomas, 9th Earl of Mar in the Celtic line, son of the Regent, must have been a small boy in 1332, for he was still a minor when his mother died in 1347-8 and Edward III. appointed his stepfather, William Carsewell, to be his guardian (*Rot. Scot.* i. 708).

time. And whereas the same King of England had assisted him in reclaiming and possessing his said realm of Scotland, whence for a season he had been expelled by the Scots, and had supplied large funds [for that purpose], the King of Scotland ceded to him the five counties of Scotland which are nearest to the English March, to wit, the counties of Berwick and Roxburgh, Peebles and Dumfries, the town of Haddington, the town of Jedburgh with its castle, and the forests of Selkirk, Ettrick and Jedworth, so that all these should be separated from the crown of Scotland and annexed to the crown of England in perpetuity.[1] Thus there remained to the King of Scotland on this side of the Scottish sea[2] nothing but the other five counties, to wit, Ayr, Dunbarton, Lanark, Stirling, and Wigtown in Galloway beyond the Cree. All these aforesaid things were publicly confirmed by oath, script and sufficient witnesses, and after they had been duly settled, the king returned to England.

Howbeit after a short lapse of time, to wit, about the feast of S. Mary Magdalene,[3] the Earl of Moray newly created by the Scots, the Steward of Scotland, Lawrence of Abernethy and William de Douglas, who had been taken by the English earlier and ransomed, having gathered a great force of Scots, raised rebellion against the king,[4] and violently attacked the Galwegians who adhered faithfully to him. Also they attacked others of Scotland who dwelt in the aforesaid five counties subject at that time to the King of England, and levied tribute from them. Also a certain knight of Galloway, Dugald de Macdouall, who

[1] In the deed of surrender Dumfries and Linlithgow are included (*Fœdera*, 12th June, 1334).

[2] The Firth of Forth.

[3] 22nd July.

[4] Edward Balliol.

had always hitherto supported the King of Scotland's party,[1] was persuaded for love of his newly-wedded wife to raise the Galwegians beyond the Cree against the king and against others on this side [of the Cree],[2] who offered strong resistance; and thus they mutually destroyed each other.

About the same time came the Lord of Brittany to England, to render his homage to my lord the King of England for the earldom of Richmond after the death of John of Brittany, earl of the said town.

Meanwhile David, whom the Scots had formerly anointed as their king, and who had remained in the strong castle of Dunbarton, betook himself to France, and did homage to the King of France, so that he should hold his realm from him as from a Lord Paramount, on condition that he should assist him in recovering his kingdom from the aforesaid Kings of England and Scotland. Rumour of this being spread through Scotland, the number of Scots in rebellion against their king[3] increased daily, so much so that before the feast of S. Michael,[4] nearly the whole of Scotland rose and drove the king to Berwick, which belonged to the King of England. Even the Earl of Atholl, who had borne the chief part in bringing the King of Scotland to his kingdom, now deserted him, and the Earl of Dunbar did the same

[1] And who soon returned to it, as appears from a deed printed in *Rotuli Scotiæ*, i. 608, showing that Macdouall had rejoined the English party in May, 1341.

[2] The river Cree (Gaelic, *Criche*, a boundary) divided Eastern Galloway (now the Stewartry of Kirkcudbright) from Western Galloway or Wigtownshire. The people of Eastern Galloway adhered to the Balliols, whose principal messuage was at Buittle.

[3] Edward Balliol. [4] 29th September.

to the King of England, to whom he was bound by oath.[1] Then the whole of Scotland rose as one man, except the Galwegians on this side of Cree and except the Earl of Buchan, who was not of Scottish birth and whom they kept in captivity. When the King of England heard this, he called parliament together in London, arranged for an expedition against Scotland, and before the feast of All Saints[2] arrived with an army at Newcastle-on-Tyne, where he remained until the feast of the holy Martyr and Virgin Katharine.[3] Then he entered Scotland, coming to Roxburgh, where he repaired the castle, which had been dismantled, as his headquarters.

On the fourth day of December of the same year Pope John XXII. died at Avignon, to wit, in the eighth year from his creation. A certain monk Albur[4] succeeded him in the pontificate, and was named my lord Benedict XII. Now my lord John, his predecessor, had determined many questions during his lifetime and had affirmed certain doctrines not in accord with all the opinions of the doctors nor, apparently, consonant with the Catholic faith, especially in declaring that souls that had passed through purgatory could not behold God face to face before the day of judgment. Wherefore in presence of the cardinals before his death he publicly revoked that saying, and all those things which he had said, pronounced or determined which did not savour of the truth, and by a bull under his hand. . . .[5]

[1] The cession of Scottish territory was too much for the stomachs of these gentlemen.

[2] 1st November.

[3] 25th November.

[4] A Cistercian; sometimes called 'the White Cardinal.'

[5] *Nonnulla desunt.* This was the bull *Benedictus Deus*, defining the beautiful vision, declaring that the faithful departed do see God face to face before the re-union of soul and body.

On the third day after Christmas next following the King of England searched the forest of Ettrick with his men ; but the Scots did not dare to give him battle, keeping themselves in hiding. Wherefore my lord the King of England sent the King of Scotland, who was with him there, and the Earl of Warwick and the Earl of Oxford with their people, and certain barons and knights with all their people, to Carlisle, in order to protect that western district from the Scots. But on their march they turned aside to Peebles and those parts to hunt the Earl of Moray and other Scots who they were informed were thereabouts. Howbeit these [Scots] took to flight, so the English burnt and wasted everything on their march, and arrived thus at Carlisle.

After the Epiphany of our Lord[1] the forces of the counties of Lancaster, Westmorland and Cumberland assembled by command of the King of England at Carlisle under the King of Scotland[2] and the earls and barons of England who were there ; whence they all marched together into Scotland, destroying such towns and other property as they came upon, because the inhabitants had fled, and afterwards the King of Scotland returned to Carlisle.

Meanwhile the King of England, hearing that some of his subjects were holding meetings in secret as if they were plotting rebellion against him, returned to England with a very small following disguised as traders, in order to ascertain the truth ; and in a short time all matters were peacefully settled by God's help.

About the feast of S. Matthew the Apostle[3] the King of France's envoys came to the King of England to negotiate some MS. fo. 226b

[1] 6th January, 1334-5. [2] Edward Balliol. [3] 24th February, 1334-5

treaty of peace with the Scots; but they did not fare very successfully in their mission.

[*There is inserted here an instrument in Norman French, given under the hand of Edward III., 1st March, 1335, setting forth the terms upon which Edward Balliol was to hold the kingdom of Scotland under the King of England as Lord Paramount.*]

In the same year, after the death of Pope John XXII., there were affixed to the door of the church of Minorite Friars in Avignon four placards, two greater and two less, no doubt by Friar Michael of Cesona and his adherents; which Michael the said Pope John had removed from the office of Minister-General of the Order of Minorites and had excommunicated. The title of the greater placards was—'The Appeal of Friar Michael of Cesona against James of Caturco to the Catholic Pope next to be created.' And the title of the two lesser placards was—'Declaration that Friar Gerard Odo[1] is not Minister-General of the Order of Minorites'; for it was the person formerly known as James of Caturco whom the Order appointed to be Minister-General, in compliance with the will of the said Pope John.[2]

On the feast of the Ascension of the Lord[3] the King of England held his parliament at York, and made arrangements for his expedition against Scotland. Thus about the feast of the Nativity of S. John the Baptist,[4] he came

A.D. 1335.

[1] Called in French Gerard Eude.

[2] This bitter dispute is told at length in L. Wadding's *Annales Minorum*, ad ann. 1328-1334.

[3] 25th May. [4] 24th June.

with his army to Newcastle-on-Tyne, whither came to him the King of Scotland[1] from Carlisle with his people, and there it was arranged that the King of England, his brother the Earl of Cornwall, the Earl of Warwick, the Earl of Lancaster, the Earl of Lincoln, the Earl of Hereford, with all their retinues, and the Count Juliers from over the sea (who had married the sister of the Queen of England and had come to support the king with a splendid following), should march to Carlisle and there enter Scotland on the twelfth day of the month of July. But the King of Scotland,[1] the Earl of Warenne, the Earl of Arundel, and my lord Henry de Percy, a very wealthy baron, all being near of kin to the King of Scotland, were to remain with their retinues at Berwick and to enter Scotland in like manner on the aforesaid day. This was carried out as it had been arranged. Each king entered Scotland by a different route; nor did they find anyone so bold as to resist the force of either of them. Wherefore they freely marched through all the land on this side of the Forth and beyond it, burning, laying waste, and carrying off spoil and booty. Some of them, especially the Welsh, spared neither the clergy nor their monasteries, plundering regulars and seculars impartially. Also the seamen of Newcastle burnt a great part of the town of Dundee, with the dormitory and schools of the Minorite Friars, carrying away their great bell; and they burnt one friar MS. fo. 227
who formerly had been a knight, a man of wholly pure and holy life. The bell they exposed for sale at Newcastle, where it was bought by the Preaching Friars of Newcastle for ten marks, although one party had no right to sell it and the other none to buy.

[1] Edward Balliol.

Meanwhile my lord Guy Count of Nemours beyond the sea, kinsman of my lady the Queen of England, came to England with seven or eight knights and one hundred men-at-arms, to assist the King of England against the Scots, although the king did not stand in the smallest need of his assistance. Passing through England to join the king at Berwick, which was in possession of the King of England, he took certain English guides to show him the way. But while he was on the march towards Edinburgh, the Earls of Moray and Dunbar and William Douglas,[1] having been informed of the coming of the aforesaid count, waylaid him in ambush with a strong force, attacking him twice or thrice in the same day. But he and his party made a manful defence, and arrived at Edinburgh on the same day after a march of many miles. There, however, they surrendered, it is said, through want of provender. But when the Scots learnt that he was the Count of Nemours, through whose country they had often to pass in travelling to lands across the sea, they held neither him nor his knights nor his men-at-arms to ransom, but allowed him to return free to England with all his men, exacting, however, from him a solemn oath that neither he nor his people would ever bear arms against the Scots. But they made prisoners of all the English who were with him, and killed some of them. The Earl of Dunbar and William Douglas escorted them back to England, but the Earl of Moray and his men returned after these events.

[1] Son of Sir James Douglas of Lothian. Born about 1300, he became chiefly instrumental in recovering the ceded counties for King David. He was known as 'the Knight of Liddesdale' and 'the Flower of Chivalry,' and was killed in 1353 by William 1st Earl of Douglas, who detected him in treasonable negotiation with the English.

It came to pass by chance that the English garrison of Roxburgh undertook a plundering expedition into these parts; hearing of which, the Earl of Moray, being in the neighbourhood with his force, attacked them vigorously. But they made manful defence and defeated him, taking him a prisoner to England, and so at last he was brought to Nottingham. The English cared but little for the capture of the Count of Nemours, considering it a mighty piece of presumption that he should have dared to enter Scotland in time of war with so slender a force.

While these things were happening, the King of France and the King of Bohemia had fitted out seven hundred and fifteen ships to harass the southern parts of England with armed parties in the cause of the oft-mentioned David de Brus, who had done homage for the kingdom of Scotland to the King of France, in order that the King of England, hearing that his country was invaded by foreigners in the south, should desist from molesting the Scots in the north.

The aforesaid ships appeared first off the town of Southampton, eight of them seizing the harbour, while the men in two ships invaded the dry land, burning two unimportant villages on the coast. But the people of that district, forewarned of their coming, got between them and their ships, and their seamen captured those who remained in the two ships. The other six ships took to the open sea in flight, nor was any more seen in those parts of all the aforesaid ships, save one, which, having 300 armed men on board, made the land near Portsmouth and did some burning on the shore, but of all these men not one got back to his own country.

At last the Scots, feeling themselves beaten and wholly unable to resist the kings, came in to peace about the feast of the

Assumption of the Glorious Virgin ;[1] the Earl of Atholl[2] being among the first at the instance and by persuasion of the earl,[3] whose daughter he had married. Howbeit, Patrick of Dunbar, the Earl of Ross,[4] Sir Andrew de Moray (a wealthy baron), and Maurice of the same [name], William de Douglas, William de Keith,[5] and some other nobles of Scotland with their retainers, did not come into the peace, but, assembling many others, committed much injury upon those who had accepted peace. The Lord's day next before the feast of S. Andrew the Apostle[6] was appointed at their own request as the day for coming into peace, if they were willing, but very few presented themselves. Indeed, while the Earl of Atholl was occupied in besieging Kildrummie Castle beyond the Scottish sea in the cause of the King of Scotland,[7] the aforesaid Earls of Dunbar and Ross marched upon him with all those who adhered to their party, in order to force him to raise the aforesaid siege, and an encounter took place between them. In the end, many Scots who were with the Earl of Atholl having taken to flight, either through panic or treachery, the earl himself was killed together with a few others who remained in the field with him to the end.[8] William de Douglas, who was one of the chief actors in this affair, was made Earl of Atholl by the Scots.[9]

[1] 15th August. [2] David of Strathbogie, last of the Celtic Earls of Atholl.

[3] He married Katherine, daughter of Sir Henry de Beaumont, titular Earl of Buchan.

[4] William, 5th Earl of Ross and Lord of Skye, d. 1372.

[5] Second son of Sir Robert de Keith, who commanded the Scottish horse at Bannockburn.

[6] 26th November. [7] Edward Balliol. [8] Cf. Bain's *Cal. Doc. Scot.* iii. 1221.

[9] Douglas, who conveyed the earldom to Robert Stewart (afterwards Robert II.) in 1341, does not seem to have ever assumed the title.

LANERCOST

The King of Scotland[1] remained during the whole of that winter season with his people at *Elande*, in England, because he did not yet possess in Scotland any castle or town wherein he could dwell in safety. But the King of England remained in the north, and kept his Christmas at Newcastle-on-Tyne. But soon after the Epiphany of the Lord,[2] being much grieved because of the death of the aforesaid earl [of Atholl], he issued summons for the assembling of an army to quell the said earls and their power. But in the meantime there came to the King of England at Berwick envoys from the Pope and my lord the King of France to arrange some kind of peace or a temporary truce. The English army was assembled, when, by consent of the king and (MS. fo. 227b) the King of Scotland,[3] a truce was struck between the kingdoms until the middle of Lent,[4] when there should be a parliament in London, certain articles and demands having been drawn up, whereby peace might be restored if the parties could come to agreement in the meantime; if not, then the war should be renewed. This truce was struck about the Purification of the Glorious Virgin;[5] the first and most important demand being on the part of the Scots, that there should be a fresh investigation by learned and impartial men of both realms as to who had the strongest claim to the kingdom of Scotland—to wit, Edward de Balliol or David son of Robert de Brus, or whether David should succeed Edward in the kingdom if he [Edward] should not have an heir born of his body. It had been adjudged, however, after manifold and long controversy among the people and clergy that the inheritance of the kingdom of Scotland went to Sir John de Balliol, the father

[1] Edward Balliol. [2] 6th January, 1336. [3] Edward Balliol.
[4] 10th March, 1336. [5] 2nd February, 1336.

of Edward, because he was descended from the elder sister (as has been explained above in the year of our Lord 1292), notwithstanding that Sir Robert de Brus was the senior in equal degree from the line as the Lady Devorguilla, mother of the aforesaid John de Balliol, and Sir Robert was male heir in that female [line], because neither in England nor Scotland doth the inheritance of the kingdom run according to the laws of the Empire.

During this parliament the aforesaid Maurice de Moray by treachery slew Sir Godfrey de Ross, a Scottish knight, the King of Scotland's[1] sheriff of Ayr and Lanark, because he had killed his brother in fair fight. Wherefore in the said parliament no terms of peace were arranged, owing to the pride of the Scottish partisans.

At Christmas in the same year, my lord Philip, son and heir of the King of Aragon, and brother of Lady Sanxia, Queen of Sicily, took the habit of a Minorite Friar in the convent of Naples, with great solemnity, my lord Robert, King of Sicily, preaching in the mass of his (Philip's) taking the habit, and the lady Queen Sanxia serving at table. Mention is made above (1292) about the admission of the King of Aragon and other kings and sons of kings to the same Order.[2]

Before the feast of Ascension the king sent the said King of Scotland[3] to Scotland, and with him sundry earls, to wit, Lancaster, Warwick, Oxford and Angus, and barons and an army; but he himself remained in the south. Meanwhile the Scottish knight, Sir John de Stirling, the King of

A.D. 1336.

[1] Edward Balliol.

[2] No such mention is made in the chronicle as it has come to us.

[3] Edward Balliol.

England's governor of Edinburgh Castle, hearing that the Earls of Dunbar, Fife and Sutherland were besieging with an army the castle of Cupar in Fife (in the hands of the King of England and the King of Scotland), beyond the Scottish sea, took with him forty men-at-arms of the garrison of his castle and eighty archers and other men, crossed the firth secretly, set fire one morning to a couple of villages near the aforesaid castle, and suddenly attacked those who were besieging the castle. When they saw the neighbouring villages in flames, a body of men charging fiercely upon them, and those in the castle making a sortie, they took to instant flight, abandoning their siege engines, arms, stores, and all that they had ; for they thought that the aforesaid English earls, of whose approach they had been well informed, had suddenly arrived with their army. Sir John hotly pursued them with his party, reinforced by those in the castle, killing those whom he could catch, and driving the others away. Afterwards he returned, seized their baggage, and burnt their engines. After this successful exploit, he marched back to Edinburgh.

Throughout all these transactions the King of France was fitting out warships and preparing an army of his own kingdom, besides the King of Bohemia and his mercenary troops, with stores and arms, in aid of the Scots against their true and rightful king, my lord Edward de Balliol, and against his kinsman the King of England, who was his ally and defender, supporting him in all ways, and this because David, son of the late Sir Robert de Brus, had done homage to him [King Philip] as holding his kingdom (if he could obtain it) from him as Lord Paramount. This action of the King of France was not concealed from the King of England ; wherefore, as, although young, he was able and warlike, he sent word inviting them to come freely, if they would, to land in England, and allotted to them a space of four-and-twenty miles wherein to rest their forces unmolested until the day of battle should be fixed, after which each should abide by the fortune which should befal him. But whereas the king [of England] is lord of the sea, possessing far more ships than all other Christian princes, the seamen of England undertook on peril of their heads that, if the foreigners made good a landing, they should never afterwards enjoy the use of a single one of their ships; wherefore the king should do his best against them on land, because at sea they would never afterwards return to their own country in their ships. And the sailors most vigilantly watched all approaches by sea.

Soon after Pentecost[1] the King of Scotland[2] entered Scotland, crossed the Scottish sea to the town of S. John (which is called by another name Perth), which he found to have been burnt by the Scots, because they dared not await his coming there. But he repaired it with his troops, surrounding it with a solid mud wall and a deep ditch as the headquarters of the English.

About the feast of St. Barnabas the Apostle[3] the King of England, who hitherto had been waiting in the south to see whether any French ships should happen to land in those parts,
MS. fo. 228 came to Newcastle with a very small following, boldly entered Scotland with them, not without danger, and reached Perth. Having waited there for a short time, he took part of the army and marched beyond the Scottish mountains, burning Aberdeen and other towns, taking spoil and destroying the crops which were then nearly ripe for harvest, trampling them down with horses and troops, nor did he meet with any resistance.

[1] 19th May. [2] Edward Balliol. [3] 11th June.

About the Ad Vincula of S. Peter[1] the king's brother, my lord John of Eltham, Earl of Cornwall, came from the south with the men of Yorkshire, whom the men of Northumberland went to reinforce, and likewise Sir Antony de Lucy with the men of Cumberland and Westmoreland, and they all marched together into Carrick and the western parts of Scotland which were not in the king's peace, laying them waste as much as they could, burning and carrying away splendid spoil, but the people of the country fled before them. Howbeit William de Douglas hovered craftily on the skirts of the English army, inflicting upon it all the injury he could; but the army quickly marched back with the plunder to its own country, the Earl of Cornwall taking his column to Perth to meet the king, who had just come back from beyond the mountains. Nevertheless the king did not remain long in Perth, but, having dismissed the King of Scotland[2] and his people, marched with a detachment of his army to Stirling in the west country, where in place of the ruined castle he caused a fort to be built—a pele, as it is called in English. But whereas he had spent a great deal, not only upon the army under his command, but also upon the King of Scotland's army, which he maintained entirely at his own expense, therefore he commanded a council or parliament[3] to be held at Nottingham in order that he might demand an aid for recovering both past and future expenditure from all the people of his realm. In which council or parliament there was granted to him the fifteenth penny from the community of the country, and a tenth from the cities, the boroughs and the

[1] 1st August. [2] Edward Balliol.

[3] The chronicler seems doubtful what was the exact nature of this assembly, whereof the proceedings were not entered in the Parliamentary Roll.

clergy, during six years to come, providing that what was due by the clergy might be discharged by the payment within a year to come of one mark on every sack of wool.

Meanwhile, sad to say, the said Earl of Cornwall died at Perth within the octave of the Nativity of the Glorious Virgin,[1] and was carried to England for burial.

The king, taking account of what was the common opinion of experienced men, that the land of Scotland could never be conquered unless in winter, marched with his army to Bothwell Castle and those western parts about the feast of S. Luke the Evangelist.[2] When the men of those parts heard of his sudden and unexpected coming, not being strong enough to resist him they submitted to his peace, more through fear than for love. He received them to peace, repaired the said castle which the Scots had formerly destroyed and abandoned, and he left a garrison there. Howbeit William de Douglas, hovering about the army with his following, killed some of the king's men from time to time.

Meanwhile the Baron of Stafford, a very accomplished soldier, marching with his following to join the king, passed through Douglasdale, which had not come into peace, and carried away much spoil therefrom.

The King of England returned to England before Christmas, and the King of Scotland[3] remained throughout the winter at Perth with an extremely modest following.

At the beginning of Lent[4] following the king held his parliament in London, at which six new earls were created in addition

[1] 15th September.

[2] 18th October.

[3] Edward Balliol.

[4] 5th March, 1337.

to the old ones, to wit, Sir Henry, son of the Earl of Lancaster, was made Earl of Derby; Sir Hugh de Audley Earl of Gloucester; Sir William de Bohun, brother germane of the Earl of Hereford [became] Earl of Northampton; Sir William de Montagu Earl of Salisbury; Sir William de Clinton Earl of Huntingdon; Sir Robert de Ufford Earl of Suffolk; and Sir Edward,[1] elder son of the king, was made Duke of Cornwall, which since the time of the Britons never had been a dukedom, but only an earldom.

Now the Scots, being aware that the King of England and the nobles of the country were in distant parts, assembled and besieged Bothwell Castle which the king had lately repaired; and because the aforesaid Sir Robert de Ufford, to whom, as well as to the warden, that castle had been committed by the king, was absent at the time, the castle quickly surrendered to the Scots upon these terms, that all those therein should be secure in life, limb and all their possessions, and receive a safe-conduct to England: all which was done.

Also at that time the Scots seized several towns and fortresses in the land of Fife, and thereafter once more destroyed the wretched Galwegians on this side of Cree like beasts, because they adhered so firmly to their lord King Edward de Balliol.

It was also decided in the aforesaid parliament of London that, whereas the King of France had taken and occupied certain of the King of England's towns and castles in Gascony, especially the province of Guienne, one army should be sent to Gascony and another to Scotland, at a suitable time, and that the king should

[1] The Black Prince, who was then but six years old. The Prince of Wales still bears the title of Duke of Cornwall.

remain in England. My lord William Montagu, Earl of Salisbury, was appointed to command the expedition to Gascony, with certain earls as arranged; and my lord the Earl of Warwick, was appointed to command the expedition to Scotland, represent-
MS. fo. 228b ing the person of my lord the King of England, and with him marched all the nobles between Trent and Scotland.

After Easter,[1] however, the King of England sent for the King of Scotland,[2] who came to him in England for reasons to be explained presently.

In the same year Friar Peter, Patriarch of Jerusalem, the Pope's legate to the Holy Land to negotiate with the Sultan for restoration of the Holy Land to the Christians, reported thus—that the Sultan with the assent of all his people was prepared to restore to the Christians the whole of the Holy Land and whatsoever they had at any time possessed oversea which was known to appertain to the spiritual power, and this gratuitously and without payment of any kind, so that they [the Christians] might have possession of the Lord's sepulchre, and the stable, and all the oversea churches, with oblations, tithes, and all rights belonging to them, and that their prelates should exercise spiritual authority in them, according to the custom in churches, and that they should hold and dispose of these and all the other holy places at their will, and might solemnly celebrate the divine office in them with open doors, administer to their people the sacraments and all sacramental rites and ecclesiastical sepulture, and freely preach the Word of God in churches and cemeteries, make wills, build houses without defences round the holy places, rebuild, add to and construct afresh ruined churches in any place. But that neither

[1] 31st March, 1337. [2] Edward Balliol.

prayers nor price, fear nor favour would induce him to give up the kingdom of Jerusalem—neither the city nor any town, castle, house, field, garden, gate, nor a foot of ground which he or his predecessors had hitherto taken from the Christians, so far as pertaineth to the temporality, jurisdiction, dominion, property, expenditure or revenue. But it pleaseth him that all Christians who wish to do so should come to the Holy Land and to all his dominion freely to travel and trade, to go, to stay or to return, and that pilgrims should be free from all tribute. Also he is willing reasonably to abate the tax upon traders, so that they may not be oppressed, but rather encouraged. All the aforesaid grants he offereth upon this condition, that my lord the Pope shall revoke all the sentences and writings promulgated against merchants going thither to trade. And thus he concedeth all the aforesaid [points] from his own free will and not ours.

Now about the feast of the Lord's Ascension,[1] the Scots, seeing that they had captured Bothwell Castle, assembled in great numbers and laid siege to Stirling Castle; but met there with a stout defence. The King of England, being A.D. 1337. occupied in distant parts, when he heard of that siege, hastened at high speed by day and night to Stirling Castle, believing that the Scots would offer him battle. But when the Scots heard of this, they raised the siege and would not meet him, wherefore he returned immediately to England.

About the same time Sir Eustace de Maxwell, a knight of Galloway and lord of Carlaverock Castle, false to the faith and allegiance which he owed to my lord the King of England, went over to the Scottish side (notwithstanding that the King of

[1] 29th May.

England had just provided him with a large sum of money, flour and wine for the greater security of his castle) and caused the Galwegians on this side of Cree to rise against the king, using similar authority to that which he had formerly employed for the king.[1]

Dunbar Castle[2] at that time was still in the hands of Earl Patrick, having been neither besieged nor taken by the English, the whole of the surrounding district of Lothian, although it was then in the King of England's peace, paid each week one mark to those within the castle, more, it is thought, out of fear lest it should be forced from them than from love. Also Dunbarton Castle was still in the hands of the Scots, and a few small towns.

About the feast of SS. Peter and Paul[3] three Scottish knights who had been with the King of Scotland[4] came to England; to wit, Sir Geoffrey, Sir Alexander and Sir Roger de Mowbray, and were arrested and imprisoned; for they were accused of having endeavoured their utmost to persuade the King of Scotland to break faith and allegiance to the King of England, and to put his trust in the Scots, regardless of the homage he had done to the king. The King of Scotland affirmed that this was so, making this grave accusation against them, and announced it to the King of England when he came to England.

When the king heard that Sir Eustace de Maxwell had joined the Scots, he gave his castle[5] to the Lord of Gillesland, who,

[1] Or perhaps 'serving the king the same baseness as he had practised before.' *De consimili servitio servierat regi ante.*

[2] *Comes de Dunbar* in Stevenson's edition ought obviously to read *Castrum de Dunbar*.

[3] 29th June. [4] Edward Balliol.

[5] Carlaverock, which, however, is not in Galloway, but in Nithsdale.

having assembled a force of English, invaded Galloway and burnt his [Maxwell's] lands, driving off cattle, wherefore the Scots retaliated by invading England in force by way of Arthuret. On the third day, before the feast of S. Lawrence,[1] marching towards the east, they burnt about twenty villages, taking prisoners and an immense number of cattle ; but, having met with some opposition from the men-at-arms who were in Carlisle and the surrounding country, and having lost some of their men, they returned on the same day into Scotland.

About the feast of the Assumption of the Glorious Virgin,[2] two Scottish ships returning from France were taken at sea by the English, wherein were my lord Bishop of Glasgow, many ladies, soldiers and arms and 30,000 pounds of silver, besides charters, conventions and indentures which had been concluded between the King of France and the Scots. The men were either killed or drowned in the sea ; but my lord Bishop of Glasgow[3] and some of the said ladies, refusing through excessive vexation to eat or drink or accept any consolation, died at sea before reaching the land and their bodies were buried at Whitsand in England. The other things which were in the ships were preserved for disposal by my lord the king.

Now in the beginning of September, when the Scots were reaping their harvest, my lord the Earl of Warwick, representing in all respects the person of the King of England and maintaining his state, invaded Scotland by way of Berwick, with MS. fo. 229
the barons, knights, esquires, and troops drawn from all places on

[1] 7th August. [2] 15th August.

[3] John de Wischard, consecrated in 1325, not to be confounded with Bishop Robert Wischard, the strenuous supporter of Robert Bruce.

this [north] side of Trent. At the same time the noble baron Sir Thomas Wake, lord of Liddel, my lord de Clifford, and my lord of Gillesland, invaded Scotland by way of Carlisle, together with my lord Bishop of Carlisle, taking with them the men of two counties, to wit, Westmorland and Cumberland. Within two days they formed a junction with the Earl of Warwick's army, as had been previously arranged between them; and so they marched together into Teviotdale, Moffatdale, and Nithsdale, driving off cattle and burning houses and corn, which had then been stored in the barns; but they killed few men, indeed they found hardly any. But Sir Antony de Lucy, taking with him a detachment of the army, turned aside into Galloway—killing, plundering, laying waste all that he could find to the best of his power, returning afterwards to the main body. And whereas, because of the excessive rain and flooded rivers they could not advance into Douglasdale and to Ayr and those parts as had been intended, on the twelfth day they all returned to Carlisle.[1] On that occasion the King of Scotland[2] remained in England and was not with them.

Five days later, however, hearing that the Scots had led an expedition to the east in order to plunder Coquetdale and Redesdale, they marched together against them; but they lingered too long, for the Scots had re-entered their own land before they could overtake them. Howbeit the Scots lifted but few cattle, because the people had been forewarned of their coming, and had removed their cattle to distant parts. But they did some burn-

[1] The chronicler refrains from attributing the floods to the direct interposition of the Almighty in favour of the Scots, as undoubtedly he would have done if a Scottish invasion of England had been cut short in like manner.

[2] Edward Balliol.

ing, and would have done much more had not the Earl of Angus, lord of Redesdale,[1] offered them bold resistance with his small force.

About the middle of October the Scots invaded England again by way of Carlisle, and on the first day marched round that town towards the east, showing off before the town in three bands, on the chance of any one or more daring to come out and engage them. But whereas there was not in the town at that time sufficient troops to oppose such a strong force, some archers and a few others went out to harass them in the field. Of these they made no account, but marched round the town, and, having burnt the hospital of S. Nicolas in the suburbs, they went off the same day to the manor of Rose, because they held my lord Bishop of Carlisle, who owned that manor, in utmost hatred through his having marched against them in war, as has been described above. Therefore they destroyed that place, and everything else on their march, with fire. But in that first night of their coming into England, Sir Antony de Lucy beat up their quarters and severely harassed them. Next day, however, the Scots burnt the villages throughout Allerdale, and detached part of their force against Copeland to lift cattle. But on the third day, to wit on the vigil of S. Luke,[2] the noble barons, Lord de Percy and Lord de Nevill, came to the relief of the district with their following of men-at-arms; although, as described above, they came too late, although the leading men had written to them to move with speed, because

[1] Gilbert de Umfraville, 4th Earl of Angus in the English line. He inherited the title from his great-grandfather, a powerful Northumbrian baron, who married Matilda, Countess of Angus in her own right, in 1243.

[2] 17th October.

the Scots had sent their booty and wounded men before them into Scotland, the armed troops following soon after. For they had lost a great number of their men, among whom the brother of William de Douglas[1] was taken alive and brought to Carlisle Castle. Howbeit it had been commonly, but secretly, reported for a long time that a certain noble in the north country was unduly favourable to the Scottish side, and that he did on that occasion, as on other occasions, inform them beforehand at what time they might safely invade England with their army, and afterwards sent them word when they should leave it. Which, if it be true, may God make known to king and country these cunning traitors.

About the feast of All Saints the Scots mustered and laid siege to Edinburgh Castle, in the absence of Sir John de Stirling, warden of that castle. Hearing this, my lord Bishop of Carlisle and Sir Rafe de Dacre, lord of Gillesland, assembled the forces of the counties Westmorland and Cumberland, to relieve that siege, and at Roxburgh there joined them my lord the King of Scotland[2] and Sir Antony de Lucy with their forces which they had brought from Berwick, and so they marched together to Edinburgh, broke up the siege, put the Scots to flight, and re-established Sir John de Stirling, by birth a Scot, for the safer custody of the King of England's castle. Somewhat later, however, when he went forth with his people from the castle to take some booty, he was captured by William de Douglas and taken to Dunbarton Castle, as will be shown presently.

Now after the aforesaid feast of All Saints the King of England sent ambassadors to France to arrange peace with the King of

[1] The Knight of Liddesdale. [2] Edward Balliol.

France, offering to the said king for free possession of the land of Guienne, just as he held the other parts of Gascony, that his elder son, the heir of England, should take a wife from the King of France's family, whom that king should accordingly give him in marriage, and that the King of France should possess the land of Gascony with all its revenues for seven years, and after seven years should restore it without dispute to the King of England, as formerly. Further, that the King of England should accompany the King of France, with one thousand men-at-arms, to the Holy Land against the Saracens. These, I say, were the conditions offered by the King of England to the said king, MS.
but that proud and avaricious person rejected them all, wherefore fo. 229b
the King of England prepared to fight him, hiring and making alliance with the following nobles oversea as his mercenaries, to wit, my lord the Emperor Louis, who was then King of Germany and Duke of Bavaria, and had married the Queen of England's sister, and was at dire enmity with the King of France; *item*, the Duke of Brabant, son of the King of England's maternal aunt; *item*, the Count of Hainault, the queen's brother-german; *item*, the Count of Guelders, who had married the King of England's sister; *item*, the Count of Julers, the Queen of England's uncle; *item*, the Archbishop of Cologne; *item*, the Count of Trèves;[1] *item*, the Dauphin de Vienne; *item*, my lord William de Chalons; *item*, my Lord de Faukemounde. The emperor had 50,000 helmed men under arms, the Duke of Brabant 15,800, the Count of Guelders 20,000, the Count of Hainault 15,000,

[1] *Sic* in Stevenson's edition, but further on he is referred to as Bishop of Trèves. In fact he was Archbishop, and, as Chancellor of Burgundy, was one of the Electors of the Empire.

the Count of Julers 5,000, the Archbishop of Cologne 4,000, the Bishop of Trèves 2,000, the Dauphin of Vienne and my lord William de Chalons 15,000, my lord de Faukemounde 3,000; in all, 129,000 helmed men.

The Count of Artois-Arras, whom the King of France had expelled from his country and of whose lands he had taken possession, was in England at that time under protection of the king, who treated him courteously in all respects.

The King of England sent to the aforesaid lords across the sea my lord William de Bohun Earl of Northampton, the Earl of Huntingdon, and the Earl of Suffolk, with 15,000 men-at-arms, archers and spearmen. Also he sent the Bishop of Lincoln with 14,000 sacks of wool to defray the wages of the troops for the meantime. Afterwards there were granted to him in the next parliament in London 20,000 sacks of wool of the English merchants for the fitting out and supporting his war. He himself purchased from the English merchants one sack out of every two sacks of prime wool for half a mark, and inferior wool at less price and value; for he was obliged to spend an almost incalculable sum for the maintenance of so great an army. Thus it was said that he spent a thousand marks a day, according to others two thousand pounds.

It so happened that my lord William aforesaid and the other earls with the army, encountered in their voyage over sea eighty French ships, which they captured and disposed of at will. The brother of the Count of Flanders was found in these ships and taken to the King of England, who received him with so much honour, setting him free, that peace was made between England and Flanders. But when they arrived in a certain town of

Flanders, they found armed men who gave them battle, but were soon put to flight by the English archers. Then they raised the surrounding district to fight our people, but some of them were again put to flight, and some took shelter in a certain church; and because, trusting in the strength of the place, they refused to surrender, the English set the church afire, and they were burnt in the church.

After Christmas two cardinals came to England, sent by my lord the Pope to the King of England in order by God's grace to make peace between him and the King of France.[1] They had first been to the King of France and had heard all that he desired. Therefore the King of England commanded that all the archbishops, bishops and nobles of the country should be summoned to a parliament in London, which was to begin on the morrow of the Purification of the Glorious Virgin.[2] But meanwhile, pending whatever might happen about the said peace, he sent my lord William de Montagu Earl of Salisbury, the Earl of Gloucester, the Earl of Derby, three barons, de Percy, de Nevill and de Stafford, and the Earl of Redesdale, with 20,000 men, to the King of Scotland[3] in Scotland, commanding them to besiege closely and effectively the castle of Dunbar—the castle of Earl Patrick, traitor alike to himself and the kingdom—because it was irksome and oppressive to the whole district of Lothian, as has been explained above.

Close siege, therefore, was laid to the castle: those inside were surrounded by a deep trench, so that they could not get out;

[1] The bull with which they were provided is set forth in Raynaldi, A.D. 1337, § 15.

[2] 3rd Feb., 1338.

[3] Edward Balliol.

wooden houses were constructed before the gate, and pavilions or tents were set up for the lodging of the chief persons in the army. Meanwhile it happened that Sir John de Stirling, warden of Edinburgh Castle, going forth with the intention of lifting some booty, was captured by craft by Sir William de Douglas and a large party which he had brought with him ; [Stirling] himself and two or three knights and about twenty men at arms [being captured], of whom some were killed and some were taken alive and brought to Edinburgh Castle by William de Douglas and his people. When they arrived there, William summoned the castle to surrender, promising faithfully if those within would do so that both Sir John whom they had captured and all those who were outside the castle with him, as well as all those within the castle, should preserve life and limb and all their goods, and a safe-conduct to go whither they would; but that if they refused to do so, he declared that he would cause Sir John to be drawn there at the tails of horses, and afterwards to be hanged on gallows before the gate, and all those who were prisoners there with him to be beheaded before their eyes. But those who were within made reasonable and conciliatory reply, saying that that castle was a fortress of the King of England, and that, let what might befal Sir John and the others with him, they would not surrender it to Douglas or any other living man unless at the king's command. When William heard this, he did not carry his threat into effect, but sent all those prisoners to Dunbarton Castle, because there
MS. was no other good castle in possession of the Scots at that time
fo. 230 except that and Carlaverock Castle, belonging to the traitor Sir Eustace de Maxwell, who afterwards killed the knight Sir Robert de Lauder, the most intelligent man among the Scots.

When my lord William de Montagu who was besieging Dunbar Castle, heard of these events, he took a strong force and came to Edinburgh, appointed another warden of the castle with a sufficient garrison to hold and defend it, and then he returned with his men to the siege of [Dunbar] Castle.

In the following Lent[1] Sir Andrew de Moray, Guardian of Scotland, died in his bed of dysentery, as some say; others, however, declared that he mounted an unbroken colt which threw him from the saddle, that one of his feet caught in the stirrup, and thus he was dragged by his foot and leg to death. The Steward of Scotland was chosen Guardian in his place.

Dunbar Castle held out stoutly and made a gallant defence, in despite of the close siege; and whereas the Countess of Dunbar,[2] who was in chief command of the castle, was sister of the Earl of Moray, he had been taken in Scotland, carried off to Nottingham Castle in England, and there placed in ward, as mentioned above, [to await] the King of England's pleasure.

In the same year my lord Pope Benedictus XII. commanded that twelve wise and discreet friars of the Order of Minorites, should be chosen to regulate discipline, together with the cardinals, certain bishops and masters of theology;[3] which was done accordingly. The constitution having been considered approved, my lord the Pope placed them in a bull, and sent them in the bull to the Captain General that they should be scrupulously observed throughout the whole Order; howbeit he willed not that the rule of the Friars nor their other constitutions should be modified in any respect. Now the said bull contained

[1] 25th Feb.–12th April, 1338.

[2] "Black Agnes."

[3] The true date was in November, 1336.

nine-and-twenty minor chapters, wherein, among other things, it is provided that the custodians and wardens of the said Order shall be canonically elected.

After Easter[1] the said Earl [of Moray] was taken back to Scotland, on the chance that his sister would surrender her castle in order to save his life; but she replied that the castle belonged to her lord and had been committed to her custody, nor would she surrender it except at his command; and when the besiegers told her that then her brother should die, she answered them—'If ye do that, then shall I be heir to the earldom of Moray,' for her brother had no children. Howbeit the English would not do what they had threatened, but [decided] rather to take him back to England and keep him in ward, as before.

A.D. 1338.

Forasmuch as the King of France refused to agree to any good and reasonable terms of peace, the King of England directed his journey to France, and undertook himself a campaign with the aforesaid nobles in his pay. He took with him from England a great army of helmed men, archers and spearmen, in addition to those whom he had sent already with my lord William Earl of Northampton, which, as was commonly said, amounted in all to 30,000 men.

When the Scots perceived that the King of England was preparing himself to make war against the King of France, they besought a truce from him, and truce was granted them by the king to last a year from the next feast of S. Michael, provided, however, that if the King of England at any time within that term should feel dissatisfied with the truce granted, he might

[1] 12th April.

break it at his pleasure. But whereas the king, as aforesaid, determined to cross the sea, my lord William de Montagu and the other earls engaged with him in besieging the said castle of Dunbar, being unwilling that he should incur any danger without them, whom he had promoted to such high rank, granted truce to those within the castle, on condition that during the truce no change should be effected either around the castle, within the castle, nor in the buildings built by the English outside (albeit this condition was not afterwards observed); and so they returned to the king in England.

The king embarked with the aforesaid army at Portsmouth, about the middle of the month of July, a little before the feast of S. Mary Magdalene[1] in the year of the Lord aforesaid. Also the lady Queen of England went with him, in order that she might have intercourse with her kindred and friends beyond the sea. After the king had crossed, the Flemings left the King of France and adhered to him.

Shortly after the departure of the King of England across the the sea, the King of Scotland[2] entered Scotland with a small following, the truce granted to the Scots notwithstanding, and there remained for some time at Perth.

[*Here follows Edward III.'s letter to the Court of Rome, the people of France, etc., setting forth his complaint against King Philip, etc. It is printed in Fœdera as if issued on 7th or 8th February, 1340, but Father Stevenson observes that the Lanercost chronicler is probably right in assigning it to a date (not mentioned in the chronicle) soon after King*

[1] 22nd July. The actual date was 16th July, and the port of embarkation was Orwell, not Portsmouth (*Fœdera*).

[2] Edward Balliol.

Edward's arrival in Flanders. The original draft was destroyed by fire among some of the Cottonian MSS.]

In the year of the Lord one thousand three hundred and thirty [ ],[1] Edward the third after the Conquest, King of England, crossed the sea against the King of France, [having] with him Queen Philippa, the Earls of Derby, Northampton and Salisbury, and a large army. He landed at Antwerp, where he did not meet such good faith among his German allies as the Germans had promised to his envoys; but he remained there a year and more, exposed, with his people, to great dangers and at excessive cost, accomplishing nothing of importance except that he travelled to [visit] the Duke of Bavaria,[2] by whom he was received with honour. After a conference had been held, he was appointed Vicar of the Empire.[3]

When Pope Benedictus XII. heard thereof he wrote to him a letter of rebuke for having made a treaty with the enemies of the Church, in the following terms.

[*Here follow the Pope's letters dated from Avignon, according to the chronicler, 1st November, 23rd December, 1338, 12th October, 1339; but there is considerable confusion in the chronology of this part of the Annals, and the dates do not correspond with those given in Fœdera, where these letters may be found. However, the exact sequence of the correspondence is not of much moment. The Pope remonstrates with King Edward for entering into alliance with the Emperor, who is*

[1] Blank in original. This passage seems to be taken from another chronicle.

[2] The Emperor Louis.

[3] Walsingham (i. 223) states that Louis desired that Edward should kiss his foot on appointment, but that Edward refused, on the ground that he was an anointed king.

excommunicated, for his proceedings against the Bishop of Cambrai, for assuming the title of Vicar of the Empire. He denies that he granted the tenths to the King of France to aid him against the King of England, and offers to mediate in person between the two kings.]

The King of England sent to the said Pope by his ambassadors a letter justifying his alliance and declaring his just dealing with the realm of France. During the king's absence two cardinals, accompanied by the Archbishop of Canterbury and the Bishop of Durham, crossed the sea to promote the peace of the kings and their kingdoms. Having endured many hardships and perils, even under protection of the aforesaid cardinals, and having suffered from famine while remaining in Paris and Arras until the month of November, without effecting anything towards the peace of the kings and their kingdoms, they returned to the King of England in Brabant.

In the year of the Lord one thousand three hundred and thirty [ ],[1] while the king was in Brabant, the Scottish leaders broke the truce they had accepted, inflicting much injury both by sea and land upon the English and their confederates in Scotland. A.D. 1339.

Early in July, Cupar Castle and the county of Fife were surrendered to William de Douglas, who had returned from France to Scotland with a strong armed force. Thence the aforesaid William marched to Perth with Earl Patrick and French mercenaries, laid siege thereto, and within five weeks, without much fighting, received the surrender of that town from its governor, to wit, Sir Thomas de Houghteryth. After the surrender, taking with them the booty obtained there, they

[1] Blank in original.

embarked on the sea with a company of both French and Scots, and perished in a sudden storm which arose at sea.

In the same year, on the third day before the feast of the Assumption of the Glorious Virgin,[1] a marvellous flood came down by night upon Newcastle-on-Tyne, which broke down the town-wall at Walkenow for a distance of six perches, where 160 men, with seven priests and others, were drowned.

At the same time the King of England (the Duke of Brabant[2] having left him), invaded the realm of France at the end of September with a large army, and carrying his arms against the district of Cambrai, he caused it to be burnt. On the feast of S. Michael[3] he entered Vermandois, where he had been informed the King of France was lying with his army, intending to give him battle. And on the appointed day of battle, to wit the morrow of S. Luke the Evangelist,[4] the King of England, having been assured that the King of France was willing to fight, took up his appointed position, distant about two leagues from the King of France, and waited there a whole day. But as the King of France and his army did not come to battle, as he had promised, the King of England, after mature deliberation, marched back into the duchy of Brabant. Howbeit he traversed parts of France with his army, killing, plundering, and burning over a space eight-and-twenty miles broad and sixty miles long, to

[1] 14th August.

[2] The chronicler names the Duke of Bavaria, but that is evidently wrong. The Emperor Louis was Duke of Bavaria. Brabant, however, did not desert Edward.

[3] 29th Sept.

[4] 19th October.

wit, in the counties of Cambrai, Vermandois, Meuse, Tierache, Blois, Artois and La Flamengriá.[1]

After the King of England returned from his expedition, many of his troops, English as well as German, returned to their homes; but the Earls of Derby, Northampton, Salisbury and Suffolk remained with him. At this time my lord Pope Benedictus XII. sent two cardinals to the King of England to convey his paternal exhortation that peace or truce should be concluded with the King of France. The King of England wrote to him in reply setting forth the grievances, injuries and annoyances he had endured from Philip, who was in occupation of the realm of France, and who had declined to negotiate reasonably with him either about a truce or a peace, which if he would do, he [King Edward] would be ready to come to reasonable agreement with him.

[*Here follows a long letter from King Edward to the Pope, setting forth his grievances against King Philip, the advances he had made to him from time to time, Philip's refusal of his offers and the many injuries he had received from him. Printed in Fœdera, 8th February. Also a declaration to the people of France as to the King of England's title to the crown of France and his intentions in regard to the same. Printed in Fœdera.*]

Meanwhile, the King of England, having prepared to sail back to England, being entreated by the community of Flanders, remained several weeks at Ghent, where the Flemings acknow-

[1] Father Stevenson observes that the general narrative of King Edward's operations in this campaign is confirmed by an eye-witness, Johannes Hocsemius, a canon of Liége, whose history covers the period 1251-1348, and was printed at Liége in 1630.

ledged him as rightful heir, King and Lord of France, and swore fealty and homage to him as to the rightful King of France. In compliance with their suggestion and advice the King of England assumed the title of King of France and the arms of each realm, to wit, of England and France, whereof he claimed dominion, and entitled himself King of England and France,[1] in consequence of which he caused public letters given at Ghent to be displayed and published throughout England and France, and he besought the Supreme Pontiff for letters of absolution for the invasion of the realm of France. After which, with the consent and advice of the Flemings and the Duke of Brabant, he sailed for England with the Earls of Salisbury and Suffolk, leaving Queen Philippa in Flanders. After his departure William de Montagu was captured on the frontier of Flanders by some of the King of France's army and placed in prison.

In the same year on the sixth of the Ides of March,[2] my lord Henry de Beaumont died at Luthburg and was buried in the Abbey of Valle Dei on the morrow of S. Gregory the Martyr.[3]

In the year of the Lord MCCCXXX [ ][4] died William de Meltoun, Archbishop of York, and was committed to the tomb on the morrow of S. Gregory.[5] My lord William de la Zouche succeeded him.

King Edward, the third of England after the conquest and first of France, held his parliament in London, demanding and obtaining

[1] The title of King of France was retained by the Kings of England and Great Britain until A.D. 1801, when it was discontinued and the lilies of France were removed from the royal arms.

[2] 10th March, 1340.

[3] 13th March.

[4] Blank in original.

[5] 13th March, 1340.

a large subsidy from clergy and people in aid of [the wars] against France and Scotland, taking a ninth of all produce from the people and a triennial tenth from the clergy, in recognition of which welcome concessions my lord the King of England and France granted and published a new charter, ratified the liberties of the Church in England and also renewed many, as is contained at length in his charter. In the same parliament he decreed and specially confirmed by his charter that, in regard of the claim which he made to the realm of France as rightful heir, king and lord, devolving upon him by the death of his uncle my lord Charles King of France, the realm of England should in no respect be subject to the realm of France, neither through him nor any his successor whatsoever, but that as regardeth divine things the succession and liberties should remain freely and totally separate. Parliament having ended he assembled a fleet and sailed for Flanders from the port of Orwell on the day before the eve of S. John the Baptist[1] (which in that year was a Thursday), with a few nobles, to wit, the Earls of Derby, Gloucester, Northampton and Huntingdon, and only a few other nobles. Arriving off the coast he was informed that the fleet of Philip de Valois, at that time occupying the realm of France, was in hostile array with a great force of Normans and French to attack him and his people. He sent forward the Bishop of Lincoln and Sir Reginald de Cobham to Sluys to stir up the Flemings (as they themselves had proposed) to fight the King of France's fleet on the morrow. On the morrow, therefore, to wit the vigil of S. John the Baptist, about the ninth hour, he prepared for battle, and, albeit he had no more than 147 ships against the immense fleet of the French, by

A.D. 1340.

MS. fo. 238b

[1] 22nd June.

God's grace he obtained the victory he hoped for, killing, drowning or capturing 30,000 of the French. But on the English side they killed but some four hundred men, with four noble knights, to wit, Sir Thomas de Mouhermere, Thomas de Latimer, John Butler and Thomas de Poynings.[1]

After this victory the King of England and France remained at sea for three days, and then landed in Flanders, all men shouting, 'Long live the King of the French and of England! Blessed is he that cometh in the name of the Lord!' And although they had been some little incensed with him by reason of his long stay in England (the queen remaining in Ghent exposed to many risks, together with her English there who were in Flanders supporting the King of England and France) yet all those afflicted with king's evil who came near him were immediately made whole by his touch.

After this, the King of England and France, having rested in Ghent and held counsel with his people, marched with a strong force to Tournay and laid close siege to that city, to relieve which, Philip de Valois, occupying the kingdom of France, assembled a large army. To him the King of England and France wrote from the siege works, sending [the letters] by his ambassadors, giving him a triple alternative—to wit, that, as a means of deciding the dispute between himself and the aforesaid Philip, they two themselves should fight a duel for the settlement of their rights; or that Philip [should choose] one hundred of the most valiant knights of France, Philip himself being one of their number, and Edward [should choose] as many English knights, Edward him-

[1] Confirmed by an entry in the Close Rolls, but the date was 24th June (*Fœdera*).

self being one of their number, and thus the slaughter of Christian people might be avoided. Or again, should neither of these [proposals] be agreeable to the aforesaid Philip, then, after receiving the aforesaid letters of the King of England and France, let him appoint a certain day for battle between power and power before the city of Tournay to which he [Edward] had laid siege; so that God who removeth kingdoms and establisheth them should make justice manifest through whichever of the three plans might be chosen, and bring the conflict to an end.

When Philip received this letter and understood the alternatives, he would not reply to King Edward about his proposals because the letter had not been addressed to him as King of France; but he wrote back to the King of England and France to effect that whereas he had unreasonably and injuriously invaded the realm of France and had rebelled against him to whom he had done homage, he [Philip] proposed to expel him from his kingdom for the honour of the realm and welfare of the people.[1]

Meanwhile, during these transactions, seeing that the aforesaid Philip dared not encounter the King of England and France in any manner, and that the funds required by the King of England for maintaining the siege were far short of what was necessary, a truce between him and the aforesaid Philip was agreed to through the mediation of the cardinals; whereupon the king suddenly came to England and [imprisoned] the warden of the Tower of London, to wit, Sir Nicholas de Beche (who was also guardian of the king's son), Sir John de Pulteney, William del Pole, and several other knights and justiciaries, as well as some clerks of the

[1] Edward's challenge and Philip's refusal are printed in *Fœdera*.

Treasury.[1] A serious dispute had arisen between him [King Edward] and John de Stratford, Archbishop of Canterbury; all of which was caused by their not having supported him with proper funds when he was going to war, but frustrated his just right and purpose.

While these things were going on, David de Brus, returning from France to Scotland, and collecting an army, wasted Northumberland with sword and fire as far as the river Tyne, returning home without any opposition. After this he[2] marched to Scotland and kept Christmas at the Abbey of Melrose in Scotland, where he was exposed to much danger by cunning assaults of the Scots, losing several of his men, and he retreated to England without [performing] any notable exploit.

MS. Preceded by certain nobles, the King of England invaded
fo. 239 Brittany, where he took several castles and fortresses by storm, closely besieging the city of Vannes, which he would have taken within a few days, had not a truce for three years and more been struck at the earnest mediation of my lord the Supreme Pontiff and by the intervention of the two cardinals, which truce proved to be rather a betrayal than a settlement.

[*Here follow the terms of truce at great length. They are not in Fœdera.*]

In the same year the King of England incurred many dangers in returning from Brittany to England, especially from flashes of lightning and unprecedented storms, whereby nearly all his ships were scattered from him and several were sunk in the sea. How-

[1] Sir Nicholas de la Beche must have cleared himself, for he was appointed Seneschal of Gascony, 20th July, 1343 (*Fœdera*).

[2] King Edward.

beit it is said that not one of the sailors or soldiers was so cheerful amid these storms and dangers as himself, who ever remained fearless and unperturbed through them all; whence he was delivered by God's grace and the Blessed Virgin's intercession (whom he always had invoked and chosen as his peculiar patron in all dangers), and so was happily carried to that part of the kingdom of England which he desired.

The truce in Brittany having been concluded, several nobles of England assembled at Carlisle under my lord Bohun[1] Earl of Northampton, in order to fortify Lochmaben; but they went no further, as the Scots gave leave that the aforesaid castle should be peacefully fortified. A.D. 1344.

In the same year the King of England held a round table of three hundred knights and as many ladies at Windsor, for which immense expense was incurred as befitting the royal dignity.

The King of England on the eve of the kalends of July[2] went to sea at Sandwich with *a large army for the protection of his* people, and kept at sea with the aforesaid army until the ninth of the kalends of August,[3] and then returned to the kingdom of England at Sandwich, without performing any notable exploit. A.D. 1345.

In the same year, while [the king] was at sea, the Flemings, who were then believed to be faithful to the King of England, attacked [ ][4] at Ghent and cruelly put him [?] to death.

In the same year the Scots with a large force invaded England by way of Carlisle on the eighth of the kalends of November,[5] and also burnt Gillesland and Penrith in Cumberland, with the adjoining

[1] *Wowen* in MS. [2] 30th June. [3] 24th July.
[4] Blank in original. [5] 25th Oct.

villages; but as they suffered from hunger, they returned without any gain to themselves or much loss to us.

Afterwards, on the eighteenth of the kalends of January,[1] certain nobles invaded Scotland in revenge for the deeds they had endured, and, having burnt Dumfries with many adjacent villages, returned to England without much gain or loss on their part on the fifteenth of the kalends of the same month.[2]

In the month of July, David King of Scots entered England under the banner of the Earl of Moray, harrying Cumberland, the hills of Derwent and the moor of Aldstone,[3] with slaughter and fire, and returning to Scotland with great droves of cattle without [sustaining] any loss to his army.

A.D. 1346.

In the same month of that year Edward, renowned and illustrious King of England, sailed from Portsmouth with fifteen hundred ships and a great force of soldiers upon an expedition against the King of France to vindicate the inheritance which was his, due to himself ancestrally and through his maternal uncle. On the twelfth of the same month he landed at la Houge in Normandy, whence he marched to Caen, sacking the city to the bare walls thereof, killing and capturing many knights and an immense number of soldiers.

'Edward, by the grace of God King of England and France and Lord of Ireland, to the honourable Father in God William, by the same grace Bishop of York, Primate of England,—Greeting.

'Forasmuch as we know well that you would wish good news from us, we make known to you that we arrived at la Hougue near Barfleur on the 12th July last, with all our people safe and sound, praise be to God, and remained there while our troops and horses disembarked and our troops

[1] 15th Dec. [2] 18th Dec.

[3] Not to be confused with Alston in Lancashire.

were being victualled, until the following Tuesday; on which day we marched with our army to Valognes, where we took the castle and the town; and then on our march we caused the bridge of *Oue*, which our enemy had destroyed, to be rebuilt, and we passed over it and took the castle and town of Carentan, whence we held the straight road to the town of Saint-Lô. We found Herbert bridge near that town broken down, in order to prevent our crossing, so we caused it to be repaired, and next day we took the town. Then we pressed forward to Caen without halting for a single day from the hour that we left la Hougue until we arrived there. MS.

'And so soon as we had gone into quarters at Caen, our people began to fo. 240b
deliver assault upon the town, which was very strongly fortified and garrisoned with about 1600 soldiers, besides about 30,000 common people armed for its defence, who fought very well and boldly, so that the mellay was very hot and lasted a long time. But, praise be to God, the town was taken by storm in the end without loss to our people.

'There were taken there the Comte d'Eu, Constable of France, the Chamberlain Tankerville (who on that day had been proclaimed a Marshal of France), of other bannerets and chevaliers about one hundred and forty, and a great crowd of esquires of the wealthy burghers. Also there perished many noble chevaliers and gentlemen and a great number of the commonalty.

'And our fleet, which kept in touch with us, has burnt and laid waste the whole seacoast from Barfleur as far as the Fosse de Colleville near Caen, and likewise has burnt the town of Cherbourg and the ships of la Havre, so that either by us or our people there have been burnt one hundred or more great ships and other vessels of the enemy.

'Wherefore we beg that you will devoutly return thanks to God for the exploit which he has enabled us to perform, and continually beseech him that he will grant us further success; also [we desire] that you write to the prelates and clergy of your province that they act in like manner, and that you ratify these events to our people in your district, for their comfort, and that you apply yourself diligently to resist our enemies of Scotland by all the means in your power for the safety of our people in your parts, for which we rely confidently upon you.

'Forasmuch as we have already obtained the assent of all our principal officers, who show themselves to be of excellent spirit and willingness we have firmly resolved to press forward with all our might against our adversary, wheresoever he may be from day to day, and our firm hope is in God that he will assure us good and honourable [results[1]] of our enterprise, and that you will shortly receive good and agreeable news of us.

'Given under our privy seal at Caen, the 30th day of July, in the twentieth year of our reign in England.'

Hereafter the province of Bayeux surrendered voluntarily, fearing lest it should suffer in the same manner, whence he [King Edward] pursued his march as far as Rouen, wasting all around with fire and sword. He took possession without any resistance of all the great villages through which he passed; he captured castles and fortifications, even the strongest, without difficulty and with very small attacking columns. At that time the enemy was in Rouen with a very strong armed force, and, notwithstanding his superiority in numbers, he caused the bridge over the Seine to be broken lest the King of England should reach him. And so it was all the way to Paris—on one side of the Seine the King of England plying fire and sword, and on the other side the King of France breaking down and fortifying all the bridges of the Seine, to prevent the King of England crossing over to him; nor would he dare anything for the defence of his people and realm, although he could have crossed the Seine, but fled towards Paris.

When the King of England reached Poissy, he found the bridge broken and guarded by 1000 knights and 2000 cross-bowmen, so that it might not be repaired to enable the King of England to cross. But the King of England, having killed the guards, speedily repaired the bridge, and crossed over with his army. Then he proceeded through Picardy to Ponthieu; his enemy followed him to Crécy-en-Ponthieu, where, on the seventh of

[1] Blank in original.

the kalends of September,[1] by the help of the Lord, he defeated his enemy in a great battle. For the action began on the aforesaid day, to wit, the Saturday after the feast of S. Bartholomew, and continued until noon on the following day, and was brought to a close, not by human, but by divine, power. Among those slain and captured there were the King of Bohemia[2] and the King of Majorca, also the Duke of Lorraine, the Archbishop of Sens and [the bishop of] Nimes,[3] the Comte d'Alençon, who was the King of France's brother, the Abbot of Corbeil, besides the Count of Flanders, the Comte d'Albemarle [?],[4] the Comte *Sauvay*, the Comte de Blois, the Comte de Mont Villiers, the Comte de *Sainiers* and his brother, the Prior-in-chief of the Hospital of Jerusalem, the High Lord of Rosenburg and chief man in all France after the King, the Vicomte de Turnas, the Lord de Morles, the Lord of Righou, the Lord of Saint-Vinaunt, and many other knights and esquires. More than 20,000 were killed,

[1] 26th August.

[2] Froissart describes thus the death of this gallant old King Charles of Bohemia. 'Having heard the order of battle, he enquired where was his son the lord Charles. His attendants answered that they did not know, but believed he was fighting. The king said to them—"Gentlemen, you are all my people, my friends and brethren in arms this day; wherefore, as I am blind, I beseech you to lead me so far into the battle that I may deal one blow with my sword." The knights replied that they would lead him forward at once; and, lest they should lose him in the mellay, they fastened all the reins of their horses together, and put the king at their head, that he might gratify his wish. They advanced against the enemy; the king rode in among them and made good use of his sword. He and his companions fought most gallantly; but they pressed forward so far that they were all killed; and on the morrow they were found on the ground, with their horses all tied together.' (*Froissart*, ch. cxxix.).

[3] *Archiepiscopus Senonensis Neminensis.* Nimes was not an archiepiscopal see.

[4] *Comes Daumarle.*

and people without number of other nations; many were captured and imprisoned, King Philip [saved himself] by flight in arms.

After this the King of England undertook the siege of Calais, which was from old time most hurtful to the English.

Blessed be the Lord God of Israel! who hath visited and redeemed his people and raised up a horn of salvation for us in the house of David, from our enemy!

In the same year, that is 1346, to wit on the vigil of S. Luke the Evangelist,[1] from the root of iniquity in Scotland sprang a stem of evil, from which tree certain branches broke forth, bear-
MS. fo. 241 ing, I trow, a crop of their own nature, the buds, fruit and foliage of much confusion. For in those days there went forth from Scotland the sons of iniquity, persuading many people by saying, 'Come, let us make an end of the nation of England, so that their name shall no more be had in remembrance!' And the saying seemed good in their eyes. Wherefore on the sixth day of October, the Scot assembled, children of accursed Belial, to raise war against God's people, to set a sword upon the land, and to ruin peace. David, like another Ahab deceived by an evil spirit [ ],[2] strong men and eager and most ready for war, earls, barons, knights and esquires, with two thousand men-at-arms and 20,000 commonalty of the villages, who are called 'Hobelers' among them, and of foot soldiers and archers it was calculated there were ten thousand and more. Impelled by pride and led by the devil, these invaded England with a lion-like rush, marching straight upon the fortress of Liddel. Sir William of Douglas arrived with his army at the said fortress in the morning, and David in the evening, laid siege thereto on the aforesaid day.

[1] 17th October.

[2] Words missing in original.

For three days running they lay there in a circle, nor did they during the said days allow any attacks to be made on the threatened[1] fortress. But on the fourth day, having armed themselves before sunrise with spears, stones, swords and clubs, they delivered assaults from all quarters upon the aforesaid fortress and its defenders. Thus both those within and without the fortress fought fiercely, many being wounded and some slain; until at length some of the Scottish party furnished with beams and house-timbers, earth, stones and fascines, succeeded in filling up the ditches of the fortress. Then some of the Scots, protected by the shields of men-at-arms, broke through the bottom of the walls with iron tools and many of them entered the said fortress in this manner without more opposition. Knights and armed men entering the fortress killed all whom they found, with few exceptions, and thus obtained full possession of the fortress.

Then Sir Walter de Selby, governor of the fortress, perceiving, alas! that his death was imminent and that there was no possible means of escape for him, besought grace of King David, imploring him repeatedly that, whereas he had to die, he might die as befitted a knight, and that he might end his last day in the field in combat with one of his enemies. But David would not grant this petition either for prayer or price, being long demented with guile, hardened like another Pharaoh, raging, furious, goaded to madness worse than Herod the enemy of the Most High. Then the knight exclaimed, 'O king, greatly to be feared! if thou wouldst have me behold thee acting according to the true kingly manner, I trust yet to receive some drops of grace from the most felicitous fountain of thy bounty.'

[1] Prælibato.

O, infamous rage of this wicked king! Alas! he would not even allow the knight to confess, but commanded him to be beheaded instantly; and he had hardly ceased speaking when those limbs of the devil, the tyrants torturers who were standing by, carried out in act what he had ordered in speech. And thus these evil men, shedders of blood, wickedly and inhumanely caused human blood to flow through the field. Wherefore shortly after God poured forth upon them abundantly his indignation. Thus, therefore, did these wretches, *ut alteri filii*, bragging over the fate of a just man, stamp their feet and clap their hands, and they marched forth rejoicing, horse, foot and men-at-arms, David and the devil being their leaders.

Coming then to the priory of Lanercost, where dwell the canons, venerable men and servants of God, they entered arrogantly into the sanctuary, threw out the vessels of the temple, plundered the treasury, shattered the bones, stole the jewels, and destroyed as much as they could. Thence these sacrilegious men marched by Naworth Castle and the town of Redpath, and so the army arrived in Tynedale. But the English of the Carlisle district had a truce with the Scots at that time, so that in that march they burnt neither towns nor hamlets nor castles within the bounds of Carlisle. David then came to Hexham Priory, where the Black Canons dwell, and, as is to be deplored, on that occasion and on others David utterly despoiled the aforesaid priory; for the Scottish army lay there for three whole days, and David took delight in burning, destroying and wrecking the church of God.

Not this the David whom the Lord
To honour did delight;
But quite a different David who
To Christ did show despite.

HEXHAM ABBEY CHURCH

CHANTRY CHAPEL OF PRIOR ROWLAND LESCHMAN, OB. 1491

LANERCOST

He proved his evil kind when he
  God's altar did defile ;
Blacker his guilt when to the flames
  He gave the sacred pile.[1]

It was, then, not David the warrior, but this David the defæcator who, for some reason or other, strictly ordered that four northern towns should not be burnt, to wit, Hexham, Corbridge, Darlington and Durham, because he intended to obtain his victual from them in the winter season; but a certain proverb saith, 'The bear wanteth one way and his leader another.' Wherefore, although the man himself had laid his plans, we were patiently hoping for something different.

The Scots marched from Hexham to the town of Ebchester,

[1] *Non tamen ille David quem Christum sanctificavit,*
Sed erat ille David qui Christum inhonoravit.
Quod bene probavit cum super altare cacavit;
Sed plus peccavit quando sacra templa cremavit.

The reference is to an accident which, it was alleged, happened to the infant David at his baptism. It is characteristic of the monkish spite against everything Scottish that this little mishap was made the subject of unseemly reproach throughout King David's reign. The following lines, which will not bear translation, and seven others which I do not care to quote even in the original Latin, occur in a monkish poem on the Battle of Neville's Cross. (*Political Poems and Songs of the 14th Century*, vol. i. p. 48. Rolls Series. 1859.)

Dum puerum David præsul baptismate lavit,
Ventrem lavavit, baptisterium maculavit.
Fontem fœdavit in quo mingendo cacavit;
Sancta prophanavit, olei fæces reseravit.
Brus nimis emunxit, cum stercore sacra perunxit,
Se male disjunxit, urinæ stercore junxit.
Dum baptizatur altare Dei maculatur,
Nam super altare fertur mingendo cacare,
Fac singularis puer hic cælestibus aris
  Optulit in primis stercora fœda nimis.

MS. fo. 241b ravaging all parts of the country. Thence, praised be God! they crossed toward the wood of Beaurepair[1] for our deliverance and their confusion. David abode in the manor of Beaurepair, sending forth his satellites in all directions, bidding them drive off cattle, burn houses, kill men and harry the country. In like manner as [that other] David seized the poor man's lamb, although he himself possessed sheep and oxen as many as he would; wherefore, according to Scripture, his son died; so did [this] David, a root of iniquity, believing himself like another Antiochus, to possess at least two kingdoms,[2] suddenly attack towns and hamlets, inflict injury upon the people, gather spoil, destroy houses, carry women into captivity, seize men and cattle, and, worst of all, command churches to be burnt and books of law to be thrown into the flames, and thus, alackaday! did he hinder work in the vineyard of the Lord. He caused, I say, a great slaughter of men, and, uplifted in pride, he declared that he would assuredly see London within a very short time; which purpose the Searcher of Hearts caused to fulfil his fate.[3] Thus this most cruel David was ill at ease, being inspired by the devil and destitute of all kingly grace through his exceeding moroseness.

Who can describe the pride of old men? Scarcely can any one now living reckon up the scourges of the feeble mourners, the groanings of the young people, the weariness of the weepers, the lamentation and wailing of all the humbler folk; for thus [the Scripture] had been actually fulfilled, 'A voice is heard in Rama, and would not be comforted.' Goaded by memories sad and joyful[4]

[1] Now Beaupark. [2] 1 Maccabees, ch. 1.

[3] *Ad suum fortunum disposuit implere*, appears to be a misreading of *suam fortunam*.

[4] *Præ memoris stimulo jam dolens gaudendo*, seems to be a corrupt reading.

I shall not waste time in many words, but pass on briefly to the course of events. Every husband uttered lamentation, and those who were in the bonds of matrimony mourned cheerlessly; young and old, virgins and widows, wailed aloud. It was pitiful to hear. Little children and orphans, crying in the streets, fainted from weeping. Wherefore when the [arch] bishop of York beheld the extreme grief of the people together with the lamentations of the commonalty, he, like, for instance, that other noble priest, the mourning Mattathias, with his five sons, Abaron and Apphus, Gaddis, Thasi and Maccabeus, did not take to flight like a mercenary, but like a good shepherd went forth against the wolves with Sir Henry de Percy, Sir John de Mowbray, Sir Rafe de Neville, Sir Henry de Scrope and Sir Thomas de Rokeby, and chose out of the north men prudent and apt for war, in order to deliver his sheep from the fangs of the wolves. He went to Richmond, and lay there several days with his army; but my lord de Percy, with many other valiant men from all parts remained on watch in the country.

The [arch] bishop, then, moved out of Richmond with his army on the day before the Ides of October,[1] and directed his march along the straight road to Barnard Castle, and on the morrow he and the other commanders reckoned up their force of men-at-arms, cavalry, foot-soldiers and fighting men upon a certain flat-topped hill, near the aforesaid castle. Also the leaders did there set their army in order of battle, etc., as was proper. They arranged themselves in three columns, whereof Sir Henry de Percy commanded the first, Sir Thomas de Rokeby the second, and the [arch] bishop of York the third—a wise father, chaste and

[1] 14th October.

pious, shepherd of his flock. These men marched cautiously to the town of Auckland, in no spirit of hatred as Cain [felt] when he slew Abel, nor inflated with any such pride as Absolom's who hung in the tree, putting their trust, not in swords, helmets, lances, corselets, or other gilded armour, but only in the name of Christ, bent upon no invasion but only upon resisting the invaders. Pitching their tents in a certain beautiful woodland near the aforesaid town, the English army spent the whole night there.

At dawn next morning, that is on the vigil of S. Luke the Evangelist,[1] William de Douglas rode forth from the Scottish army with 500 men to harry the country and gather spoil. Thus the Scots seized their prey in the early morning, but in the evening the English divided the spoil.

On that morning, while the Scots were plundering the town of Merrington, suddenly the weather became inclement, with thick fog. And it came to pass that when they heard the trampling of horses and the shock of armoured men, there fell upon them such a spasm of panic that William and all those with him were utterly at a loss to know which way to turn. Wherefore, as God so willed, they unexpectedly stumbled, to their astonishment, upon the columns of my lord the Archbishop of York and Sir Thomas de Rokeby, by whom many of them were killed, but William and two hundred with him who were on armoured horses, escaped for the time, but not without wounds. Then Robert de Ogle, who is of great strength and not without skill in the art of war, followed them over hill and dale, killing many of the enemy with his own hand, and would not stop until beside a great pool in a certain deep woodland glen his charger, being utterly at a stand-

[1] 17th October.

still, was quite unable to go further. Now came William, greatly heated, to the Scottish army, crying aloud with much excitement, 'David! arise quickly; see! all the English have attacked us.' MS. fo. 242 But David declared that could not be so. 'There are no men in England,' said he, 'but wretched monks, lewd priests, swineherds, cobblers and skinners. They dare not face me: I am safe enough.' But they *did* face him,[1] and, as was afterwards evident, they were feeling his outposts.

'Assuredly,' replied William, 'oh dread king, by thy leave thou wilt find it is otherwise. There are diverse valiant men [among them]; they are advancing quickly upon us and mean to fight.'

But just before he spoke two Black Monks came from Durham to treat with David for a truce. 'See,' said David, 'these false monks are holding conference with me guilefully. For they were detaining me in conclave in order that the English army might attack us while we were thus deceived.'

He ordered them, therefore, to be seized and beheaded at once; but all the Scots were so fully occupied at the time that the monks escaped secretly, serene and scatheless, footing it home without any loss.

On that day David, like another Nebuchadnezzar, caused the fringes of his standard to be made much larger, and declared himself repeatedly to be King of Scots without any hindrance. He ordered his breakfast to be made ready, and said that he would return to it when he had slain the English at the point of the sword.[2] But soon afterwards, yea very soon after, all his

[1] *Sed illum respexit*, should be *respexerunt*.

[2] Reminding one of Napoleon's taunt to Soult on the morning of Waterloo. 'Parceque vous avez été battu par Wellington vous le regardez comme un grand

servants had to hurry, allowing the food to fall into the fire. Thus David, prince of fools, wished to catch fish in front of the net, and thereby lost many and caught but few. Therefore he failed to carry out the plan he had laid, because, like Aman and Achitophel, that which he had prepared for us befel himself. So David, having reckoned up his forces, called the Scots to arms—the folk that were eager for war and were about to be scattered; and like Jabin against Joshua, he marshalled three great and strong columns to attack the English. He set Earl Patrick over the first division; but he, like an ignorant fellow, refused to lead the first line, demanding the third, more out of cowardice than eagerness.[1] The Earl of Moray forthwith undertook his [Earl Patrick's] duty, and so held chief command in the first division of the army, and afterwards expired in the battle. With him were many of the valiant men of Scotland, such as the Earl of Stratherne, the Earl of Fife, John de Douglas, brother of William de Douglas, Sir Alexander de Ramsay,[2] and many other powerful earls and barons, knights and esquires, all of one mind, raging madly with unbridled hatred against the English, pressing forward without pause, relying on their own strength, and, like Satan, bursting with over-weening pride, they all thought to reach the stars.

King David himself commanded the second division—not, however that David of whom they sang in the dance that he

général. Et, moi, je vous dis que Wellington est un mauvais général, que les Anglais sont de mauvaises troupes, *et que ce sera l'affaire d'un déjeuner.*'

[1] This seems to be the meaning of the passage, whence some words have probably dropped out. *Sed ipse, sicut sciolus abnegans principium fiet postulavit.*

[2] He means Sir William de Ramsay. Sir Alexander had been starved to death by 'the Flower of Chivalry' in Hermitage Castle.

had put ten thousand to flight in battle, but that David of whom they declared in public that his stench and ordure had defiled the altar. With him he took the Earl of Buchan,[1] Malcolm Fleming, Sir Alexander de Straghern (father and son without the holy spirit),[2] the Earl of Menteith,[3] and many others whom we do not know, and whom if we did know, it would be tedious to enumerate. In the third division was Earl Patrick, who should have been more appropriately named by his countrymen 'Non hic.'[4] He was late in coming, but he did splendidly, standing all the time afar off, like another Peter; but he would not wait to see the end of the business. In that battle he hurt no man, because he intended to take holy orders and to celebrate mass for the Scots who were killed, knowing how salutary it is to beseech the Lord for the peace of the departed. Nay, at that very time he was a priest, because he led the way in flight for others.[5]

[1] There was no Earl of Buchan at this time. Sir Henry de Beaumont was recognised as Earl in 1312 in right of his wife, a niece of John Comyn, last Earl of Buchan in the Comyn line; but Sir Henry died in 1340, and his son, Sir John, never claimed the title.

[2] Sir Malcolm Fleming of Cumbernauld was created Earl of Wigtown in 1341. The name of his son is not known. Sir Malcolm survived him, and was succeeded in the earldom by his grandson Thomas.

[3] Sir John Graham, Earl of Menteith in right of his wife, who inherited from her uncle Murdach, eighth earl in the Celtic line, killed at Dupplin Moor in 1332. John Earl of Menteith was taken prisoner at Neville's Cross and executed in London in March, 1347.

[4] Patrick, 9th Earl of Dunbar. In Stevenson's text the sense of this pleasantry is marred by the misplacement of a comma after *patria*. The passage should run, *Comes Patrik, sed melius vocaretur de patria non hic.*

[5] Another sarcasm, which cannot be rendered in English, the play being on the words *Presbyter* and *præbuit iter*.

His colleague was Robert Stewart;[1] if one was worth little the other was worth nothing. Overcome by cowardice, he broke his vow to God that he would never await the first blow in battle. He flies with the priest [Earl Patrick], and as a good cleric, will assist the mass to be celebrated by the other. These two, turning their backs, fought with great success, for they entered Scotland with their division and without a single wound; and so they led off the dance, leaving David to dance as he felt inclined.

About the third hour the English army attacked the Scots not far from Durham, the Earl of Angus[2] being in the first division, a noble personage among all those of England, of high courage and remarkable probity, ever ready to fight with spirit for his country, whose good deeds no tongue would suffice to tell.

Sir Henry de Percy, like another Judas Maccabeus, the son of Mattathias, was a fine fighter. This knight, small of stature but sagacious, encouraged all men to take the field by putting himself in the forefront of the battle. Sir Rafe de Neville, an honest and valiant man, bold, wary and greatly to be feared, fought to such effect in the aforesaid battle that, as afterwards appeared, his blows left their marks upon the enemy. Nor was Sir Henry de Scrope behindhand, but had taken his post from the first in the front of the fight, pressing on the enemy.

In command of the second division was my lord the Archbishop of York, who, having assembled his men, blessed them all, which devout blessing, by God's grace, took good effect. There was

[1] King David's nephew and heir-presumptive: afterwards Robert II.

[2] Gilbert de Umfraville, 4th Earl of Angus in the English line, g.-grandson of Matilda, who succeeded to the earldom from her uncle Malcolm, 5th and last earl in the Celtic line

also another bishop of the order of Minorite Friars, who, by way of benediction, commanded the English to fight manfully, always adding that, under the utmost penalty, no man should give quarter to the Scots; and when he attacked the enemy he gave them no indulgence of days from punishment or sin, but severe penance and good absolution with a certain cudgel. He had such power at that time that, with the aforesaid cudgel and without confession of any kind, he absolved the Scots from every lawful act. MS. fo. 242b

In the third division Sir John de Mowbray, deriving his name *a re*, was abounding in grace and merit. His auspicious renown deserves to be published far and wide with ungrudging praise, for he and all his men behaved in such manner as should earn them honour for all time to come. Sir Thomas de Rokeby, like a noble leader, presented such a cup to the Scots that, once they had tasted it, they had no wish for another draught; and thus he was an example to all beholders of how to fight gallantly for the sacred cause of fatherland. John of Coupland dealt such blows among the enemy that it was said that those who felt the weight of his buffets were not fit to fight any longer.

Then with trumpets blaring, shields clashing, arrows flying, lances thrusting, wounded men yelling and troops shouting, the conflict ended about the hour of vespers, amid sundered armour, broken heads, and, oh how sad! many laid low on the field. The Scots were in full flight, our men slaying them. Praise be to the Most High! victory on that day was with the English. And thus, through the prayers of the blessed Virgin Mary and Saint Cuthbert, confessor of Christ, David and the flower of Scotland fell, by the just award of God, into the pit which they themselves had dug.

This battle, therefore, as aforesaid was fought between the English and the Scots, wherein but few Englishmen were killed, but nearly the whole of the army of Scotland was either captured or slain. For in that battle fell Robert Earl of Moray,[1] Maurice Earl of Stratherne, together with the best of the army of Scotland. But David, so-called King of Scotland, was taken prisoner, together with the Earls of Fife, of Menteith, and of Wigtown, and Sir William of Douglas and, in addition, a great number of men-at-arms. Not long afterwards, the aforesaid David King of Scots was taken to London with many of the more distinguished captives and confined in prison, the Earl of Menteith being there drawn and hanged, quartered, and his limbs sent to various places in England and Scotland. But one of the aforesaid captives, to wit, my lord Malcolm Fleming, Earl of Wigtown, was not sent to London by reason of his infirmity, but, grievous to say! was allowed to escape at Bothall through the treachery of his guardian, a certain esquire named Robert de la Vale, and thus returned to Scotland without having to pay ransom.

After the aforesaid battle of Durham, my lord Henry de Percy being ill, my lord of Angus and Ralph de Neville went to Scotland, received Roxburgh Castle on sure terms, patrolled the Marches of Scotland, exacting tribute from certain persons beyond the Scottish sea, received others to fealty, and returned to England, not without some losses to their army.

Explicit Chronicon de Lanercost.

[1] His name was not Robert, but John. He was second son of Thomas Randolph, 1st Earl of Moray, and succeeded his brother Thomas as 3rd Earl in 1332.

INDEX

INDEX

INDEX

INDEX

INDEX

INDEX

INDEX

INDEX

INDEX

INDEX

INDEX

INDEX

INDEX

INDEX

INDEX

www.ingramcontent.com/pod-product-compliance
Lightning Source LLC
Chambersburg PA
CBHW022057150426
43195CB00008B/174

* 9 7 8 1 8 4 5 3 0 0 9 4 4 *